To Jonathan More[illegible]
brilliant son of a [illegible]
father and mother, [illegible]
love.

Martin R. Haskell

SOCIOANALYSIS: SELF DIRECTION *via* SOCIOMETRY *and* PSYCHODRAMA

SOCIOANALYSIS: SELF DIRECTION *via* SOCIOMETRY *and* PSYCHODRAMA

by MARTIN R. HASKELL, Ph.D.
California State University at Long Beach

ROLE TRAINING ASSOCIATES OF CALIFORNIA

Library of Congress Catalog Card Number 75-31418

Printed in the United States of America
by Anderson, Ritchie & Simon, Los Angeles

To the Memory of Jacob L. Moreno, M.D.
1891 - 1974
My teacher, intellectual father, and friend

and for Rochelle J. Haskell, M.A.
My wife, lover, and colleague

APOLOGIES

I apologize for the repeated use of the masculine pronouns "he" and "his" to represent persons who may be male or female. Habits maintained throughout over half a century of one's life are difficult to change. I hope my readers will understand.

I also apologize for the repeated use of the word "subject" referring to a person engaging in his Socioanalysis. The Socioanalytic process requires one to view himself as both subject and object. When applied to a person in interaction with a professional Socioanalist the term "client" would be more appropriate. However, I have used the term "subject" to facilitate identification of the persons. No inferiority in status is implied.

MARTIN R. HASKELL

CONTENTS

CHARTS

FIGURES

PREFACE

One of the most innovative and influential leaders in the field of the personality studies, whose work in Europe and the United States has spanned most of the century until his death in 1974, was Jacob L. Moreno. The immediate source of the main ideas developed by Professor Haskell in this volume is the long association of the author with Moreno over a period of more than twenty years. It would serve no useful purpose to attempt to draw a line between the Moreno position and the development which Haskell presents in this study, except perhaps to note that the former would be the first to support the further probing and development of his ideas.

It may be helpful to look at the stage setting for this study of what Dr. Haskell calls SOCIOANALYSIS. What sets it apart is its image of man, its underlying philosophy; its formulation of a set of concepts drawn together to constitute a frame of reference or "theory"; and its provision of a series of procedures for practice in the application of its philosophy and theory.

At the outset, its image of man is not dominated by a view of an organism with instinctive demands in distorting conflict with the psyche. The conflict model with its image of man as the victim of the organism's instinctive drives, even when tempered by the distant goal of the psyche's achievement of its own relative autonomy, is rejected. Whatever the instinctive drives of the organism, the psyche has its own order of reality. The metaphor which most fully locates the image of man is that of the explorer, the discoverer, the creator. Basically the image of man is optimistic rather than pessimistic—it is not man the victim but man the maker.

The psyche thus imaged is viewed in terms of several primary concepts to provide a frame of reference. First the psyche of the person, potential and achieved, is constituted out of its relationships with other persons as individuals and in collectivities. Personality is structured in the bendings of the individual to others as they are integrated into a whole, in action forming. The reality world of the psyche is interpersonal. The reality world of the psyche and the identity of the person is never fixed and final but is always generating its own reconstruction and growth. This process has its own dynamics. It is the immediate action which is crucial. The future is built on the past accumulation, but that past, whether private or embodied in the culture, is a resource to create the future. Merely to repeat, to stop and rest upon that past accumulation of experience is destructive. That in fact is a major source of conflict to be overcome. The main process manifest in this endless making of the psyche's reality is communication. The person discovers and constitutes his identity and achieves his autonomy in forming actions out of that kind of communicating with others which is possible when he projects himself into the thinking and feeling and intending of others in their own unique experiencing and forming of their actions.

From this set of concepts, one then goes on to a specification of procedures appropriate in dealing with problems of the person with such a structure and dynamics. Structurally, the organization of the psyche is constituted of the sets of relationships of the individual to others, and therefore one kind of procedure is to trace out these relationships as they manifest themselves in the bendings of the actor to others—social configurations as they are integrated into a personality structure. That structure is in its nature continuously changing in the individual's experience of forming actions—it is the continuous making and discovery of his identity in his autonomy in dependency upon those others. The process is communicating in interaction but specifically that kind of communicating in which the actor projects his experiencing into the experience of the others with whom he enters into relationships in forming his actions. One level of that activity is called "taking the role of the other," but its most complete manifestation is in "becoming the other." In both, the actor undertakes to perceive, experience himself as the others experience him as they form their own actions to express and execute their motivations. What is called "Psychodrama" is a procedure devised to enable actors to participate in that kind of dynamic communicating.

It is important to note that this way of thinking about human nature is designed not only to provide procedures to treat the disordered or sick person but to provide directives for the healthy psyche in its development and the continuing fulfilment of its potentials.

Thus, this "system" is at once a philosophy of the person in an interpersonal reality, a set of ideas making up a framework of address, a theory, and a series of procedures to implement that set of ideas in practice. In this volume, Professor Haskell brings into focus all three of these three interrelated components. Out of his own long, rich experience and his innovative scholarship, his exposition is informed with the clarity and directness of one who is making accessible to the public a report of what he has found both as an investigator and a successful practitioner. To the inquiring reader it brings the information and insights necessary to make an evaluation of the position it represents. To the practitioner it will serve as an invaluable resource and directive for guidance in further testing and developing both the underlying theory and the achievement of more effective practice.

WELLMAN J. WARNER

PART ONE

THE SOCIOANALYTIC PROCESS

Socioanalysis as described in this book offers a way of examining our social relationships, understanding them better and experimenting with change. Awareness of self, self-confidence and a realistic approach to interpersonal relationships are the desired goals. Socioanalysis is offered as an alternative to psychoanalysis to those disenchanted with or indifferent to psychoanalysis or any other form of psychotherapy. It may also be used as a supplement to psychoanalysis or any other form of psychotherapy by those who find the insights gained in psychotherapy insufficient to produce changes desired by them. Finally, techniques used in socioanalysis may be applied by psychotherapists with different theoretical positions in an effort to achieve their objectives. In essence, however, Socioanalysis is, a form of sociotherapy for the individual. To many if not to most people this sociotherapy can provide an alternative to any form of psychotherapy.

In Chapter I, I describe Socioanalysis as a system of sociotherapy and provide a theoretical basis for such a system. Chapter II is devoted to a discussion of Spontaneity Development and Chapter III to Sociometry, a method of evaluating one's relationship to others. In Chapters IV and V the Socioanalytic Process is outlined in detail for use by one undertaking self-analysis or by an expert, a Socioanalist, who assists one in his self-analysis. Each person, however, is responsible for his own analysis. Each must evaluate his associations of the past and present and his goals for the future. The Socioanalist can only provide the tools.

In a review of the book by Frederick Perls, *Gestalt Therapy Verbatim,* Eric Berne, the founder of Transactional Analysis said:

"Dr. Perls is a learned man. He borrows from or encroaches upon psychoanalysis, transactional analysis, and other systematic approaches, but he knows who he is and does not end up as an eclectic. In his selection of specific techniques he shares with other "active" psychotherapists the "Moreno problem": the fact that nearly all known "active" techniques were first tried out by Dr. J. L. Moreno in psychodrama, so that it is difficult to come up with an original idea in this regard."

I do not have a Moreno problem. For twenty years I had the rare privilege of being associated with Dr. J. L. Moreno and I consider him my teacher, intellectual father, and friend. I fully recognize his influence on my work and would gladly concede his paternity to any of the ideas contained in this book. However, I fully accept responsibility for the particular combination of Moreno methods and techniques which I have chosen to call Socioanalysis as well as for variations and additions to these methods and techniques.

Chapter I

WHAT IS SOCIOANALYSIS?

"The Platform of the *third psychiatric revolution* consists of a medical sociology," J. L. Moreno.

In 1955, Dr. J. L. Moreno, the man whose genius and hard work was largely responsible for the creation and development of Group Psychotherapy, Psychodrama, Role Playing, Sociodrama, and Sociometry, suggested that those who based their "therapeutic" approach on sociometric theory, whether engaged in group psychotherapy, individual therapy, or psychodrama, apply the term "Socioanalysis" to describe their work. He sought consensus around a single term which could clearly differentiate work inspired by him from psychoanalysis. The term, "socioanalysis" seemed most appropriate to him because it had always been his position that in psychotherapy it was essential that one dealt with the "socius," the whole man, in interaction with others. He felt that since the entire man, and not a segment of a man, is involved in any action, a reduction to simpler elements of abstraction must of necessity prove inadequate. In an article published in 1962, entitled "Socioanalysis and Psychoanalysis," I undertook to differentiate the Moreno system from psychoanalysis and adopted the term "Socioanalysis" to encompass it. The term socioanalysis has not been widely used since that time. I regard the analysis of one person by another, regardless of the method used, as improper and ineffective. Each person, as I see it, is responsible for himself and to himself. He must experience and choose for himself and it is in his interest that he examine the alternatives available to him and the relationships in which he is participating. He must therefore be his own analyst. Diagnostic categories, I consider largely irrelevant. Psychiatrists, psychologists, and others who label people neurotic or psychotic base their diagnoses largely on behavior. They do not agree on treatment. The socioanalist is an expert in the methods and techniques employed in socioanalysis. He does not deal with a person as a "neurotic" or "psychotic" but as one who behaves in a certain way and is involved in certain relationships. Because he perceives each person as a unique human being, responsible for himself, the socioanalist has no need to place people into categories or affix labels to them.

A person wishing to examine his past behavior, his past, present, or potential relationships or prepare for possible future situations is encouraged to do so. If he can communicate with a socioanalist he may be furnished tools available for his socioanalysis. He, however, is his own analyst. No effort is made to solve his problems for him nor does a socioanalist select or reject relationships. It is anticipated, that each person in socioanalysis will, with the assistance of others in groups, including skilled directors, increase his awareness of alternatives available to him. He should then be better prepared to choose both behavior patterns and persons to relate to.

As I define it, *socioanalysis is an exploration in depth of the relationship people have with other people and the problems they encounter in the course of such relationships.* It may be employed in the study of the structure of groups and even of societies but the focus of this book is on the relationships of individuals to others and the problems they experience. Furthermore, the position taken in this book is that people can and should become investigators and experts in the social relationships that include them. Socioanalysis provides methods which make it possible for each person to be a researcher into his social roles and relationships. These include Sociometry, Psychodrama, and Role Training.

With respect to problems in social relationships, people vary on each of the four following levels:

1. In their ability to recognize the existence of a problem.
2. In their ability to recognize alternative solutions to problems.
3. In their ability to choose between alternatives available to them.
4. In their ability to act on available alternatives.

Socioanalysis may be employed to quantify increases and decreases in spontaneity as evidenced by the ways in which people deal with problems in social relationships on all four levels. It may also be used in efforts to increase spontaneity and the ability to deal with problems in social relationships. The theoretical basis for socioanalysis represents a combination of Spontaneity Theory and Sociometric Theory. The principal method of measuring change is provided by Sociometry. The principal methods used to produce change are Psychodrama, Sociodrama, and Role Training.

Dr. J. L. Moreno, a medical doctor, neurologist, and psychiatrist, contributed greatly to the treatment of people labeled "mentally ill," applying all of the elements of his system to their problems. To Dr. J. L. Moreno, *the first psychiatric revolution* was symbolized by the emancipation of the "insane" from chains. The establishment of psychotherapy as a part of a medicine and the development of a "medical psychotherapy" he characterized as the *second psychiatric revolution.* In pioneering a medical sociology, Moreno from the 1920's on was in the forefront of the *third psychiatric revolution,* which had as its goal a therapeutic society. He contributed to that revolution by introducing and expanding the uses of group psychotherapy psychodrama, sociodrama, and sociometry, all of which led to the decline of individual methods of psychotherapy. Psychodrama, for example, has been used by Moreno, and many other psychiatrists and others who employ it, as a deep action method for treating "psychoses" and "neuroses." However, he did not overlook, the potential contribution of his system to preventive psychiatry and continually encouraged the use of sociometry, psychodrama, sociodrama, and role playing in the fields of education, religion, industry, marital counseling, delinquency, race relations, and other human relations. In addition, he encouraged their use by people who wished to examine their own relationships, and the problems they encounter in the present or to prepare them for future encounters and relationships. He felt that groups of people could themselves get together and employ his techniques to assist each other in gaining a better understanding of their relationships and roles. Such self-helf groups as Alcoholics Anonymous, Synanon, TOPS, and others were urged to employ action methods. In my view, people who, for any reason seek to arrive at a better understanding of their roles and relationships or to improve their social skills might very well form socioanalytic groups. In the process they would provide themselves with a form of preventive psychiatry. I avoid using such terms as "mental illness" and "therapy" for reasons which will become obvious before the end of this chapter.

The methods and techniques available to those interested in using socioanalysis are described in detail in the chapters on Sociometry, The Psychodramatic Method, and Role Training for Spontaneity. The writings of J. L. Moreno and his followers and the training institutes established by them provide a wealth of additional material.

Since socioanalysis as here defined is limited to the exploration of the relationships of people to other people, the therapist-patient relationship applicable to the medical model and characteristic of psychotherapy, individual or group, is inapplicable. A more appropriate model is that of a laboratory in which one or more persons, preferably in groups, examine roles and relationships, and experiment with alternative courses of action and alternative relationships. Although some of the people in the laboratory may have more technical skills than others, each participates as a researcher. Hopefully, one day, there will be an institute in every city to which an individual can go if he wishes to participate in Psychodrama or Role Training Sessions directed by an expert. Moreno Institute, New York, The California Institute of Socioanalysis in Long Beach, California, and Psychodrama institutes in many cities and many countries already provide sessions which are open to the public at nominal costs.

Traditional understandings of "mental illness" have been challenged by many psychologists, and sociologists and have been constantly undergoing reevaluation and change. Moreno challenged them within Psychiatry. His spontaneity theory and sociometric theory give support to a model at variance with medical and psychoanalytic models. In my view the use of the medical model and even the term "mental illness" is counterproductive. The term mental illness first gained acceptance in the 16th century. During the period of the Inquisition, from the 13th to 15th century, a great number of people were tortured and killed because they were believed to be possessed by the devil. Saint Teresa D'Avila, a nun, coined the phrase "mental illness" and applied it to sisters who were charged before canonical courts with being possessed by the devil. Prior to her intervention those convicted were killed as witches. Her contention was that they were acting "as if sick and therefore, were mentally ill." Thus, the concept "mental illness" was introduced for the most humanitarian of reasons. The term, however, represents a combination of two unrelated concepts; mind and illness.

The concept "illness" is ordinarily applied to an individual who complains of discomfort and an associated somatic disfunction which renders him incapable of performing in some of his customary and expected roles. A person categorized as "ill" is regarded as curable, and may be treated for the illness. The assumption is made that if he recovers fully, he will reassume his former roles and if not fully cured, he can be trained for new roles. In my view, the term "mind" was best explained by George Herbert Mead, as a mechanism of control over meaning. Seen in this way it is a social phenomenon made possible by language and emerges when an individual is able to point out meanings to others and to himself. *Thinking,* then, is a function of the "mind" and is in fact conversation of the individual with himself. It is a mental process by which one takes *various roles* and chooses between alternative courses of action. *Intelligence* represents the ability to use "mental processes," in order to solve problems of the present in terms of possible consequences based on past experiences. A characteristic of the mind, therefore, is *reflective intelligence.* Since the "mind" is not a somatic phenomenon it cannot logically be considered "ill." It either functions well or functions poorly or on a level somewhere in between.

According to Barbara Brown, one of the leading proponents of Biofeedback, new and important links between mind and body have been discovered by her and other researchers. Through Biofeedback, it is claimed that man can master his physical and mental destiny as mind assumes control over body. Since thought goes on by one assuming the roles of others and controlling one's behavior in terms of taking of roles, mind and thought are essentially social phenomena. They are developed in interaction with others in social relationships. Biofeedback is recommended by its proponents as a way in which mind can be used to determine our physical well being. Socioanalysis is recommended as a way in which man can influence his social well being and indirectly his physical well being. It provides each of us with a method of selecting relationships with those others who can contribute most to the development of self, self confidence, and self direction.

It is my position that man can be understood and can arrive at an understanding of himself largely by studying his relationships to other persons, particularly the significant others (father, mother, close friends, wives, husbands, children) within a social context. "Mental illness" to me is a form of social deviance, deviant conduct, differing only in form from other forms of deviant conduct such as juvenile delinquency, criminality, drug abuse, and sexual deviance. All these forms of deviant behavior I consider to be social problems, having social origins and influenced greatly by the relationships of the "deviant" to other people. Once we label a person, once we classify him as mentally ill, a delinquent, a criminal, a sex deviant, or a drug addict, we assume power over him, manage his affairs, make decisions for him, and determine his treatment. We may subject such a person to incarceration, degradation, isolation, and in many instances, psychiatric or psychological treatment.

A person who is physically ill, one who suffers some somatic or bodily complaint which makes it difficult or impossible for him to function in any of his occupational, family or community roles is generally encouraged to assume other roles or to perform in his customary roles with some acceptable modifications. There is no reason why the same principle should not be applied to the stigmatized persons (mentally ill, delinquent, etc.). The present tendency is to regard the disabilities attributed to stigmatized persons as permanent. Newspapers headline a heinous crime committed by a parolee, ignoring the fact that there are literally hundreds of thousands of persons on parole at a given time. When an atrocity has been committed by one who has been in a mental hospital or under psychiatric treatment, the media do not fail to emphasize the "mental illness." The implication is that this sort of behavior is to be anticipated from one so labeled. Furthermore, when one is stigmatized as mentally ill, criminal, or otherwise delinquent, he tends to develop a self-image that confirms the stigmatization. He often comes to accept the social definition and the prediction of failure that goes with the label. The result is a self-fulfilling prophecy. The stigmatized person may become what society says he is and behave in accordance with what is expected of him.

To summarize: The effects of applying stigmatizing labels to people who deviate from societal rules of behavior are:

1. *The degradation of the individual by society.* The meaning of the label is known to most people in the society and they tend to fear him, reject him, and discriminate against him in employment and other social relationships.

2. *The stigmatized person develops a concordant self-image.* He

sees himself as others see him and this image is reinforced by the way he is treated by others. He begins to regard himself as "mentally ill," a "criminal," a "delinquent" etc.

3. *The self-fulfilling prophecy operates.* The stigmatized individual tends to behave in the ways predicted by those stigmatizing him. He becomes a repetitive delinquent, a criminal, a chronic mental patient, etc.

4. *We seek an explanation for the deviant's behavior within him. We tend to ignore the effect of his environment and his social relationships and roles. Furthermore, we turn the stigmatized individual inward.* We encourage him to blame himself—reexamine his own personality and character rather than his relationshiip to others.

5. *The stigmatizing label gives society control over the individual.* With control goes responsibility. The individual, deprived of responsibility, becomes more and more dependent. The role of "mental patient," "delinquent," "criminal" involves leaving important decisions to others. After a time the stigmatized person is unable to assume responsibility for his actions.

Obviously, if I reject the medical model I have another model that I would like to substitute for it.

Man according to the Socioanalytic Model is:

1. A social being who must confront others in relationships and deal with problems in relationships along with other problems on a daily basis.

2. Man learns how to solve problems in relationships early in life and acquires patterns of behavior which he uses to solve relationship and other problems. He has adopted solutions that have been satisfactory for him. If he engages in deviant behavior patterns he has learned them and can learn other patterns of behavior. However, before we can expect him to adopt them he must be convinced that they will be more successful for him than the ones he is now using.

3. Deviant behavior represents attempts to solve problems resulting from social relationships.

4. The success or failure of an individual in our society depends greatly on the way he functions in his important occupational, family and community roles. Because we are a highly materialistic society failure in occupational roles frequently results in failure in family roles and community roles. Successes achieved in oc-

cupational roles (teacher, worker, student, professional) while they do not necessarily guarantee success in family roles, or community roles are *the first step* in improving chances for success in those roles. If a man is deprived of employment or other ways of occupational achievement he has little opportunity to conduct himself in such a way as to be considered successful by himself or by others close to him, his significant others.

What occurs in the process of Socioanalysis?

1. *Social Relationships* are examined in an effort to find the influence of such relationships on problems experienced by an individual. Persons are encouraged to turn outward to reexamine existing relationships, abandon unsatisfying ones, and to seek satisfying relationships. Persons are not turned inward in an effort to find causes in mythical internal processes.

2. The emphasis is on relationships in the *present,* the *here* and *now.* Relationships with persons out of the past, particularly significant others, are considered only insofar as they directly influence present behavior.

3. *Socioanalysis provides methods by which people can examine their relationships with others, explore possibilities for change, and experiment with alternatives.* A qualified Socioanalist is recommended for those desiring expert direction. Self-help socioanalytic groups may be formed. However, each person employing socioanalysis must himself examine and reexamine his relationships and explore alternatives available to him.

4. *An important goal is the development of spontaneity.* As one increases his awareness of alternatives available to him he becomes more free to choose, more secure, and therefore more spontaneous. Spontaneity will be discussed in detail later in this chapter.

5. *The responsibility for change in his behavior rests with each individual.* A Socioanalist, a Psychodramatist, or a Role Training Director is responsible only for expertise in applying the methods and techniques. The responsibility for his behavior rests with each individual. Some people reading this book may be eager to apply Socioanalysis to the examination of their relationships. Others are uncertain and may experiment with some of the techniques described. Others may be satisfied with their relationships and be averse to any changes. Still others may be reading this book solely for the purpose of finding fault with the author. What you do with

the book and the techniques described in it is your responsibility. I am responsible, as author, for presenting my ideas in as clear and honest a manner as I can.

As previously noted, people are viewed as having problems in social relationships on four levels; in their ability to recognize problems, recognize alternatives available to them, choose between those available, and act on available alternatives. It is not considered abnormal for a person to have a problem in relationships on any or all of the four levels. In fact, it is safe to assume that every person alive has been dissatisfied with some of the relationships in which he was involved and that others were dissatisfied with him in some roles or relationships. Since this becomes readily apparent when we examine our relationships in interaction in groups, people experiencing difficulties in some area feel less isolated. As each removes his mask and presents himself to a group as he really is he is likely to experience existential validation. He may find that people accept him, even like him, as he really is without a mask. As others accept him the individual becomes better able to accept himself. One finds that others have similar problems, and learns that there are many ways of dealing with relationships.

Sociometric techniques, Psychodrama, Sociodrama, Role Training may be applied to problems and relationships on all four levels. Psychodramatists and Role Trainers have in the past employed some of these methods and techniques in combination and are doing so now. In my view, the application of the most frequently employed techniques in any combination will result in increased spontaneity and in the improvement of social relationships. In all likelihood few, if any, employ them exactly as I am suggesting in this book. Each director adopts methods and techniques most compatible with his personality, life style, and experience. The combinations suggested in this book are tentative and should be considered only as guides to socioanalytic exploration. As experience demonstrates the effectiveness of other sociometric, psychodramatic, or other action techniques, these can be readily incorporated. I am committed to the scientific method and the experimentation with relationships in Socioanalytic, Psychodramatic, Role Training, or other synthetic groups. Experimentation in such natural groups as the family or work groups may be dangerous. One cannot fully express anger or dissatisfaction to an employer without risking his job. One can, however, experiment with all sorts of behavior in interaction with a person *playing the part* of his employer on a Psychodramatic or Role Training stage. The same holds true with experimental behavior in such natural groups as the family. There is far less risk in experimenting with changes in behavior toward a spouse if the experiment takes place in a synthetic group in the absence of the spouse than if tried for the first time at home in his natural group, the family.

THE THEORETICAL BASIS FOR SOCIOANALYSIS

Spontaneity Theory

Socioanalysis is based on a combination of Spontaneity Theory and Sociometric Theory, both developed by Dr. J. L. Moreno. Since Moreno died in May, 1974, and was ill for some time prior to his death at the age of 85, I had no opportunity to discuss this chapter with him. In his long and productive life Moreno wrote a great deal on the subjects of Spontaneity and Sociometry. The portions of his work I refer to in this and the ensuing chapters were selected because they give support to Socioanalysis as I use it.

Moreno viewed man as a creative being, a fact which sets him apart from all other beings. The creation he saw, as a continuous process with man creating the miracles in the world. In the course of this process man, in interaction with other men, is continuously participating in the creation. The world we live in is a creation in continuous development with every new individual born having a part to play in the creation of the world of the future. The world which man finds at birth is one which billions of his fellow human beings have aided in creating, and to which he has a contribution to make. In every venture it is man that determines success or failure. Man, therefore, is not viewed as opposed to society nor is society regarded as hostile to man. On the contrary, man is seen as a *willing* and *active* participant who shares in the creation.

Active participation in the creation he viewed positively. One who does not participate with others he regarded as isolated and alienated. The isolation or alienation of an individual to me, is evidence of a deficiency in his social relationships. The deficiency may be due in part to the behavior of the "isolate" and in part to the response of others to his behavior. As I see it, an important task of Socioanalysis is to identify the isolate and then stimulate him into active participation in social relationships. The development of spontaneity, is an important step toward such participation. The child at birth possesses a great deal of spontaneity and repeatedly reaches out for new experiences. As he does so he may experience trauma. The trauma results in a reduction of movement toward new experience, and a retreat toward security, a situation already experienced as safe. This process, as I see it, continues throughout one's life. As one becomes more secure he may become more spontaneous. He may dare to take more risks. An important goal of socioanalysis is to help the individual to find groups that will afford him security and encourage his spontaneity.

A dictionary of psychological and psychiatric terms defines spontaneity as the quality of behavior that is self-initiated. While outside stimulation acts as a *cue,* the behavior reflects the inner state of the person rather than that of the demands of the environment and tends to disregard restrictive social controls or remote consequences. *Impulsiveness* is listed as an approximate synonym. The dictionary contains a notation that J. L. Moreno uses the term in a restricted sense. Consistent with Moreno's use of the term, I use it here to represent *the ability* to provide an adequate response to a novel situation and a novel response to an old situation particularly where the customary response is no longer adequate or effective. Spontaneous behavior is experienced by the individual as his own state, free from any internal experience he cannot control. Thus, *spontaneity is defined as the variable degree of adequate response to a situation with a variable degree of novelty.* Novelty of behavior alone is not a sufficient measure of spontaneity. The behavior must also be *adequate and appropriate to the situation.* This means that the individual is expected to bring into the situation a knowledge of the roles appropriate to that situation and the limits of permissible deviation.

Before the individual learns to take the role of other (place himself in the position of other) he must *play the role.* Man is a role player. After acquiring the cultural definition of the role, *he acts, improvises, exercises spontaneity,* and at times, *creates.* It is important to remember, however, that unless the individual is familiar with the *cultural definition of the role* and is aware of the limitations society places on it, his spontaneous act may be pathological.

The following example will serve to illustrate this point:

An experienced chauffeur, driving an automobile along a major highway sees a vehicle, out of control, coming toward his vehicle from the opposite direction. To avoid a head-on collision, he may swerve to the right, swerve to the left, or, under certain conditions engineer a fast u-turn. He has very little time to organize his thoughts or consider alternatives as he is required to react to the situation almost instantaneously. A high level of spontaneity is required. The experienced chauffeur, because he is secure in the role of automobile driver, is likely to provide a response which will be both novel and adequate. In a similar situation a person who is driving a vehicle for the first time, or a driver with very little experience, is less likely to produce a novel response that is adequate. He might respond by jamming his brakes, a course of action which could lead to a disastrous head-on collision. He might fail to take any action and ride headlong into the other vehicle. He might swerve to the right and collide with a barrier or post. Any of these actions could lead to disaster. Yet, a person without experience in the role might not be aware of the dangers and what is even more likely, might be unfamiliar with alternative courses of action which might be less dangerous. Inexperience in the role and the accompanying insecurity make it less likely for a person to produce a response that is both novel and adequate.

When confronted with a situation requiring immediate action an individual may provide the following types of response:

1. *A novel response occurring without adequacy.* The inadequate response may be described by others as undisciplined or pathological. Several of the responses mentioned in the foregoing example could be so categorized. Swerving to the left into a collision with cars in opposing traffic, driving straight ahead throwing his car into a head-on collision or jumping out of the car would all be novel responses which could lead to disaster.

2. *An adequate response occurring without significant novelty or creativity.* In the foregoing example stepping on the brakes to reduce the impact of the collision would represent such a response.

3. *An adequate response occurring with characteristics of novelty and creativity.* In the foregoing example swerving to the left or right in such a way as to avoid a collision or minimize the effects

of one would be a response, which evidenced healthy spontaneity. To be spontaneous in this way man must know his capabilities and limitations and be able to choose between alternatives, some determined by his limitations and others inherent in the situation. The more alternatives an individual is aware of the more he is able to provide solutions that are novel, adequate, and creative. Thus, knowledge of alternatives and security in a role enhance the possibilities of spontaneity and creativity.

Spontaneity and creativity are not identical or even similar processes. One may have a high degree of spontaneity and be low in creativity. However, to be creative, one must be spontaneous. Perhaps I should clarify the relationship between the two concepts. To *create* has been defined as to cause to come into existence, or to make a new form out of a pre-existing substance. Musical compositions, synthetic fabrics, and atom bombs are all forms of creation. All represent combinations of substances and ideas. In interpersonal relations creativity involves the ability to invent or improvise new roles, or alternative courses of action in relation to others and to elicit novel behavior from others when required by a situation.

Alternatives to spontaneity are conflict, evasion, rigidity or isolation, each of which disrupts the free flow of interaction. The result of such interruptions, of such lack of spontaneity, is pathological both for the individual and the group. If he is in conflict with others, the pathology for the individual and the group is obvious. However, if he evades interaction with others, is rigid, or isolates himself from others, the trauma may be equally severe. He, as an individual may suffer from the loneliness and alienation which may result from the isolating pattern. The group, in effect, loses a member to all intents and purposes. Increased spontaneity, as it enhances the free flow of interaction makes life more pleasant for the individual and improves the relationships within the group.

For the individual actor, action is a learning process. In a series of stages his social perception is sharpened and his motive patterns continuously shaped. When the actor (individual) brings to any situation his initial perceptions and motives (based on his life experiences) and gears into the responses, perceptions, and motives of others, there occurs the *development of perception and motive patterns of each member of the group.* This sort of development is functional to the integration of the personality of each of the individuals in the interaction and to the integration of the group. To act out one's perceptions and motives under these conditions is both *reality producing* and *reality testing*. Order depends upon change. Not to change produces disorder. The individual does not internalize the cultural patterns of a group in a fixed way. He encounters them in accordance with his own variable perceptions and in the forms presented to him by the groups in which he operates. He acts upon them. *The way he performs in each role is unique*. At every stage there is a reformulation and fresh construction. The product is a creation. Creativity is the quality of the action that is thus "reality" producing. *Creativity is a property of the act itself. Spontaneity is related to readiness for the act.*

The implications are clear. To counter the negative categories of *anxiety, fear,* and *defense,* Moreno proposed a positive category *spontaneity*. To deal with frustration he presupposed a positive category, *creativity,* rather than such negative categories as projection, substitution, or sublimation. All men are endowed with spontaneity and creativity although there may be considerable individual differences in the degree of endowment. They exist *sui generis*. They are not identical with intelligence, or memory. They are not derived from conditioned reflexes nor are they reducible to instinctive sexual responses. Socioanalytic goals center around the development of spontaneity and creativity, with the qualification that spontaneity in roles be developed along with or subsequent to the development of adequacy. An auxiliary goal would therefore be to develop adequacy of response where this is lacking. In other words, I recommend that the individual first be made aware of as many alternative courses of action as possible before he is encouraged to become spontaneous in a role. *He is free when he can choose*. He can choose most effectively when he is aware of the alternatives available to him. Role Training is recommended to familiarize the individual with the alternatives and at the same time encourage the development of spontaneity that is potentially creative. Psychodrama may be used to provide a laboratory for experimentation in roles and relationships, and in the expression of feelings and emotion, all contributing to the development of spontaneity.

Theory of Sociometry.

Sociometry is well established in social psychology and sociology as a technique for the measurement of social configurations. Sociometric measures have been devised to determine the structure of groups and may be directed toward the discovery of the structure of society. Sociometry may also be directed at promoting change based upon the facts revealed by sociometric measurement. Sociometric measurement accurately reflects the extent of involvement and isolation of every member of a group. The basic unit is not an individual in isolation (a psyche bound up within an individual organism) but an individual in relation to other individuals. Sociometric theory places a strong emphasis upon group dynamics and group action as well as upon measurement and evaluation. It is based on the idea that we never deal with an individual in isolation but with the individual in social relationships. The individual appears to seek persistently for recognition, esteem, and affection toward himself as a person. When he meets with reciprocation, he shows himself able to relate well to others, and to their goals. He can participate with them in the efforts to attain these goals and in the creative tasks related to the development of new goals and actions to achieve them. If, however, he is blocked from fulfillment on a person to person level, he is less likely to accept group goals. While fulfillment comes first in intimate groups such as the family, it has been demonstrated that it may also come in less intimate groups such as work groups, school groups, and other interest groups. The individual who finds satisfaction in such groups may change his patterns of behavior to those required for membership in the satisfying group or groups.

Psychoanalists and others have emphasized the idea that individuals develop personalities and patterns of behavior in the family very early in life, and that they carry the developed personality and behavior patterns with them into all groups they subsequently enter. However, there is evidence to support the conclusion that attitudes, behavior patterns, and even personalities undergo change in those groups in which an individual desires to gain and maintain membership, his reference groups. Furthermore, great changes may occur in the course of a lifetime. Studies of inter-generational conflict in families of immigrants to the United States indicate that children acquire attitudes and ways of behaving in school and bring them into the home. In such immigrant families the children often reject the behavior, values, and attitudes of their parents. The same process has been seen to operate in families of various sub-cultures. Applying the standards learned in school the child of such a family may find his parents on the low end of the scale of education, occupation, and social position. To the extent that he imports these standards into the home he tends to reject his parents. The more the child deviates from the values and attitudes of his parents, the lower his sociometric position in the family. The more he deviates from the values and attitudes prevalent in his school group the lower his sociometric standing in the school. With lowered sociometric standing in both family and school, the deviant experiences less security in family and school roles. I would hypothesize that it is this insecurity in roles which accompanies lowered sociometric status that inhibits spontaneity. Participation in groups in which he is accepted and recognized as an asset frees the individual to be more spontaneous. If in the course of one's socioanalysis he finds that he is not associated with a reference group, one in which he receives sustenance, recognition, approval, and acceptance for just being himself, he can learn how to find such a group or create one.

Anxiety may be viewed as any operation that blocks spontaneity. It arises when the individual wants to move toward a new experience but is afraid to take a risk. A predominance of anxiety tends to prevent one from realizing his potential. *As anxiety is diminished spontaneity increases.* Security in a group, because it reduces anxiety, leads to an increase in spontaneity. As the individual has less need to worry that his behavior may adversely effect his acceptance by his reference group, he becomes more free to explore new patterns of behavior. As he can take for granted the *continuation of the satisfying relationships and experiences* that go with membership, he can move more freely into creative action. His sociometric position, since it greatly influences his security in his roles in a group as well as the nature of his experiences in the group, has an important effect on his spontaneity. Ideally, the first primary reference group of the child, his family, may serve him well, throughout life. However, I maintain that even if it does not, even if it was unsatisfactory from the very beginning, one can find or develop other constructive primary reference groups.

There are three concepts essential to an understanding of sociometric theory. Familiarity with these concepts will make clear the relevance of sociometry to socioanalysis. They are: the social atom, sociometric choice and tele.

The *social atom* consists of all individuals towards whom the person is significantly related and who, at the same time, are related to him. The relationship may be emotional, social, or cultural. The social atom, then may be defined as the sum of interpersonal structures resulting from choices and rejections centered about a given individual. It is dynamic. Changes are in process with or without the active intervention of the individual. Membership in one's social atom may be diminished as a result of the death or departure of some. The social atom may increase as a result of marriage, births, or added friendships. The individual, however, may initiate changes in his social atom by modifying his behavior or by withdrawing from some groups and/or affiliating with others. Socioanalysis seeks to provide an understanding of the group affiliations of the individual and can lead to a modification of his social atom, if he discovers the need for change.

Sociometric choice provides us with an instrument for determining the social atom of the individual. All interpersonal actions manifest themselves in the forms of attractions, repulsions, or indifferences. We may, therefore, chart the tendencies of a person to move toward another or away from him. To chart these choices, we may employ formal methods such as sociometric tests and relationship tests, or we may observe them informally. Every individual is attracted to some others and feels repelled by some, as he performs in the many roles which are related to the roles of other individuals. Thus, he may be positively or negatively related to a number of others who in turn may be related to him, positively or negatively. Sociometric research indicates that people tend to view positively the people, who view them positively and tend to reject those people who reject them. Furthermore, the image the individual has of himself is developed while he is performing in various roles and experiencing the responses of others to him.

Some social psychologists have identified the "self" as a reflection of the attitudes of other significant persons. Certainly relationships with others close to us are important factors in the development of the self. It is in the process of interacting and intercommunicating that one's self is constituted and one's personality developed. When one takes the role of other in action and views himself from the point of view of the other he experiences himself as an object and he also experiences others as subjects. In other words, he begins to see himself from the point of view of other. If he takes the role of other well he sees himself as other sees him. He also gets some idea as to how the world looks, and particularly how he looks, from the point of view of other. On the Psychodrama stage and in Role Training an effort is made to encourage this process through use of the technique of Role Reversal described in detail in Part *II* of this book.

The development of the self is, therefore, related to the specific roles in which the individual functions, and to the sociometric positions he occupies in the groups in which he maintains membership. The individual also develops a self-image closely related to his sociometric status in the groups which are important to him. The person with low sociometric status in a group may become insecure in his roles. He may be threatened by the possibility of loss of membership. If that group is a reference group, one in which he desires to maintain membership, this danger may inhibit his spontaneity. He will be under pressure to avoid new experiences and creative efforts and conform strictly to established rules of behavior.

Tele represents insight into and appreciation of feelings of other persons. It is more than empathy which has been described as the ability to take the role of another in a given situation. It is the ability to assume the *feelings* of the other in every situation including the situation involving the self. A confidence man with a great deal of empathy may be able to take the role of a potential victim, and understanding the role of the victim, more effectively exploit him. A person with a high degree of Tele would *feel* as the potential victim and therefore would be less likely to exploit him. He would rather be inclined to help him.

The self described by certain social psychologists is a "looking-glass self." The individual, as he develops empathy, acquires a "self" in the significant groups in which he operates. It is reflected by the significant others. Tele, on the other hand, requires that "I look at you with your eyes and that you look at me with mine." Where there is Tele, there is not only empathy but sympathy as well, and even love. Since one ordinarily perceives others *only* through his own eyes he cannot fully understand them or fully meet their needs. However, as he develops Tele, he comes closer to such understanding. Tele is responsible for increased mutuality of choices in sociometric tests and increased rates of positive interaction in real life situations. At the outset of Socioanalysis one may determine the extent of Tele present. Changes in tele are noted as the socioanalytic process continues. The development of increased tele is a goal of socioanalysis.

According to sociometric theory expansion of the social atom, improvement in Tele and improvement in sociometric position all lead to increased spontaneity, increased freedom to choose between alternatives, and increased ability to create. Changes in sociometric position are, therefore, considered important criteria of success in Socioanalysis if they indicate more positive social relationships. Evidence of such improvement in social relationships would be expansion of the social atom and an increase in the number of mutual choices. If, in Socioanalysis the individual learns to choose more people, the likelihood of his being chosen by others increases. The increase in Tele should result in an expansion of the social atom of the individual. Furthermore, as he rises sociometrically in groups which are important to him, his self-image is likely to improve.

In Socioanalysis, sociometric instruments are used first to identify the individual's place in the natural groups of which he is a member. Through them he learns as much as he possibly can about his relationships, particularly why he chooses the people he does choose and why others choose him or fail to choose him. In socioanalytic groups focusing on social relationships he gains a greater understanding of his relationship to others; ways of improving them, and alternatives available to him. Sociometric instruments may be used periodically to supply information relative to changes in relationships. Thus, Socioanalysis includes both methods and techniques useful in producing change and the instruments needed to measure change.

The descriptions of Sociometry, Psychodrama, and Role Training presented in this book are considered to be sufficient to provide the reader with an understanding of their interrelatedness. For those interested in learning more about them, there is a considerable body of knowledge reported in the literature. The bibliography presented in this book incorporates by reference other published bibliographies listing over a thousand books and articles dealing with aspects of sociometry, psychodrama, sociodrama, and role training. Applying the techniques described in this book an individual may undertake his socioanalysis with confidence. With the assistance of a trained socioanalist he should be able to employ sociometric techniques in an analysis of his social relationships. By attending and participating in Psychodrama and Role Training Sessions he should be better equipped to understand them and experiment with change. Reading alone, however, will not adequately prepare a person, no matter how well qualified he may be in psychiatry, psychology, social work, or any other profession, to effectively direct Psychodramas or Role Training sessions. Training by a skilled director and experience under the direction of a skilled director are essential. It is hoped that this book will in some way encourage people to seek such training.

Chapter 2

THE DEVELOPMENT OF SPONTANEITY

"Conscious evolution through the training of spontaneity opens a new vista for the development of the human race." J. L. Moreno

Most everyone would agree that ours is not the best of all possible worlds and that our society falls somewhat short of approaching the ideal. We engage in endless wars and even those of our leaders who recommend their continuance find it difficult, if not impossible to justify them. In the midst of unparalleled affluence, a large percentage of our population lives in poverty. Despite an enormous potential for medical care, we have large numbers of people afflicted with disease going unattended or poorly attended. Our atmosphere is heavily contaminated by noxious gases cast into it by the exhaust mechanisms of millions of motor vehicles and factories. The countless tons of chemicals which we add to our soil to increase the size of crops render many of our food products harmful. Some of these chemical additives have found their way into our rivers and lakes and, together with chemical wastes dumped directly into them by our industrial enterprises, have polluted our waters. Yet, somehow, despite our tremendous technological capability and affluence we do little or nothing to protect our air, waters, soil, or other natural resources and far less than we can to maintain our health and raise the level of living of our poor. Knowledgeable people in our society bring these problems to our attention and warn us of the dangers of inaction. Yet, we appear to be immobilized.

Pressures for change are great within our society and as frustrations increase more and more people strike out against it in rebellion. The affluent, threatened by the rage of the have nots, expressed in riots in our cities and crime on our streets, react with demands for increased repression. Although the possibilities for orderly social and political change are provided for in our constitution, laws, and traditions, neither those who desire change nor those who tend to resist seem to seek solutions to problems. On the one hand, we appear to have a striking out against the establishment by a relatively small number of frustrated people, and on the other, a violent repression by the "establishment" directed against the "protestors." The vast majority of the people appear to be indifferent or apathetic.

Blame for our inertia has been placed on alienation, the mediocrity of our political leaders, the machinations of a military-industrial complex, the greed of our economic imperialists, the mass media, etc. Regardless of where we place the blame, it is evident that most people do little or nothing to alter the course of events. Prevailing attitudes of those who do not act to promote change may be viewed as on a continuum from the conservative to the passive. At one extreme are the conservatives,[1] people who like things as they are and would like them to continue regardless of the lot of others. They resist all change.

Not all conservatives are wealthy people who live without working, nor is the conservative philosophy limited to persons in professions or in upper or middle management. Many white collar and blue collar workers share in the conservative view which places self-interest far above and often to the exclusion of societal interest. They too oppose change which may be disadvantageous to them and tend to favor unrestrained self-interest. They see the unemployed, particularly those who are members of minority groups, as persons who may replace them on their jobs. They also resent having to pay taxes to support those in need. While this view of life is often attributed to the American ideal of "rugged individualism," it is espoused by many who do not share this ideal but who resist all change simply because they are satisfied with their lot, or are in fear of change lest in some way change may reduce their relative position in our society.

Then there are those who may be called *indifferent*. Such people

[1] The term "conservative" as here used is limited to the above definition.

tend to recognize the dangers inherent in continuing along our present course. They appear to be aware of the serious cleavages in our society created by war, poverty and racism. They do not like cleavages and would prefer to see things improve. However, they do not modify their behavior nor do they wish to do anything that might jeopardize the benefits now accruing to them. They want to hold on to their desirable jobs, neighborhoods, and social advantages, at the same time regretting the disadvantages to others. They do little or nothing to promote change but in their inaction give comfort to those who actively resist change by remaining a part of the "silent majority."

The next category on our continuum are the *apathetic.* These people are not ambivalent. They recognize the dangers of continuing on our present course and occasionally give lip service to the need for change. However, they are neither ready nor willing to take any action to bring it about. They spend a great deal of their time as onlookers at spectator sports or watching television. Action on the important issues of our times they leave to others.

At the other end of our continuum are the *passive.* In this category are those who clearly recognize the danger to all of us, yet take no action. Helplessness, powerlessness, and the overwhelming superiority of establishment power are given as reasons for inaction.

This failure on the part of most people to take action to deter society from moving toward its destruction is paralleled by a failure to take action to change the course of their own unfulfilling lives. They remain in occupational, family and community relationships regardless of whether or not they are satisfying or rewarding, acting as though there were no alternatives available to them. Escape from their dilemma is often provided by addiction to alcohol, drugs, music, television, or spectator sports. Action to promote change in a relationship is taken only when that relationship (marital, occupational or societal) is on the verge of disaster or after the disaster has occurred. Marriage counselors may be consulted when a war of nerves has reached its last stages. Psychiatrists and psychologists may be called upon only after an emotional breakdown has occurred or when one is deemed imminent. Changes in employment or occupations are sought only when discharge from employment has occurred or appears inevitable.

The same patterns of behavior that characterize our response to societal problems appear to apply to the ways in which we deal with our personal problems. The conservatives continue in the behavior patterns that satisfy them regardless of the effect on others (wives, children, colleagues, employees, etc.). They take no action in the direction of change. The indifferent, apathetic, and passive fail to take action that might result in change in their personal relationships for reasons similar to the ones advanced for their failure to act toward the solution of societal problems.

In my view, conservatism, indifference, apathy, and passivity, evidenced in personal or societal roles, are symptoms indicating varying degrees of deficiency in spontaneity. This failure to deal with personal problems and relationships as well as the inertia displayed in dealing with the malaise in our society, I attribute to a deficiency in *spontaneity.* The more spontaneous a man is the better is he able to deal effectively with problems arising in the course of any of his relationships, personal or societal. He demonstrates an increased awareness of the many alternatives available to him. This awareness of alternatives makes him *free to choose* and *free to act.* Increased spontaneity enables man to improve his relationships with his wife or move to an alternative solution of his marital problems. He is also better able to derive satisfactions in his occupation or choose another.

Is spontaneity a generalized ability or is it limited to one's specialized role? To put this question another way, does one who becomes more spontaneous in his societal roles also become more spontaneous in his occupational roles and family roles? The results of an experiment which I directed in 1956-1957 led me to conclude that Role Playing ability was a generalized skill. People who subsequent to a Role Training Program, showed improvement in performance of occupational roles also improved in family and community roles. Subsequent experiments indicated that this resulted even though the Role Training was limited to training in occupational roles. These findings convinced me that the subjects did not simply learn to perform in roles that were emphasized in the Role Training Program, but actually increased in their ability to perform in all sorts of roles. Would we obtain the same results following spontaneity training? I am convinced that we would. My observations indicate not only that Role Training increases Role Playing ability but also that increased Role Playing ability is accompanied by an increase in spontaneity. I have not found a way to quantify the changes in spontaneity but my observation of the persons who increase in Role Playng ability support the conclusion that they are also more spontaneous. My observations of the behavior of college students tend to confirm this conclusion. Those more spontaneous in societal roles (those more willing to examine the possibility of political and social change) are also more spontaneous in interpersonal roles. They appear to experiment more freely in innovative dating and mating patterns, family structures, and styles of life. I would therefore expect an increase in spontaneity in occupational and family roles would be accompanied by an increase in spontaneity in societal roles.

I would hypothesize that man can go a long way toward solving his problems, both personal and societal, by increasing his spontaneity. Most of the problems referred to above, were observed in Twentieth Century American society. The fact that so many problems remain unsolved and so little is done to resolve them leads me to conclude that the deficiency in spontaneity is widespread. Is American man less spontaneous than his forebears?

There is considerable evidence to support the contention that American man of today is far more spontaneous than his forebears, and compares favorably in spontaneity with his contemporaries in other societies. He has created an economics of plenty, has developed cures for a great many diseases and immunization processes to prevent many others. He has developed pills to inhibit pregnancy and others to soothe the sleepless and emotionally disturbed. He has constructed canals across large land obstacles, dams across swift rivers, bridges over some and tunnels under others. He has built large and powerful airplanes and ships which successfully navigate in the skies and seas. He has invented instruments of war which enable him to defoliate forests, poison waters, burn down cities, and destroy potential enemies many times over. He has successfully exploited the potentials of nuclear fission, nuclear fusion, and biological and chemical warfare. He has moved into the orbit of earth and moon and soon may orbit other planets. Indeed, he has even walked on the moon and returned to talk about the experience.

Any of the above achievements required an enormous amount of spontaneity. Instead of regarding each obstacle encountered as insurmountable because it had never been overcome, he sought and found *new* ways to overcome them, and yet I have attributed his failures to a deficiency in spontaneity. Does not this indicate an important inconsistency in my position? I do not see it that way. As I see it, the problems man faces have increased more rapidly than his spontaneity. To paraphrase Malthus, we might say that man's spontaneity has increased in arithmetic progression while his problems have increased in geometric progression. Thus, the need now is for even greater amounts of spontaneity. The tremendous increase in population alone presents us with many problems. Combined with the constantly increasing levels of aspiration of the people and the high levels of consumption deemed desirable and even "necessary," the problems become enormous.

The Spontaneity of Children

For us to better understand our own spontaneity or lack of it, we shall consider at this time the development of spontaneity first in children and then in adults. The two men who have contributed most to an understanding of the ways in which children develop spontaneity are Jean Piaget and J. L. Moreno. The discussion of the spontaneity of children contained in this chapter is based on a synthesis of their conclusions.

An infant, at birth, comes into this world irresponsible at both ends. Although born approximately nine months after conception, he steps into a world that is far too complicated and too dangerous for his organism to cope with unaided. His brain, in particular, is not sufficiently developed to solve a significant number of the problems he encounters. At birth his forebrain is incomplete, his capillary system is inadequate and his circulation incomplete. Muscular coordination necessary for walking is not developed, neither are speech centers. Despite all of these inadequacies he moves from a situation in which he is provided with a safe equilibrium to one which requires him to develop an equilibrium of his own. Furthermore, this change from one world to a totally different one occurs with great suddenness. In a matter of minutes he encounters a completely new set of relationships and each situation that faces him is, to him, a new situation.

Some psychologists assume that the moment of birth provides a traumatic experience. They tend to equate novelty with suffering. In this view a child emerging from the security of his mother's womb into a vastly enlarged environment cries out in pain. While there are certainly some traumatic aspects to so tremendous an experience some of it may very well be perceived as pleasurable. The infant leaves a world that is damp, humid, and constricted for one in which he has far greater freedom of motion and one in which every experience is a new one. The world he enters is a theater of action in which he can not only enjoy new experiences but also a changing panorama of objects and people that appear before him. In my view new experiences need not be considered traumatic but rather exciting and pleasurable. Furthermore, when the infant encounters a traumatic experience, mother is frequently available to provide security. The infant can quickly move from the trauma of the new experience to the security provided by mother. He does not have to reenter the womb to experience that security. She can give it to him in so many ways.

The world which the infant enters provides new experiences in rapid succession. He has no past experiences to provide the basis for solutions and has little or no knowledge on which to base predictions for the future. He has no model to help him formulate solutions or lead him toward solutions. In order to act he must be endowed with spontaneity. *The spontaneity of the child involves immediate response to a new situation.* The infant warms up to spontaneous acts with every part of his being participating. He is totally involved and totally absorbed. He does not permit any part of his being to function in any reference except that of the immediate situation. Each activity, while it is in progress excludes every other activity. The child reaches out to discover the world for himself. He warms up to the immediate situation and lives entirely in the "here and now." He involves himself with such a degree of intensity that every part of him participates fully. According to Moreno, for him to remember what happened would require, that while engaging in an act, a part of his ego function as an internal participant observer, not involved in the act, to register the events. *If the event is not registered there can be no memory of it. If it cannot be remembered it cannot be forgotten.* Based on the foregoing, Moreno concluded that the child, warmed up to a spontaneous act, cannot remember what had taken place, and therefore, cannot repress memories he never had. *Infantile time has only one dimension, the present.* During the early years of life his being is organized around the things he can sensually experience. The first childhood experiences are of contact, support, and communication through give and take on a physical contact level. He slowly learns time and space arrangements by eye and ear, and learns to respect the abstractions and logic of the outer world.

For a personality, such as that of the infant, who lives predominantly in action, the unconscious cannot exist. It is only in relation to a past that concepts such as "unconscious" can have any relevance. Dreams related to events of the past are also excluded if the infant has no memory of the past. The infant may thus be viewed not as a psyche bound up in an individual organism, but as *an individual organism moving about in space in relation to objects and other individuals who are also moving in space.* Even his spontaneous movements are influenced by the movements of his mother. In his early fantasy world, he is master. The free flow of fantasy occupies his mental activity. He sees himself as in control of all objects and persons about him, including his mother. He sees her responding to his wants and moods. As far as he is concerned, his spontaneous act is free from any external influence and also from any internal influence he cannot control. However, the flow of feeling between two spontaneous states (in the infant and his mother) results in an interpersonal situation. *In this relationship we see the beginning of the development of spontaneity which includes the ability to meet each new situation with adequacy.* The infant, very early in life, begins to become aware of alternatives and the degree of spontaneity he displays may be measured by his ability to adequately choose between alternatives. His random behavior, at first free of external influences, may result in pain, injury, or frustration. Social support provided by mother and others not only help him to achieve his goals (food, warmth, attention, etc.) but also reduce or prevent the pain or injury.

An infant needs others to help him eat, sleep and move around. He is helped by others to establish safe contacts with the world surrounding him. Indeed, he would not survive for long without such help. Nevertheless, his anxiety is never entirely eliminated. He tends to fear any situation he knows nothing about. He is secure only in the known. He spontaneously employs Role Playing to encounter and solve problems created by novel situations. He learns in action that stimuli outside himself such as hard and sharp objects, glaring lights, loud noises, and blows inflicted by others may hurt him in some way. He becomes aware of social needs in his earliest experiences. As he obtains social guidance, from mother and others, he gains the needed security and safety. Once secure he strikes out again in search of new experiences. From the very beginning, then, we can see that *spontaneity develops best when the individual achieves security in a role.*

As I see it, Spontaneity, the drive for new experience and the need for security are interrelated throughout one's life. As one becomes secure he becomes more spontaneous and can strike out toward new experiences. Each time he fails or suffers trauma in the move toward new experience, he becomes less spontaneous. He seeks to return to a previously secure position. We can observe this more clearly when we study adult behavior. The experienced and secure pilot may test out new planes, attempt new maneuvers and experiment effectively with the use of new instruments. The spontaneity of the inexperienced pilot is greatly inhibited. He must follow strictly the instructions given by the manuals. Experience in any role, security in any role, increases spontaneity in that role, whether it is an occupational role such as the pilot role described above or a social relationship role—role of mother, teacher, writer, or lover.

Based on extensive research with children, Jean Piaget traces child development through four stages. Movement from one stage to another appears to him to be closely related to security or mastery in the earlier stage. His efforts to determine the ways in which morality is developed by children provide additional support for our explanation of the development of spontaneity. He points out that all morality consists of a system of rules. How do children come to respect rules? Most rules learned by children early in their lives were developed by adults and passed down to children. The degree of respect given to them is highly correlated with the degree to which the child respects the adults. The child starts by receiving rules from his parents and regarding them as obligatory or sacred. Deviating from these rules makes him a sinner. As the child develops autonomy he arrives at a stage when he feels that he should have a voice in making rules and in changing those handed down by adults. In checking out the child's orientation from heteronomy where rules are considered final, to autonomy where children felt they had the power to change the rules, Piaget found that there was a continuum involving four stages. Although no child was clearly in one of the stages, and children exhibited characteristics of two or three stages, the characteristics of one predominated.

The first stage he called motor and individual. Here the child was more or less governed by his own desires and motor habits. Actions became almost ritualized and when he started doing something he kept on repeating the behavior. The second stage he refers to as egocentric. This was characteristic of children between the ages of two and five years old. Here the children tend to play on their own, rules are not clear and behavior tends to be experimental. The third stage he refers to as incipient cooperation. This is characteristic of children between seven and eight years of age. In this stage each child tries to win but they have contradictory versions of the rules. They argue about the rules and settle their arguments by agreeing on a pattern. Then they play according to the pattern they had agreed upon. Children at this stage are developing cooperative behavior patterns. The fourth stage which is characterized by the clarification of rules, was reached by children between eleven and twelve years of age. Here the rules are fixed by the children and everyone knows the rules. Let us note, however, that these stages are on a continuum, and the levels are approximate. Some of the seven year olds play according to clarified rules, some of five and six year olds are capable of some cooperation.

In stage one rules are not considered coercive. They are perceived as interesting. In stage two rules are regarded as sacred emanating from adults and final. In stage three rules are regarded as law due to mutual consent and alterable only by mutual consent. *A characteristic of stage four, reciprocal cooperation, is that each has some voice in making the rules and tends to accept them only if he had had a hand in making them.* Rules established through reciprocal cooperation become the basis of a *new morality.* Obedience to such rules becomes spontaneous when incorporated into the mind of the individual. Since each had a voice in deciding on the rules, each could initiate change. The tyranny of moral restraint which supports rules laid down by parents inhibits spontaneity. When this tyranny yields to a new morality based on reciprocity and freedom, spontaneity is increased.

We see, then, that the child develops two kinds of social relationships. Early in life he is ruled by a "primitive" morality based on restraint and a respect for authority acquired as a learned expectation. Later on he develops cooperative relationships with peers. In Psychodrama with adults who have many serious problems, we find that moral restraint is dominant. They still have respect for parental authority and when they deviate from the rules imposed by their parents, they see themselves as rebelling against that authority and feel guilty about it. Moral restraint still seems to regulate their behavior. One goal of Socioanalysis is to encourage the individual to develop social relationships on the basis of mutuality, interchange on an equal footing, or what Piaget calls reciprocal cooperation.

As we trace the development of spontaneity from infancy to adolescence we note that Piaget emphasized equilibrium while Moreno emphasized spontaneity. Piaget sees intellectual equilibrium developing in stages, each at a higher level, each beginning with a sort of experimental period of preparation and culminating in achievement. The evidence seems to support the conclusion that the child is secure in a role in which he has had considerable experience and insecure and unstable in new ones. Thus, each stage begins with security achieved in an earlier stage and the search for new experience in a new one. As a child becomes more secure in new roles his fear of trauma diminishes. As adults help to construct an order in which he is safe, the child shows greater willingness to accept the guidance and authority of adults. The drive for new experience is egocentric. However, when the child fails, he needs and seeks support to regain security. This is the basis of love, of hate, and of morality.

In the process of exploring for new experience, the child moves from stability and equilibrium. He then strives to establish a new stability, a new equilibrium. However, what does he do when he attains that equilibrium? Is he content to remain as he is, secure in that state of equilibrium? Apparently not. As soon as he is relatively secure in the new stage he again appears to seek out new experience. In Moreno's terms the child becomes more spontaneous. This would indicate that the basic drive is toward new experience. When this results in frustration or trauma, the individual retreats to the security he previously enjoyed.

Piaget's conclusions are based on the results of his experiments with children. Mine are far less scientific. They are based largely on observation and interpretation of the behavior of adolescents and adults on the Psychodrama stage. Piaget limited his studies to the development of children through the stages he observed. It is logical to assume, however, that people continue to pass through stages of development from birth to death.

Let us now consider the development of spontaneity in adolescence. We have seen that in every stage of the development of the child, moral restraint is a factor. The application and effect of moral restraint on the young child differs greatly from its application and effect on the adolescent. Physical and moral constraint applied to the young child is applied to protect him from the dangers that surround him. Mother keeps him from touching fire, running in front of automobiles, falling off chairs, etc. The child, when he does not obey, frequently suffers trauma. These experiences render his mother's admonitions meaningful and valuable to the child. He becomes aware of the value of her advice and love. The warnings passed out to him in the exercise of constraint become internalized and equip him with *safe alternatives.* His spontaneity may actually be increased as he moves to other new experiences. Based on his own previous experiences and the admonitions communicated to him by significant adults, he is *freer* to choose experiences not likely to produce trauma. *He becomes less dependent and more spontaneous.* Even the annoying experiences of toilet training and cleanliness training are relevant to his welfare.

In adolescence the moral restraints imposed by adults take different forms. At a time when the child is physically ready to assume sexual roles and prepare for life as an adult, the parents and other adults in society deliberately inhibit spontaneity. The adolescent is denied a meaningful social status. No longer a child, not yet a man, he remains in an in-between status. While preliterate societies have elaborate "rites de passage" designed to train the individual to fulfill the role of a full member of his society our society simply waits for the adolescent to "grow up." Parents and other adults inhibit spontaneity in sex life. They do not approve of premarital sexual activity and often actively discourage it. Although there is considerable evidence to indicate a conflict between publicly expressed ideas regarding premarital sexual behavior and actual practice, the moral constraint imposed by parents is directed at inhibiting spontaneity in sexual relationships. Knowledge about the sexual role of adults is withheld or distorted.

Sexual activity is "repressed," distorted, refined, or "sublimated," due to the inhibitions placed on it by adults.

From the point of view of the adolescent, this moral constraint is not imposed to protect him from danger but to frustrate his search for new experiences. To parents raised in the Judaic-Christian tradition open approval of premarital sexual activity would be in direct contradiction of the Christian sexual ethic. Yet, adolescents are aware of the fact that adults engage in sexual relations outside of marriage despite the taboos of that same Christian ethic. The rules for appropriate sexual behavior are imposed upon adolescents by the authority of adults, *moral constraint,* after they, the adolescents, have reached the stage of *reciprocal cooperation.* The adolescent has three alternatives. He may obey the rules laid down by his parents and inhibit his spontaneity. He may accept the rules laid down by his parents but violate these rules. The resulting guilt feelings interfere with his spontaneity. He may reject the rules laid down by his parents and substitute the ones he has developed with his peers through reciprocal cooperation. Here greater spontaneity is possible with less guilt. However, those who do not accept the morality of their elders and instead develop a new morality based on reciprocal cooperation, may find their spontaneity forcibly inhibited. This outcome results in conflicts between the generations.

According to Kinsey, virginity at marriage will be close to the vanishing point for males born after 1930, and for females born after 1940. If his estimate is correct and the moral constraint imposed by parents cotinues to lay down rules against premarital sexual activity, it is not surprising that a great many of the people participating in such sexual activity have to cope with guilt feelings for having rejected parental morality. Family counselors and psychotherapists are frequently required to deal with men and women who lack spontaneity in their sex relations. Premature ejaculation and impotence are common characteristics of men whose adolescence was marred by all sorts of inhibitions to spontaneity. Non-orgasmic women recount similar adolescent histories.

It is not only in sexual activity that adolescents find their spontaneity inhibited. Our society does not permit the adolescent to assume meaningful occupational or community roles. Our laws forbid his working in industrial or commercial enterprises. These laws are promulgated and enforced by adults who claim they are established to protect the young. The adolescent tends to reject adult explanations and often with good reason. A young man without money cannot aspire to any meaningful social or community role. Thus, excluding him from occupational roles relegates him to inferior status in the society. Again we find moral constraint dominating the scene. Here, as in so many other areas, we find the youth rejecting the limitations on his spontaneity. How often do we hear young people use the phrase, "that's *your* bag," when they are asked by adults to comply with a rule or law they had no hand in establishing?

We find, as a result of the inhibition of spontaneity, evidence of a great deal of pathological spontaneity on the part of adolescents. Some appear to violate rules almost at will. Rules against drinking alcoholic beverages, using marijuana and dangerous drugs, engaging in premarital sexual behavior, and leaving home, are ignored by many even though these activities are defined by adults as delinquent or criminal. As adults continue to impose moral constraint and adolescents continue to disregard the rules imposed upon them, the generation gap turns into a chasm.

THE SOCIALIZATION PROCESS AND SPONTANEITY

Socialization is the process by which man acquires his culture and his social behavior patterns. The parents are the first socializing agents of society with whom the child comes into contact. At the time the child arrives on the scene the parents may have already decided how they want him to behave and what sort of person they want him to grow up to be. The socialization process begins as they prepare him to behave in ways they want him to, do the things they want him to do, think in the ways they want him to, and what is more important, *choose to do all these things in ways approved by them.* The child has little influence on the way in which he is socialized. He learns to want to do some things and not to want to do others. He also acquires values—ideas of right and wrong, good and bad. Not all learning involves direct social interaction. As one acquires significant symbols (verbal and nonverbal) mind develops. Then through the manipulation of significant symbols in the mind (thinking), the individual begins to arrive at independent decisions. One also learns in the course of unique experiences and in experimentation. However, all learning is influenced by the significant symbols, values, and attitudes acquired in early socialization. The individual thinks with the words he acquired then and tends to view things as he had been taught to view them.

Socialization continues throughout one's life. Despite early family influences on behavior patterns change is possible at any age. Social behavior is a dynamic process and as the individual becomes a part of other reference groups he is likely to make the changes in his behavior required to maintain membership in such groups. The principal socializing agencies are the family, the school and the peer groups. As society has become more urbanized and complex parental influence has diminished while peer group and school influence have increased. However all three continue to exert important socializing influences.

In the course of socialization the child learns his *roles,* what is expected of him by his parents and other adults, by his siblings and other peers, and by his school and other institutions of the society. He also learns the norms or rules of behavior defined by the socializing agencies and comes to accept as his own *their standards of behavior.* In effect, he learns to control or inhibit his spontaneity and adapt to the standards of those exercising power. Knowing his *roles* helps him to determine what he is supposed to do in a given situation. Knowing the *norms* helps him select a right way of doing it. When the norms of the three major socializing agencies reinforce each other, his choice of appropriate behavior is relatively simple. It is when they are in conflict that complications arise. What is included in the socialization process? The nurture and education of children in every part of the world are determined by religious, ethical, moral, economic and political ideas and other considerations. Children are pressured to conform to the beliefs and ideas dominant in their cultures and to behave in accordance with those dominant beliefs. Every culture teaches the child to like the foods traditionally eaten in that culture and to reject certain disapproved foods. Every culture imposes some sort of cleanliness training and toilet training. Appropriate clothing, speech, sexual behavior, occupational goals and friendship patterns are also transmitted by experience of the culture. Many of those traditional patterns of child training have little relevance to the needs of the child.

Children must learn early in life to experience and accept

masculine and feminine roles and sex differences. Each child learns the appropriate response to things, and persons, what he may or may not touch or take, who he may or may not associate with, what he may or may not do. If his socialization is to be successful the child must learn how to choose between alternative courses of action. In the course of his early socialization the child loses some of his earlier kind of spontaneity. Through trial and error he learns his physical limitations, what he can and cannot do. His parents assist him in showing him alternatives. They impress on the child what he is permitted to do and what is forbidden him. His options become more restricted and limited. His performances become directed and evaluated, approved or disapproved, rewarded or punished. Impulsive action is blocked because the child cannot feel comfortable or secure in the face of parental disapproval, verbal or non-verbal. Some of the limitations on the child's spontaneity are necessary if he is to be spared serious physical and psychological trauma. Spontaneity that is pathological or dangerous to the individual acting spontaneously must be inhibited if the individual is to survive.

An illustration of pathological spontaneity is afforded by three psychologists studying aggressive behavior in nursery school children. In the course of 60 sessions, 2½ hours each, involving 18 three year old children they observed 2,585 aggressive acts. Aggressor categories included bodily attack, attack with objects, verbal aggression in the form of threats, and infringement of property or invasion of territory such as taking toys from other. Verbal aggressions occurred so infrequently that the data was not analyzed. Counter attack by the victim or intervention by the teacher temporarily suppressed the aggressive response of the attackers. The effect of the suppression led to the aggressor changing victims or changing the kind of aggressive response. Half of the children in the study were female. Girls were the least likely to be selected as targets for aggressive behavior, not because of male chivalry, but because girls were more likely than boys to counterattack as a consequence of aggressive behavior.

As the child learns to inhibit physiological impulses and substitute socially approved behavior some of his childhood spontaneity is lost. The child may even begin to fear his spontaneity and develop anxiety. While it is essential for the early spontaneity of the child to be limited, too much of it may be lost in the first ten years of the child's development. It is largely in cooperative peer groups that healthy spontaneity begins to develop. During the stage of "reciprocal cooperation" described by Piaget, the child, as a partially socialized human being can offer ideas, contribute to the making of rules, and modify his own behavior patterns when appropriate. He has learned how to define a situation in his earlier socialization and he can at this point in his development offer novel and adequate solutions to problems. Since his peer group is comprised of relative equals his spontaneity is not as likely to be crushed as it was when he was regulated by parental rules. As a rule maker he begins to develop a new kind of spontaneity.

SOCIALIZATION OF ADULTS

In our society, socialization of the child does not always prepare him to function in roles he is required to perform as an adult. Furthermore, his first socializing agents, his parents, exercise power and influence not available to subsequent socializing agents. At home he is almost completely dependent upon parents for satisfaction of his needs and there is little or no competition of others for his attention. When he gets to school he must acquire habits, beliefs, and attitudes expected of him by his teachers and peers to satisfactorily perform in the appropriate roles. He is rewarded when he conforms and made uncomfortable, rejected, and may even be expelled from school if he deviates too much. The adult has a greater number of alternative courses of action but his roles are accompanied by far more complicated interpersonal relationships. He may, for example, acquire the habits and attitudes appropriate to a work situation, or he may acquire techniques for changing working relationships, or he may seek another job. A person is faced in the course of his lifetime with a series of "self-other" relationships in which he must operate. If he is to be successful he must learn the role demands of society and internalize them. He must learn what he may expect of others and what they have a right to expect of him. He must also learn to accept himself—to be convinced that he is performing in a satisfactory manner. In the course of his socialization the intelligence and memory of the adult become controlling and his spontaneity tends to be inhibited. In the first few years of his life authority of his parents was the sole source of his moral life. As the power of the family diminished and other socializing agencies (peer groups and school) gained in importance he became emancipated. He was able to challenge rules promulgated by his parents with those set forth at school and, what is more important with rules developed by his peer groups with his participation in the decision making process. By the time he became an adult one would expect him to have developed freedom from constraint and a high degree of spontaneity. Observation of adult behavior, however, indicates considerable variation in the degree of spontaneity. The adult who in his childhood, did not associate much with persons outside his family tends to be more completely under the control and influence of his parents whether he sees them or not. The values and attitudes of a father or mother may control his behavior even after their death. He may not have developed individuality or spontaneity in the course of cooperative activities and interactions with equals, because such relations had been denied him in his childhood and adolescence. In the American society of the 1970's the child who watches television from the age of three or four may free himself from the controls and moral constraints of his parents at a very early age. By the time he is five or six he is likely to spend most of his waking hours away from parental control, at kindergarten, school, and with peer play groups.

For adults in our society, social constraint produces an effect similar to the effect of adult constraint on the child. Submission to authority which does not derive from an interchange between equals inhibits the spontaneity of the adult. He may often have to submit to such authority in his occupational, community, and even family roles. In a sense the adult who accepts the rule of unilateral respect for authority is behaving like a young child. The rigid conformist is actually displaying infantile characteristics. Those conforming against their will are compelled by economic circumstances to play an infantile role—that of obedient child. Spontaneity is narrowly restricted.

The thinking of Moreno and Piaget leads to the conclusion that throughout one's life there is a struggle within each individual between two moralities, one imposed on him by authority, past or present, and the other developed by him in cooperation with his peers. The first type of morality depends on parents, religion and social institutions external to the individual. The second is created by the individual together with his equals. As I see it man needs to create a new morality, particularly when the old morality is no longer applicable. Many people who start out as conformists become revolutionaries when they become conscious of the need for a new morality. As spontaneous men, they strive to create a new morality because they find themselves part of a society dominated by a morality requiring uncritical conformity. Such a society represses spontaneity. Pluralistic societies, those with many sub-cultures, help us to challenge the beliefs and practices of those in power. In such societies it is possible to separate the real, *what is,* from *what ought to be* as defined by others. Having done so we are better prepared to redefine the "what ought to be" to more closely resemble what we "would like it to be." Each of us in our own lives struggles to reconcile the "what we are" with "what we ought to be."

Social constraint does not really socialize if and when it tends to prolong submission to authority. Such constraint perpetuates and consecrates the existing order. We keep hearing authority figures calling for "Law and Order." What kind of order do they have in mind? Order imposed from the outside, from above? People given a voice in setting up the rules that govern their behavior are more likely to respect the resulting laws and order. If they view law and order as imposed from the outside they are more likely to rebel against it. If authority is control over us by a moral power superior to ourselves morality becomes a system of commands. The individual has no standards which he had a voice in creating, and the society is the only "legitimate" power. Discipline becomes the sole condition for the development of personality. The essence of Democracy is to replace unilateral respect for authority by the mutual respect of autonomous people. Inner discipline can flourish only when spontaneous initiative and activity are permitted. The individual must be a participant in the action: The adult who is capable of the greatest effort and energy is one who has learned as a child to make voluntary and spontaneous efforts. Meaningless obedience does not prepare an individual for life. In my view, if an adult has not learned to be spontaneous earlier in life he may undertake to develop his spontaneity as an adult.

The child is born with a great number of potentialities. In the socialization process he gives up some, and develops others. He is constantly under pressure to develop those potentialities approved of by his parents and other socializing agents. The best one can do is to develop as many of his potentialities as he can consciously choose for himself. The socialization process does not end in adolescence. It continues throughout life. When reaching adulthood many people feel that they have not realized their potentials. Some had set up impossible goals or had impossible goals set up for them, and were frustrated when they failed to attain them. Others after attaining the goals set up for them by parents and others found themselves dissatisfied and unhappy. To become aware of one's potentials requires an awareness of the alternatives available to him. It helps also in the course of experimentation to learn more about the possible consequences of one's actions and choices. The Psychodrama stage and the Role Training Session provide laboratories for such learning and experimentation.

Spontaneous man employs intelligence, memory, and experience. His spontaneity is enhanced by the ability to choose between alternatives. Each success increases security and frees a person for new experiences. Each failure discourages new experiences. Therefore success in a role tends to increase one's spontaneity. Failure tends to inhibit it. Mental health and happiness, as I see it, do not depend on the satisfaction of some drive or need but upon a person achieving a measure of success *as he defines it.* Those close to him, particularly those directly involved in his socialization contribute to his definition. Nevertheless, if it has become his definition it is his goal and he needs to achieve it. Otherwise he may be expected to be fearful, anxious, and frustrated.

The individual who lacks spontaneity in his school roles, is in our society, likely to fail in occupational roles. He tends to become a drop-out or delinquent in his adolescence and his failure in occupational roles may result in marginal employment, chronic unemployment, and in many cases a career in crime. The individual who lacks spontaneity in an occupational role may remain in an occupational rut most of his life, whether or not he is, in accordance with the Peter Principle, promoted to his level of incompetence. The individual who moves into an occupational role for which he is well prepared can act spontaneously in that role. Even if he is not too well prepared to function in his new occupational role, if it is one he desires to succeed in, and, if he has the potential, he can learn the role well. Once secure in the role he can increase his spontaneity. As we see it, then, skill in a role is prerequisite to spontaneity in that role. An individual with a consistent pattern of successful functioning in roles is more likely to move successfully into a new role and act with a relatively high degree of spontaneity in that role. He can move successfully into new experiences from a position of security. The person moving to a novel situation from a position of failure and insecurity is likely to fail again. One can learn to increase spontaneity by *spontaneity training*, practice in performing in novel situations or role training, to gain skill and security in a role. Through Psychodrama an individual may gain insight into the factors that inhibit his spontaneity. Each of us is born with a potential for great spontaneity. Much of this potential is not realized.

SPONTANEITY TRAINING FOR ADULTS

The combination of the terms "spontaneity" and "training," are terms which appear to describe contradictory principles. Those who equate spontaneity with impulsive behavior must conclude that spontaneity can never be trained. It would appear logical to maintain that any attempt to consciously use techniques to stimulate spontaneous performance is doomed from the outset, since it would present people with artificially controlled situations. This point of view was so firmly established that few dared to contest its validity. Thus spontaneity was generally viewed as a quality with which some were endowed and others not. Moreno and his associates developed Psychodramatic techniques intending to train people to become more spontaneous. He called this type of Psychodrama "Spontaneity Training." Since Moreno considered spontaneity linked to the "emergence of the creative moment," learning to be spontaneous presupposed a person capable of maintaining a flexible state. In this manner one could, at least temporarily, neglect the past and the structure of the organism which had existed prior to that moment. He encouraged the subject to act as if he had no past, and as if his actions were not determined by his organic structure. He then attempted to describe what occurred to the subject in these moments in terms of action; relying upon the evidence as it emerged.

Spontaneity Training on the Psychodrama stage is a direct, and often effective way of increasing spontaneity. In addition the Psychodramatic Method contributes to an increase in spontaneity by encouraging participants to express their feelings. Psychodramatic techniques have been developed to facilitate the expression of every emotion. Indeed, some people have, on the psychodramatic stage, learned to feel anger, hate, envy and love for the first time. Once they are in touch with their feelings it becomes a relatively simple matter to have them express these feelings in action.

We must distinguish, however, between a spontaneous act on the psychodrama stage or a creative idea expressed spontaneously, from spontaneous action in our natural groups. We can "brainstorm" ideas, permit them to flow without any consideration of past experiences or possibilities for the future. We spontaneously express our anger to a person playing the part of an employer, a wife, a husband, a teenage daughter, a policeman or a treasury agent, on the psychodramatic stage without any serious risk. The persons performing in the roles of these people cannot seriously influence our relationships in our natural groups. *Spontaneous action* in the natural group might cost us our job, wife, drive a teen-age daughter from the home, or put us in a position to be arrested or prosecuted. Before an idea involving an important change in our relationships in the future is put into action we can and should consider the effects of the action. This takes work. The simple fact of life is that if we act impulsively in our natural groups we may not be able to avoid the consequences. Those psychologists that urge a return to childhood spontaneity for adults do not often risk their own relationships so recklessly. They appear to be far braver when urging "patients" to take risks. Such counsel reminds me of the brave general who urges his men to the attack assuring them that he is behind them. Enlisted men in the military know that he is often very far behind. The psychologist or other professional who urges a "patient" to behave spontaneously in his natural groups is also very far behind. He takes no risks. The "patient" and "counselee" does.

A return to the spontaneity of the child is not desirable. A child may spontaneously defecate on the street, strike his friend, destroy his toys, and engage in other spontaneous behavior that an adult would reject in himself even if society took no action. An adult has internalized most of the norms of his society. They are *his* norms and rules. He does not desire *nor* can he condone childish spontaneity in others or himself.

One way for the adult to maintain his equilibrium in our society is continuous self-evaluation, self-therapy of a sort. In the last analysis each must be his own therapist. The professional whether psychiatrist, psychologist, social worker or counselor, can only provide tools. Each must learn how to use them, to apply them to his own problems in the light of his own life experiences. Whatever he learns from others whether in therapy sessions, classrooms, or experience in roles, he must integrate. In Socioanalysis, in a Role Training, or Psychodrama, or Group Therapy session others may contribute to his understanding of relationships and problems. Role Training sessions, in particular, provide ways of examining alternatives and learning to choose between them. The more alternatives a person has at his disposal when he acts in his natural groups the freer he is to be spontaneous. Role Training is not a brainwashing technique. It is not a way of learning the right way to do something. By increasing peoples' awareness of alternatives it contributes to their freedom to choose and to an increase in spontaneity.

Spontaneity tends to be experienced by an individual as his own state, autonomous and free from any external influence which he cannot control. For the individual spontaneity has all the characteristics of a freely produced experience. To some extent freedom and new experience involve trauma. The womb had provided a measure of security. Movement from a secure position to a new experience inevitably involves the risk of trauma. The infant in making his move out of the womb takes a risk for the first time. Man is destined to take such a risk every time he moves from a secure position to one that is novel. Yet, once secure in his life situation he tends to seek new experiences. Why? Perhaps it is that there is something exciting and rewarding in experiencing the unknown. If a new experience provides trauma, he tends to retreat to "secure" past positions.

Eastern philosophies emphasize "inner peace," the achievement of security by going inward. To an extent these approaches stifle the drive for new experience. Security becomes the goal. To establish "security" as the goal implies a rejection of new experience in favor of a conservative unprogressive life. It represents a denial of spontaneity and autonomy without which as Eric Berne has pointed out "life is mainly the process of filling in time until the arrival of death." Many young people in our society have discovered that this goal has often led to a stifling of expression, a wasted life. They take risks seeking new experiences, often heightened sensory experiences and deviant life styles. Socioanalysis, including the application of Sociometry, and the action methods I am emphasizing in this book, should be useful to anyone seeking to become more spontaneous without destroying himself.

Chapter 3

SOCIOMETRY IN SOCIOANALYSIS

"I am free because I can choose." J. L. Moreno

In an article entitled, "Your Best Weapon Against Overweight," a writer made the claim that the scale was such an instrument. If he referred to it frequently it was predicted that a person would learn how much excess weight he carried and would be motivated to diet. Once attaining the desired weight he would strive to maintain it. Several kinds of biofeedback apparatus have been developed to acquaint a subject with the workings of his mental processes. With the help of such devices a subject may modify his mental process to achieve desired objectives. Sociometry provides just such instruments to be used in modifying social relationships. Using it properly one can learn a great deal about the quantity and quality of one's social relationships, be motivated to take the steps necessary to improve those that he finds important to his well being and eliminate those that are destructive. Sociometry has been employed for many years by professionals, mainly sociologists and social-psychologists, as a way of finding out things about groups with a view to understanding them better and, if deemed useful, changing them. It has also been employed by professionals to study the positions people occupy in groups and their relative participation or isolation. When thus used it was often intended to help people to achieve greater involvement and gain increased acceptance. I am proposing here that in addition to the above uses, sociometry can provide an instrument *which each individual can employ* to gain better understanding of his position in the groups in which he functions, his relationship to other people in them, how they relate to each other, and ultimately, whether to stay in them, take the steps necessary to improve his position in them, or abandon them for others in which his needs can be better satisfied.

Some purposes to which sociometry have been applied are:

1. *To study the organization of groups and provide clues useful in restructuring them.* Based on sociometric tests the military established a "buddy system," organized compatible work groups, selected compatible airplane crews, and selected leaders. Industry applied sociometry to similar endeavors. Both the military and industrial enterprises used sociometry effectively to study morale, job satisfaction, and group integration.

2. *To classify the position of individuals in groups.* Leaders and stars can be readily identified as can the overchosen and the underchosen. One can also evaluate his own position in a group. He can also observe the characteristics common to both the overchosen and the underchosen.

3. *To aid individuals to better adjustment.* The accuracy with which an individual can identify the reactions he produces in others is closely related to personal adjustment. Research indicates that self estimates of better adjusted people are closer to the ratings of others in the group than are those of the less well adjusted. The restructuring of groups based on sociometric tests is a task for professionals. The use of sociometry to achieve better adjustment is best attained with the active participation of the individuals involved. The studied become the studiers. All become professionals.

Choices a person makes of people to be included in his natural groups are important determinants of success or failure, happiness or misery and spontaneity or the lack of it. The choices of a wife or husband, of a business or professional associate, or of close friends may greatly influence the life experience of the individual, his view of the world, and ultimately his self-image. The healthy person, the winner, chooses others who facilitate his expression and stimulate his spontaneity. If one begins by choosing people who are negative and rejecting he is unhappy in his group life. Eventually he may become reluctant to choose anyone.

Many of us do not make as good choices as we might if we analyzed them frequently. We waste too much time and energy with people who are unresponsive, hypocritical or negativistic. Efforts to please such people and maintain relationships with them add to our anxieties and reduce our spontaneity. If we can predict this outcome early in our relationship with them we can terminate such relationships quickly.

Socioanalysis as a form of sociotherapy involves us in an

analysis of our relationships, and places emphasis on ways of changing or abandoning those that are not in our interest. The emphasis in psychoanalysis and many forms of psychotherapy is on changing us, adapting us to existing relationships. To the socioanalist any relationship which interferes with the individual's acceptance of himself must be examined and altered, and in some instances terminated. Sociometry provides tools for determining whether or not others choose us, what sort of persons choose us, and whether or not our choices are reciprocated. Such data when available to us gives us an idea of where we stand in a group and can help us decide whether or not we should remain in it. Psychodrama provides techniques for determining why we choose some people and reject others. It may also provide us with clues as to why some people choose us and others reject us. Role Training provides a method for examining alternative courses of action. A combination of these methods should result in our modifying or eliminating those relationships which diminish our self-image and reduce our spontaneity.

A social group consists of two or more individuals organized around one or more specific activities. We tend to belong to and function in two kinds of groups. One, a *psyche group* consists of those persons with whom we want to associate in a person to person way. It is in this sort of group that we receive *sustenance, recognition, approval,* and appreciation for just being *"ourselves."* The family is the first such group we are part of and it is also our first *personal reference group,* one in which we are motivated to maintain membership. As long as it provides us with the sustenance, recognition, approval and appreciation we need we are relatively secure in it. When it fails to perform these functions, we seek to satisfy them in other groups, consisting of close friends, cliques, gangs, or other people we associate with in a very intimate way. Our spontaneity and creativity are dependent on such intimate social relationships so that we can say or do things without asking ourselves: "What are they thinking of me?" or "Do they still accept me?"

All of us also belong to groups organized around a particular interest. Such groups, including school groups, work groups, church groups, athletic clubs, social clubs, among many others, are called *socio groups, if they are face-to-face groups in which we get to know the other members.* In such a group concerns are shared and obligations are held in common. Our efforts are focused on objectives that are not ours alone. We are accepted into a socio group if *we* have the ability to further the objectives of the group. Our roles in the group provide an insulating factor and we can win approval as long as we contribute to the goals of the group. If the people in such groups like each other the groups are said to be cohesive. The members stick together. If there are serious cleavages they come apart.

Each individual is required to function in a set of more or less well defined social roles in each group in which he participates. As he does so he makes socio-emotional choices attaching himself to some people, rejecting others and remaining indifferent to still others. Sociometry provides a way of measuring such affective relationships in formal social systems. These measures outline for us the social atom of an individual, consisting of all those persons to whom he is significantly related, and those who are also related to him. In providing instruments for determining the structure of the social atom it also, by implication indicates ways of modifying it.

Sociometry in these ways helps us to find out the organization of groups and the positions of individuals within them, and their relationship to each other. Sociometric techniques are used to elicit responses from members of a group regarding the positive, negative, and neutral relations existing within the group. These responses provide a means of representing an important view of an individual's social relationships as perceived by *him* and also provide views of the same relationship as perceived by the other members of the group. Each member furnishes one view of the group by indicating his relationship to the others. Each is considered an expert when it comes to making sociometric judgments. We all know from experience with whom we wish to associate and whom we wish to avoid. Liking some people and disliking others, accepting some people and rejecting others are part of our daily experience.

The questions asked in sociometry are specifically directed at the attractions, rejections, and indifferences that people encounter in the groups in which they function. An individual, given access to the results of such tests administered to groups in which he participates can learn for himself a great deal about the structure of these groups and about the relationships of group members to each other. More important to socioanalysis, *he can learn where he stands in these groups.* He can learn, not only how many people choose him, but who they are. He can learn whether or not the people to whom he is attracted are attracted to him. Also, if he finds out that these people are indifferent to him or reject him, he can find out which members of the groups are attractive to them. This knowledge may serve him in good stead. First of all he may compare himself to those people and evaluate the differences. He can ask himself the following crucial questions. In what respects are they more attractive? What do I have to do to make myself more attractive to these people? Is it worth the effort? He might also learn that persons he did not choose have in fact chosen him and find him attractive. He might think about this and ask himself why he has been indifferent to or even rejected the people that have chosen him. Perhaps some prejudice of his or some superficial characteristic of his admirers have kept them apart. On one occasion I administered a sociometric test to a class at California State University at Long Beach. There were ten male and ten female students in the class. They were asked to choose the members of the opposite sex whose company they would like on a dinner date. Each was to list five choices. Bill, one of the students made five choices but none of the young women he chose reciprocated. Each of the girls he did not choose picked Bill as their number one choice. In a subsequent interview Bill expressed the belief that girls were not attracted to him. He reported that he seldom dated and was so frequently rebuffed by girls that he avoided them, and was shocked to learn that five girls in the class had made him their first choice. Apparently because he had consistently approached women who rejected him, he had developed a low self-image of himself as a hetero-social being. When we discussed his choices we found out that he invariably selected shy and withdrawn girls to ask for dates and that it was this sort of girl he chose on the sociometric test. He was reluctant to approach the more outgoing girls because they were popular with the other boys and he was afraid that they would reject him. He did not accurately perceive the feelings of women toward him.

What happened to Bill is not unusual. Research has indicated that persons who make choices that are unreciprocated tend to have inaccurate perceptions of themselves. The choice process can relate people to those who will foster and facilitate their growth, to those who will support them at their present level, or to those who may actively reinforce the negative views they hold of themselves. Bill invariably selected girls who rejected him or were indifferent to him. The choices he made in real life reinforced the negative view he had of himself. Having learned this from the results of a sociometric test he could begin to relate to people who might facilitate his growth.

A formal test in which persons are asked to choose others based on some social criterion is called a *sociometric test.* It is a way of formally measuring attractions, repulsions, and indifference. It can best be administered to a group of people who know each other for at least a few weeks and are engaged in some joint activity or share a common interest. The test provides data relative to the position of each member of the group in relation to all of the others. The total number of choices received by an individual tells us something about his social status. The total number that he chooses tells us a good deal about the extent of his involvement with others. When an individual chooses another (A chooses B) and that other person chooses him (B chooses A) we have what is referred to as a *mutual choice.* An important element in diagnosing the attachment of an individual to a group as well as his social skill is the number of choices he makes that are reciprocated. In a sociometric test the individual is asked to choose associates for some activity or relationship. The basis of choice is called a *sociometric criterion.* Wherever practicable the criterion used should relate to an actual or potential situation or activity in which the subjects may become participants. Thus, one criterion for selection for intimate association would be close friendship. The question asked might be: whom would you choose as a member of your close friendship group, the group that you hang out with or associate with regularly? The criterion may involve intimate relationships of a general or specific nature. Examples of intimate general criteria are provided by the following "who would you like most as a friend? Who would you like most as a companion on a date?" A specific criterion is employed when we ask: Who would you most like as a member of your basketball team? The possibility must exist that the person making the choice will actually engage in the activity or relationship with the person he will choose.

The individual who receives a large number of choices, a number greater than one would be expected to receive by chance, is termed a *star.* The individual with no choices is considered *an isolate.* The individual with relatively few choices, that is fewer than one would be expected to receive by chance, is referred to as a *neglectee.* If negative choices are requested the individual receiving a preponderance of negative choices is called a *rejectee.* The frequency distribution of choices obtained in sociometric test data is comparable to the frequency distribution of wealth in a capitalist society. The total number of choices is limited, for some to be overchosen others must be underchosen.

For a sociometric test to provide meaningful data it is essential that the group members have sufficient opportunity to become acquainted. A sociometric test administered to a synthetic group would have little meaning unless the group had been in session on two or three occasions prior to taking the test. If an individual is a member of an ongoing group, one that meets once or twice weekly over an extended period, the director has an opportunity to validate the results of the sociometric test by observation. The sociometric test alone does not tell us how to improve or modify our relationships. It simply identifies deficiencies in relationships or helps the individual and the Socioanalist to identify them. The action methods, Psychodrama and Role Training provide clues to the possibilities for change.

The number of choices the individual makes, as we have noted, is an indication of his social expansiveness. There has been considerable research to support the conclusion that choices tend to be reciprocated. People tend to like people who like them. Furthermore, the more people a person chooses, the more likely he is to be chosen by others. His alienation and isolation are presumed to be reduced if other members of the group indicate by their choices that they are attracted to him or he indicates that he is attracted to others in the group. This is exceedingly important in socioanalysis because, if at the outset, a person makes very few choices, and, in the course of his participation makes more choices, we may assume that his social atom is expanding and that as he continues to find more people attractive more people will find him attractive. This should be reflected in future sociometric tests. As he continues to make more choices more people will choose him. An increase in the number of choices of members of the opposite sex may be considered indicative of an increase in hetero-social interest, where lack of such interest is a problem.

The sociometric test has several limitations. For one thing, it does not tell us why an individual is an isolate, nor does it tell us how to improve his inter-personal relationships. Furthermore, it is limited to one group at a time. If administered to members of a synthetic group, it does not tell us how the individual functions in his natural groups. It does give us the patterns of attractions and repulsions in the group and reveals changes in these patterns as they occur. If a person, in his first sociometric test appears to be an isolate or neglectee and in subsequent tests chooses more people and is chosen by more people we assume that he is increasing his involvement with others and probably improving in his ability to get along with them.

Before administering a sociometric test the director attempts to motivate the group to make meaningful selections by means of a *warm-up,* a ten minute talk on the importance of having the right associates in the activity that has been selected as the criterion for the test. The director emphasizes, in the typical warm-up, that we like some people for some things, and others for other things, and we may prefer to do many things alone. He points out that the sociometric test that he is about to administer will give everyone an opportunity to indicate which persons he would like as an associate in the contemplated activity. An example of a Sociometric Test administered to members of a group is presented in Chart I.

If the director considers it useful to measure patterns of rejection he adds the following instruction:

5. In Part 2 of this Questionaire please write down the names of those persons you would choose *not* to have with you in each of the three relationships indicated. Follow the same procedures you did in Part I.

He adds as Part 2:

The persons I would choose *not* to have as my closest friends are:

1.
2.
3.
4.
5.

The persons I would choose *not* to have as companions in recreational activities are:

1.
2.
3.
4.
5.

CHART I

A SOCIOMETRIC TEST — A*

Your Name______________________________Date__________________

In the spaces below will you please write down the names of those persons you would choose to have with you in each of the three relationships indicated. It is important that you conform to the following instructions:

1. Choose no more than five persons for each of the three relationships.
2. If you like you may choose a person for more than one relationship.
3. Write down only the first names of the persons you have chosen.
4. Choose from *all* of the members of our socioanalytic group including those present and those not with us today.

The persons I would choose to be my closest friends are:
1.
2.
3.
4.
5.

The persons I would choose as members of my work group are:
1.
2.
3.
4.
5.

The persons I would choose as companions in recreational activities are:
1.
2.
3.
4.

*When used in Socioanalysis with a group of fewer than forty persons the test should be administered *orally*. After the warm-up each person is given a 3" by 5" card, asked to write his own name in the right hand corner and under it to write the names of three persons he would choose as companions in recreational activities.

The persons I would choose *not* to have as members of my work group are:

1.
2.
3.
4.
5.

Unless the members of the group know each other for some time, or associate with each other in natural groups, I do not ordinarily administer Part 2 of the Sociometric Test. There are times however, when it is useful to determine patterns of rejection. The existence and extent of such patterns are considered most relevant when:

1. Deep cleavages are observed in the group.
2. Members of different ethnic or racial groups are participating in a sociodrama or other socioanalytic group intended to improve inter-ethnic relationships.
3. Several members of the group verbalize hostility to other members and/or to the director.
4. Several members of the group avoid participation or discussion.

In the Sociometric Test illustrated in Chart I, the subjects are asked to make five choices based on each of the three criteria indicated. This number of choices is recommended for a psychodrama group, role training group or other group with fifteen members or *less*. For larger groups three choices would be easier to work with. A common practice is to suggest unlimited choices. That is, instruct the subjects to choose as many or as few as they wish to choose. This approach has the advantage of more clearly identifying the stars and the isolates. However, even where an unlimited number of choices is encouraged, the data presented in sociograms, matrices or other social maps of large groups is usually based on three choices.

When a person indicates an attachment to another this represents, in a sense, a *reaching out* to that person. Unless the reaching out is in some way reciprocated the one indicating his attachment is likely to feel rejected. In this sense, sociometric choice represents an indication of attachment. Where it is reciprocated, mutual interests are likely to develop even if they did not exist prior to the test. In the instance described before, Bill chose five girls none of whom reciprocated his choice. The five he did not choose all chose him. On learning the results of the test, Bill became more aware of the five girls who chose him. They have at least one characteristic he must approve of, their excellent judgment in the choice of a man for a dinner date!

The ability of a person to accurately predict those persons in his group who will choose him is considered indicative of a high degree of empathy. To make such a prediction requires the individual to *take the role of each other person in the group,* place himself in the position of each, and act as he would act. A sociometric test designed to measure this ability is called a Social Perception Test. The first part of the test is a sociometric test such as the one illustrated in Chart I. The second part of this test is a Social Perception Questionnaire illustrated in Chart II. Note that in the latter test each member of the group is asked to predict which persons in the group would choose him applying each of the three criteria used in the sociometric test.

For best results it should be administered no less than thirty minutes after the sociometric test. The two tests considered together, the sociometric test and the social perception questionnaire, constitute a Social Perception Test. They provide us with an opportunity of comparing predictions with actual choices. The total number of choices a person receives provides us with an indication of his popularity in the group. The total number of choices he *predicts* he will receive is a measure of his self-confidence. Unpopular people find it difficult to accurately predict the choices of other people or to recognize how others feel about them. They do not seem to correctly identify emotional responses to themselves. Perhaps it is because of this difficulty that they do not establish close and friendly relationships.

CHART II

A SOCIAL PERCEPTION QUESTIONNAIRE — B*

Your Name________________________Date________________

In the spaces below will you please write down the names of those persons who would choose you for each of the three relationships indicated. It is important that you conform to the following instructions:

1. List no more than five persons who you believe would choose you for each of the three relationships.
2. If you believe a person would choose you for more than one of the three relationships list that person's name for each relationship you believe he or she would choose you.
3. Write down only the first name of each person you believe would choose you.
4. Consider *all* of the members of the group when deciding which ones would choose you. Include those present as well as those not with us today.

The persons who would choose me to be one of their closest friends are:

1.
2.
3.
4.
5.

The persons who would choose me to be a member of their work group are:

1.
2.
3.
4.
5.

The persons who would choose me to be a companion in recreational activities are:

1.
2.
3.
4.

*When used in Socioanalysis with a small group administer this test *orally* as suggested in footnote to Chart I.

There are many ways used to score a Social Perception Test. The one most commonly employed involves comparing the predictions with actual choices and scoring five points for each correct prediction. The maximum score would be 75.

If, in the Sociometric Test, negative choices were invited, the following instruction would be added to Chart II.

5. In Part 2 of this questionnaire please write down the names of those persons who would choose *not* to have you with them in each of the three relationships indicated. Follow the same procedures you did in Part I.

Part 2 would be added as follows:

The persons who would choose *not* to have me as one of their closest friends are:

1.
2.
3.
4.
5.

The persons who would choose *not* to have me as a member of their work group are:

1.
2.
3.
4.
5.

The persons who would choose *not* to have me as a companion in recreational activities are:

1.
2.
3.
4.
5.

Predictions of rejection are scored in the same way as predictions of choice, but they are listed separately. Accurate predictions, whether of choice or of rejection, provide some measure of empathy, the ability of the individual to place himself in the position of other persons. Incorrect predictions of rejection often tell us a great deal about the self-image of the individual making such predictions. Where an individual predicts that people will reject him, and in fact, they choose him, we may hypothesize that he tends to reject himself. Such clues should be explored by the socioanalist with the person making the incorrect predictions.

If additional measures of Social Perception are desired an individual may be asked to predict the choices of every member of the group. He may then compare his predictions with the actual choices made by each member. This type of social perception testing provides not only a general measure of the individual's ability to predict the choices of others but provides clues relating to his understanding of specific individuals. He may, for example, accurately predict the choices of men and incorrectly predict the choices of women. Or, he may accurately predict the choices of young people and have difficulty predicting the choices of older people. This sort of data can provide clues to difficulties in social relationships which may be examined in psychodrama or other socioanalytic groups. Choosing is a positive force by means of which people may spontaneously assert themselves. Predicting choices has the additional requirement that the person predicting place himself in the position of others and act as they would act.

The results of sociometric tests are usually presented in specifically designed charts called Matrix Tables. Referring to a Matrix table one can quickly ascertain the number of choices each person made, the number each received, and the number of mutual choices each person was involved in. Chart III is a Matrix Table prepared from the data provided by a sociometric test. The criterion question in the sociometric test was, "Which persons would you choose as your companion at dinner?" In this Matrix table the names of the subjects are listed. Where it is desired to keep the data confidential, symbols may be employed for each name. For example, instead of using the names, Arthur, George, Henry, etc. we might use A, B, C, D, and E to represent the six male subjects and U, V, W, X, Y, Z to represent the six female subjects. The advantage of coding our data in this way is that the Matrix information would not be meaningful to unauthorized persons who happened to see the Matrix Table.

The Matrix Table presented in Chart III was prepared in the following manner:

Chart III

MATRIX TABLE PRESENTING SOCIOMETRIC CHOICES

Number of Choices made: OS	SS	Name of Chooser	No.	PERSONS CHOSEN: 1	2	3	4	5	6	7	8	9	10	11	12
2	3	Arthur	1			(1)		(2)	(3)				(4)		5
2	3	George	2	4		(3)		2			(1)			5	
2	3	Henry	3	(3)	(2)			1					4	(5)	
2	3	James S.	4	1		2		(3)					(5)	(4)	
2	3	James T.	5	(5)			(1)		(4)				(3)	2	
0	5	John	6	(5)	4	3	1	(2)							
3	2	Elizabeth	7	3		4		2			(1)				(5)
2	3	Gladys	8	(2)	(3)					4				5	(1)
3	2	Joan	9	3		2		1			4		(5)		
2	3	Mary B.	10	(2)				(4)				(3)		(1)	(5)
3	2	Mary W.	11	4		(1)	(3)			5			(2)		
1	4	Roberta	12					5		(2)	(1)		(3)	4	
		No. of Choices Received	ss	5	2	4	2	4	2	3	3	1	3	3	3
			os	5	1	3	1	4	0	0	1	0	4	4	1
			Total	10	3	7	3	8	2	3	4	1	7	7	4
		No. of Mutual Choices	ss	3	1	2	1	3	2	1	2	1	3	1	3
			os	2	1	1	1	1	0	0	1	0	2	2	0
			Total	5	2	3	2	4	2	1	3	1	5	3	3

OS = Other Sex SS = Same Sex

1. Graph paper was used, large enough so that the number of squares, vertical and horizontal, was substantially higher than the number of persons who took the sociometric test which provided the data for the Matrix Table.

2. The choices made by male and female members of the group are on separate segments of the table. This was accomplished by using the upper left hand sector for male members and the lower left hand sector for females. A line was drawn between the two, making it easy to distinguish choices of members of the same sex from choices of members of the opposite sex. The tabulation of choices on the left hand side of the table also lists same sex and opposite sex choices separately.

3. The names of male and female subjects are listed in alphabetical order. If symbols were used instead of names, they would not have been assigned in this way as it would make the code easy to decipher. If we scrambled the symbols (assigning A to Henry, B to James, C to Arthur, etc.), we could make it difficult for an outsider to decipher it, even if he knew the names of the people involved.

4. Numbers corresponding to the position of each person in the vertical listing were placed across the top of the graph page, in consecutive order. If symbols had been used, the same symbols would have appeared vertically and horizontally, in the *identical order.*

5. *The number of choices made* is summarized in the vertical columns on the left side of the table. The *number of choices received* is summarized at the bottom of the table. In each instance, we have a breakdown by six.

6. Where there was a mutual choice (Arthur chose Henry, Henry chose Arthur) the choices were circled.

7. No weight was assigned to a choice because of the numerical position given it by the chooser. The first choice was given no greater weight than the third. Where it is considered important, however, choices may be weighted. I do not use weighting unless the criterion provides some indication that the first choice has a greater social value than the others. For example, if the criterion question were, "Which of the members of the opposite sex would you choose to accompany you on a date?," it would be useful to weight the choices. Note that in the Matrix Table presented in Chart III, although all choices were treated alike; the level of

choices (first, second, third, fourth, or fifth) was recorded. It is recommended that this practice be followed because level of choice may give the subjects some idea of relative importance attached to them.

Where there are between ten and thirty members of a group, an individual receiving between five and eight choices has received more than the average and is regarded as *"overchosen,"* Arthur, Henry, James T., Mary B., and Mary W. were in that category. A person receiving nine or more choices is regarded a *"star."* Arthur is the only one with nine choices and would be considered the star of the group. Since five members of the group were overchosen it follows that, as the total number of choices is limited, other members of the group must have been underchosen. In groups of this size persons receiving between two and four choices are regarded as *"underchosen,"* those receiving only one choice are referred to as *"neglectees"* and those who receive no choices are called *"isolates."* In this group, George, James S., John, Elizabeth, Gladys, and Roberta were underchosen and Joan was a neglectee. There were no isolates as every member received at least one choice. The Matrix Table thus enables us to quickly determine the sociometric status of each person in the group. We can tell at a glance which members of the group might require assistance or encouragement to increase their attractiveness to others.

One way of portraying the social structure of a group is presenting sociometric data in the form of a sociogram. A target diagram with concentric circles drawn equal distances apart except for the outer circle, is a sociogram which, in addition to depicting the structure, helps us to identify the position of each person in the group. Figure 1 represents a sociogram plotted from the data contained in the Matrix Table illustrated in Chart III. As is customary when target diagrams are employed, each person is assigned a symbol, usually a number or letter. The symbol for each male member is surrounded by a triangle and that for each female by a circle.

The Sociogram presented in Figure 1 was plotted in the following manner:

1. Male members were placed on the right side of the diagram and female members on the left side.
2. Persons with nine or more choices were placed in the inner

circle. In this instance there was only one star, Arthur, and we find his symbol, △1, in the inner circle on the right hand side.

Figure 1.

SOCIOGRAM
(Based on data contained in Chart III)

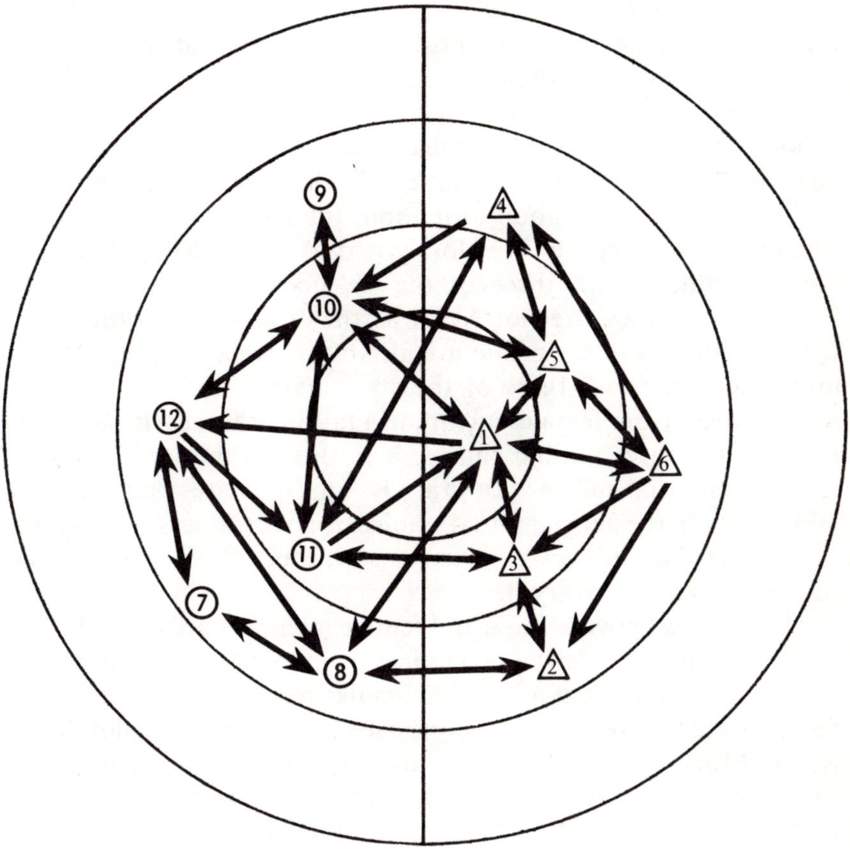

3. Symbols for the other overchosen members, those who received between five and eight choices, were placed in the second ring. We find symbols for Henry, △3 and James T., △5, on the right side and symbols for Mary B., ⑩, and Mary W., ⑪, on the left side.

4. Symbols for the underchosen were all placed in the third ring.

5. Solid lines were drawn between the chooser and person chosen. An arrow head was drawn adjacent to and in the direction of the symbol for the person chosen.

6. Mutual choices were indicated by double arrows. △1 ⟷ △3 Three persons involved in mutual choices with each other are called a triangle. Arthur, △1, James T., △5, and John, △6, constitute the only triangle in the group.

A sex cleavage exists in most every group and may be anticipated in a socioanalytic group. It is unusual for more than a third of male choices to go to females. Females are more likely to choose males. There is also a greater tendency for male choices to be reciprocated than there is for female choices. If we examine the sociogram we learn a good deal about the structure of the group. The male members are very closely tied to each other. Arthur has mutual choices with three of the six males. So has James T. Furthermore, they are not rivals as they chose each other. The female members of the group are also closely related. Mary B. has mutual choices with three of the six females. Mary W. received three choices from females including a mutual choice with Mary B. Roberta has three mutual choices with three of the six females including a mutual choice with Mary B. This indicates that the three females with the most mutual choices of the same sex were not rivals. The only neglectee, Joan, has a mutual choice with one of the female leaders, Mary B.

The choices between male and female members are limited. Two of the six females received no choices from males, while two others received only one each. One of the males received no choices from females and two received only one each. Two of the females, Mary B. and Mary W., received a total of eight choices from males, four each. Mary B. had mutual choices with Arthur and James T., two of the male leaders. Mary W. had mutual choices with Henry and James S., each of whom had mutuals with one of the two male leaders. We again see no sign of rivalry. The two female leaders do not appear to be choosing the same males and their choices are reciprocated.

We can conclude, based on our analysis, that the group is fairly cohesive and that subgroupings exist along sex lines with two subgroups across sex lines. There appears to be little sign of rivalry. So much for the structure of the group. If we are interested in increased hetero-social relationships we know where to concentrate our efforts. Two of the females, Elizabeth and Joan received no choices from males. John did not choose any females and received no choices from females. In a socioanalytic group we would try to find out why this was so and, if desired by the people concerned, take steps to modify their sociometric position.

The data presented in the Matrix Table and Sociogram we have discussed were obtained in a Sociometric test in which the subjects were limited to positive choices. When rejections are elicited each is represented on the Matrix Table by *a symbol in red.* In the sociogram rejections are indicated by drawing *a red arrow* from the symbol representing the rejector to the symbol representing the person rejected. Patterns of rejection as well as individual instances of rejection must be carefully interpreted in conjunction with all other available data. The fact of rejection may be attributable to characteristics of the rejector. He may be hostile to the person he is rejecting because of racial prejudice, class bias, or rivalry in some other context. The rejection may be a response to some undesirable attribute of the rejectee. The latter may be rude, unkempt, negativistic, or insensitive to the feelings of others. In some instances the rejection may be due to the nature of the relationship between the two people. They may be rivals for the affection of a member of the opposite sex, business or professional competitors, or persons on opposite sides of political, religious or other issues with great emotional commitments to their respective positions. Changes in patterns of rejection may be highly significant.

It should be noted that a sociogram, as well as the sociometric test on which it is based, indicates *desired associations,* not necessarily actual associations. The members of the group were asked "who would you choose as companions" not "who are your companions." The answer to the latter question and others involving actual associations might better be determined by other means. Furthermore, the sociogram is based on the criterion employed in a sociometric test and is, therefore, limited to that criterion. If the criterion question related to a specific task technical skills would influence choices. For example, if the question were, "Who would you choose as your doubles partner at tennis?," the best tennis player might be most chosen, even though he was deficient in social skills. The same would be true if the criterion question related to diverse activities as a partner or associate in dancing, bridge, a band, a work group, or other group in which the technical skills of the members was an important factor in achieving group goals.

Although the membership of a group may remain stable the status of an individual in the group may change over time. An index of sociometric choice is employed to represent the relative status of an individual in a group. The index figure is obtained by dividing the number of choices received by an individual by the number of persons in the group. The group we have previously analyzed, John received two choices. Since the total number of persons in the group was twelve, his Index of sociometric choice would be 1/6. If we desire a same sex choice index and an opposite sex choice index for each person John would have an ss index of 2/6 and an os index of 0/6. If the test is administered on successive occasions a rising index would indicate an increase in his sociometric status. The reason for computing the index in this way rather than simply stating the total number of choices received each time is that the total number of persons in the group may change. If the membership of the group doubled, for example, an increase in the number of choices received from 2 to 3 would represent a *loss* in sociometric status. Change in patterns of rejection are not ordinarily included in calculting the index of sociometric choice and are not considered a counter-balance to measures of social expansiveness.

To graphically represent the social status of an individual we use an Individual Sociogram. Figure 2 illustrates the Individual Sociogram of Arthur.

Same sex choices are indicated on the right side, opposite sex choices are on the left. The status of the people choosing Arthur is indicted by their position on the sociogram. The overchosen, Mary B., Mary W., Henry, and James T. are in the upper bracket. The underchosen are positioned in the second level and the neglectee in the third. Choices are indicated by arrows moving from the chooser to the person chosen, a double arrow representing the mutual choice. At the bottom of the sociogram is a summary of choices, same sex and opposite sex, and an *index of sociometric choice.*

Figure 2.

INDIVIDUAL SOCIOGRAM

Name—Arthur
Date__________ Group______

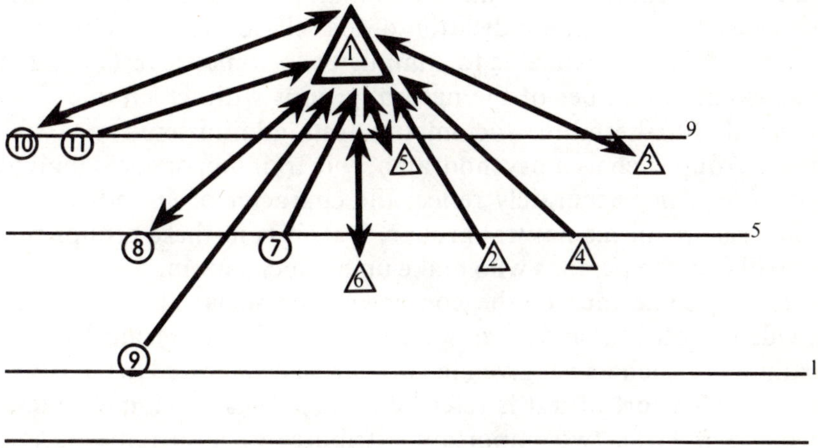

Choices	3 ss*	2 os*
Was Chosen by	5 ss	5 os
Mutual Choices	3 ss	2 os

*ss = same sex, os = opposite sex

$$\text{Sociometric choice status} = \frac{\text{number of choices received}}{\text{number in group}} = .84$$

Social Relationships Tests

While all sociometric techniques, in a sense, contribute to an appraisal of social skill, the sociometric test more directly measures the attractiveness of an individual to others in a group. The number of choices an individual receives gives some indication of his relative popularity or isolation. However, as we have noted, attributes other than social skill may influence choices where the criterion question invites the choosers to select associates in an activity requiring some specialized skill. The Social Perception Test provides us with a measure of empathy, particularly the ability to view one's self from the position of another person. . . . Also, the number of choices that an individual predicts he will receive provides us with some indication of his self-confidence. However, it is not always practicable to administer sociometric tests to all or a substantial number of the natural groups with which one is associated. Furthermore, sociometric tests administered in a synthetic group such as a psychodrama, role training, or socioanalytic group may not accurately reflect the character of an individual's relationships in his natural groups. Yet, it is in these groups that we will find the persons who make up his social atom.

To get some idea of the content of the social atom of an individual, both *real* and *ideal,* we use a Social Relationship Test. An example of such a test, given in two parts is illustrated in Charts IV and V. This sort of test is referred to as a "near sociometric test" because it lacks two important attributes of a sociometric test. First of all, the persons chosen by the subject need not be members of the same group. Thus, there is no possibility of structuring or restructuring a group based on the choices. Secondly, subjects must make choices realizing that it is very unlikely that any change in their social situation can come about as a result of the choices they express in a social relationship test. They are, in effect, being asked to make choices for their "ideal world" solely for the purpose of examining the possibilities.

As in a sociometric test each individual is asked to make choices based on general and specific criteria. In the social relationship test, however, he is asked to choose from people in the world at large for association with him in natural groups or activities in which he is involved. The number of choices he makes provides some measure of his expansiveness. Also, the total number he predicts will choose him affords some indication of self-confidence.

Before administering a social relationship test it is recommended that the director or tester deliver a ten minute warm up talk in which he expands on the printed instructions. We seek answers to the questions not merely responses to printed words. With respect to the first question an explanation would include such comments as, "You are asked to list names you would choose to be your closest friends. Include all persons you would like to associate with intimately whether or not they are members of your family, and regardless of their age or sex. All persons you care to closely associate with above all others should be listed." With respect to the second question relating to occupational roles an explanation in the warm up would include such comments as, "The question refers to work group, however, it includes any group in which you are a participant with an occupational emphasis. This would include a study group at school, a work group at your place of employment, or some other group organized around any occupational activity. List the names of those people you would most like to have work with you or study with you in the activity you have in mind."

CHART IV

A Social Relationship Questionnaire

Your Name______________________________ Date____________

In the spaces below will you please write down the names of those persons *you would choose to have with you* in each of the three relationships indicated. It is important that you conform to the following instructions:

1) Choose as many persons as you like for each of the three relationships.
2) If you like, you may choose a person for more than one relationship.
3) Please write out the full name of each person you have chosen.
4) Your choices will not be disclosed to anyone except the director.

The persons I would choose to be my closest friends are:

The persons I would choose as members of a work group of which I was a part are:

The persons I would choose as companions in recreational activities are:

CHART V

A Social Relationship Questionnaire

Your Name______________________________ Date____________

In the spaces below will you please write down the names of those persons *who would choose you* for each of the three relationships indicated. It is important that you conform to the following instructions:

1) List as many persons as you believe would choose you for each of the three relationships.
2) If you believe a person would choose you for more than one of the relationships list that person's name for each relationship you believe he or she would choose you.
3) Please write out the full name of each person you believe would choose you.
4) Your opinions as expressed in this questionnaire will not be disclosed to anyone except the director.

The persons who would choose me to be one of their closest friends are:

The persons who would choose me to be a member of their work groups are:

The persons who would choose me as a companion in recreational activities are:

An explanation of the third question would consist of the following: "Limit your choices to people you would like to have with you as companions in any recreational activities you engage in. Sports, social dancing, the theater, or any other social activity, that is of interest to you may be included. You may choose persons of either sex or any age."

If we are interested in patterns of rejection we follow the same procedures described in our discussions of Sociometric tests in the previous chapter. However, it is far more practicable to elicit rejections in a sociometric test given to an ongoing synthetic group than in a social relationship test. In the former, we have access to all of the members and have some basis for evaluating rejection, noting reciprocations, and arriving at explanations of the patterns. These possibilities are not as likely to be available to us when we give a social relationship test.

After having obtained the data, the director, tester, or subject himself should complete an initial sociogram portraying both the choices, predicted choices, and predicted mutual choices. The subject should then be asked (or ask himself) why he has chosen each of the people listed and the basis for each prediction he indicated on the test. With respect to each person listed the following questions should be answered:

1. What does he do?
2. How long have you known him?
3. Why did you choose him?
4. Why did he choose you?
5. Why did he not choose you? (Where reciprocation was not predicted)

The responses to the test and the answers to the above questions provide clues to the social atom of the individual as perceived by him. The social relationships desired by him become clear as does his perception of the relationships. If he is to become a member of a psychodrama or socioanalytic group, this test also provides clues as to which relationships may be profitably examined.

Role Tests

Sociometric and near sociometric tests provide measures of attractiveness and popularity. When a social perception dimension is added they provide measures of empathy and self-confidence. Obviously people who possess these qualities have social skill and the degree to which they possess them gives us an indication of relative social skill. However, these tests are administered to groups of which the subject is a member. The people evaluating are acquainted with him for some time and, presumably, have interacted with him. Even though their choices are related to a specific criterion, they choose him as a person, one possessing attributes other than those directly related to the criterion.

Tests have been designed which permit evaluation of behavior more specifically related to a criterion. These are called Role Tests. Individuals may be tested in occupational roles, family roles, and one or more community roles. Role Tests may be designed to measure ability to perform in a role as specific as that of insurance salesman. Studies have indicated that skill in occupational roles is highly correlated with skills in family roles and community roles. Furthermore, it was demonstrated that experience gained in playing one type of role results in improvement in the ability of the individual to play in all sorts of other roles. Skill in playing roles, role playing ability may, therefore, be regarded as a generalized social skill. Role training may be provided to assist individuals to increase this social skill, role playing ability. Although the role tests described in this book have not been validated and their reliability is not established, they have been used to measure change in Role Playing ability. Because inter-judge correlations of Role Test scores have been exceptionally high, they are used with a great deal of confidence.

A Role Test is preceded by a warm-up consisting of a three minute talk about the importance of doing and saying the things appropriate to one's role. The term "role" is explained as the part one has to play in a given situation. The remarks made by the director or tester in the warm-up are in general terms. When warming up for a test in an occupational role, he refers to the importance of saying and doing the right thing to get along with employers, foremen and fellow workers. Warming up for a test in a family role, he discusses the importance of getting along with members of one's family. *He does not mention the specific relationship involved in the test to be administered.*

A trained assistant, called an auxiliary ego, plays the part of the person who interacts with the subject in the test. Insofar as possible, he uses exactly the same words to provide stimuli to each subject and to respond to conversation initiated by the subject. As nearly as possible, the same tone of voice is also employed. Chart VI illustrates a role test in an occupational role.

CHART VI

ROLE TEST IN AN OCCUPATIONAL ROLE

The following instructions are given to the subject at the beginning of the test:

You are about to be given a Role Test. This is a test in which you will be asked to play a part different from one that you normally play. Your instructions are as follows: You are a dishwasher at a restaurant. After working in the restaurant for a month you were given an opportunity to work as a short order cook. After one week's trial the boss has called you in and asked to speak to you. Mr. Jones will play the part of the boss and you will play the part of the dishwasher.

A trained auxiliary ego or the director plays the role of the boss at this point. He asks the following stimulus questions* allowing response time after each question:

1. How did you make out as short order cook?
2. The counterman complains about the way you prepare egg dishes. How do you explain this?
3. The counterman complains that you fill the orders of waitresses before you fill his orders. Why do you?
4. I notice that you spend a great deal of time with the waitresses. What do you talk to them about?
5. This is a busy restaurant. We may have to replace you with an experienced short order cook. Why do you feel we should keep you on?

After responding to each of the above questions the subject is asked to reverse roles. He then plays the part of the boss and the auxiliary ego or the director plays the part of the dishwasher. In his role as dishwasher the trained auxiliary ego or the director asks the following, allowing response time after each question:

1. How am I doing as short order cook, boss?
2. Do you have any suggestions on how I can improve?
3. The job of short order cook is more responsible than that of dishwasher. How much more money will I get?
4. When things are slow do you think it is a good idea for me to ask suggestions from the waitresses?
5. What suggestions can you offer to help me improve?

*Stimulus Questions should be designed to require a response other than Yes or No.

In designing an appropriate test the sex, age, education, ethnicity, social class, and life experiences of the subjects should be taken into consideration. We may be interested in determining the relative familiarity of people with roles appropriate to members of sex, age, and class categories other than their own. However, we should be careful not to compare scores attained within one's category to scores attained on tests of roles outside one's category. When testing in occupational roles, we generally deal with middle class and lower class roles in the same test. This is accomplished by role reversal. For example, if a young man who is a member of the low socio-economic class is given a role test in the occupational role illustrated in Chart VI he is tested both in the lower class role of the dishwasher and the middle class role of boss.

Experience in the role might very well affect the performance. It is therefore important that the role test be given in a role which is as nearly as possible equally familiar to all of the persons taking the test. Restaurant roles such as dishwasher, waiter, bus boy, cashier and short order cook are ideal for role tests. Most everyone in our society has been in restaurants and observed people performing in these roles. We have also seen them in the movies, on television and on the stage and may also have read about them in books. Many lower class and middle class people have, on occasion, worked in part-time jobs in restaurants, either during school years or periods of unemployment. We are all more or less familiar with them. To a lesser extent the same may be said for a great many occupational roles. Most of us have some contact with people employed in retail enterprises, particularly those in sales roles. We also deal with people in service industries. Role tests in occupational roles should provide little difficulty if the focus is on a role commonly encountered in our society. Moreover, the role test does not measure relative skills in performing the tasks. It is our belief that the stimuli we use in the role tests elicit social skill. We do not ask, in the test illustrated in Chart VI, that the subject try his hand at cooking eggs. We provide him with stimuli calculated to get at *his ability to relate to his employer.* In a role reversal we have him in the role of employer and provide stimuli that requires him *to relate to an employee.* He performs in both the dominant and the subordinate roles and is required to react to stimuli posing problems in social relationships. He may have encountered similar problems in other occupational or family roles. Therefore, general experience in life situations may be of help to him. If we place him in a Role Training Program in which he is exposed to experiences in occupational, family and community roles, we can provide him with opportunities to learn how to cope with problems arising in social interaction with others in dominant and subordinate roles. He should score higher on Role Tests given subsequent to role training experiences.

Chart VII illustrates a role test in a family role. The father-son relationship tested would be appropriate with both lower and middle class boys, however, the test may be modified to accommodate to ethnic or regional cultures. While lack of experience may, in some cases, seriously affect test scores in occupational roles, virtually every young male has had some experience in father-son relationships. Even where parents are divorced or a boy is born out-of-wedlock, there is almost always some interaction with a substitute father. Furthermore, while a person with no experience in a role may be unaware of or indifferent to enactments of the role in media presentations, the same is not likely with respect to family roles. So many books, articles, movies and TV shows deal with family roles on all levels that it is virtually impossible for anyone in our society not to be aware of the cultural definitions of such roles as son, father, daughter, mother, husband and wife in every social class, and at every age level. The role test in family roles, then, measures something far more than quantitative experience in a role. Responses to the test stimuli provide clues to such matters as self-image, dependency, feelings of rejection, tendencies toward rebellion, handling of frustrations, and relationships with authority figures in general. In the role of father the young person may also provide clues relative to his perception of his father and the reaction of his father to his behavior. Thus, the role test in family roles provides us not only with a test score which might help us evaluate relative social skill but also with clues to problems in family relationships which may profitably be explored in psychodramatic or socioanalytic sessions.

CHART VII

ROLE TEST IN A FAMILY ROLE

The following instructions are given to a subject at the beginning of the test:

You are about to be given a Role Test. This is a test in which you will be asked to play a part different from one that you normally play. Your instructions are as follows: You are a seventeen year old boy attending a high school. Your grades have not been good and you want to drop out of school in your junior year and look for a job. Your father wants you to stay in school until you graduate. He has called you in to speak to you about it. Mr. Jones will play the part of the father, and you will play the part of Bill, the son.

A trained auxiliary ego or the director plays the role of father at this point. He asks the following stimulus questions allowing response time after each question:

1. I hear you are planning to quit school, Bill. Why?
2. Your grades have been poor. Why do you spend so much time running around?
3. You seem to be going out a lot with Mabel. What do you see in her?
4. If you quit school now, what kind of job do you expect to get?
5. What can I do to get you to stay in school until you graduate?

After responding to each of the above questions, the subject is asked to reverse roles. He then plays the part of the father, and the auxiliary ego or the director plays the part of the son. In the role of son, the trained auxiliary ego or the director asks the following, allowing response time after each question:

1. I have already decided to quit school and get a job, dad. Why are you trying to change my mind?
2. The stuff they teach in high school doesn't interest me. Why don't they teach interesting subjects?
3. I'd like to have enough money to buy good clothes, go out on dates, and have fun. How can I get enough money to do all this if I stay in school?
4. All the fellows I go out with have cars. Why don't you buy me a car?
5. What can you do to help me get a job now that I have decided to quit school?

Role tests in community roles perform substantially different functions than do the occupational or family role tests. In general, they are not as likely to give evidence of as much emotional involvement. More likely they measure relative involvement in or isolation from social group life in the community. Here we are likely to find tht low scores reflect lack of experience in the role. Many people in our society spend virtually all of their lives within the confines of a neighborhood and their participation in group life is limited entirely to interaction with people like themselves. Chart VIII illustrates a role test in a community role, the role of restaurant owner. Most young people have not had any experience in the role and lower class young people are not likely to have had experience as credit customers. The media provide little exposure to these roles. What then does this role test measure? In our view it provides us with a measure of general social skill. An individual that has had considerable experience interacting with people in many occupations and roles will manage to improvise effectively. One who has lived in relative isolation will have little experience on which to base his responses. Role tests may be given in community roles with which the subjects are familiar, such as the roles of teachers, policeman, clergyman, storekeeper, landlord, etc. The results of such tests provide measures of relative social skill, experience in the roles, and the quality of relationships in general. We can get some idea as to whether or not the subject has friendly relationships with people he deals with and also which relationships he finds troublesome. These can later be explored in psychodramatic or socioanalytic groups.

CHART VIII

ROLE TEST IN A COMMUNITY ROLE

The following instructions are given to a subject at the beginning of the test:

You are about to be given a Role Test. This is a test in which you will be asked to play a part different from one that you normally play. Your instructions are as follows: You are Mr. Smith, the owner of a small restaurant and soda fountain. Jim, a young man that has been a customer of yours for a long time, has asked you to extend him credit for the meal he has just ordered. He already owes you ten dollars, and you don't want to extend him any more credit. Mr. Jones will play the part of Jim, and you will play the part of Mr. Smith, the restaurant owner.

A trained auxiliary ego or the director plays the role of Jim at this point. He asks the following Stimulus Questions* allowing response time after each question:

1. I don't have any money with me today, Mr. Smith. What kind of credit arrangements will you make?
2. You've known me a long time. Why don't you trust me?
3. I expect to get a job by next week, and I'll pay you back then. Don't you believe me?
4. My friends and I have been eating here for a long time. Why do you want us to go elsewhere?
5. Do you have any suggestions that would help me out for the time being?

After responding to each of the above questions, the subject is asked to reverse roles. He then plays the part of Jim, and the auxiliary ego or the director plays the part of the restaurant owner, Mr. Smith. In the role of the restaurant owner, the trained auxiliary ego or the director asks the following, allowing response time after each questions:

1. You've owed me ten dollars for more than a month, Jim. What arrangements are you making to pay it?
2. You know I like you, Jim. Why would I give you credit if I didn't like you?
3. I have to set some limit on the amount of credit I give a fellow. How else can I pay my bills?
4. Your friends have a lot of money. Why don't you borrow some from them?
5. If I give you credit this time, what arrangements will you make to pay it back?

*Stimulus Questions should be designed to require a response other than Yes or No.

It is recommended that each person who participates in a psychodramatic, role training or socioanalytic group be given role tests in occupational, family and at least one community role prior to entering into the group experience. These tests if repeated every five sessions, or at longer intervals, will provide some measure of change. Results obtained in Role Training Programs indicate that significant change in Role Playing ability occurred in the course of fifteen role training sessions. Participation in sessions emphasizing one type of role, occupational roles for example, resulted in improvement in the ability to perform in family and community roles.

Chart IX presents a rating sheet used in scoring Role Tests. The tests are scored on the twenty variables listed on the rating sheet. One way of scoring the test is to allot five points for Superior, four points for Excellent, three points for Very Satisfactory, two points for Satisfactory, and one point for Unsatisfactory. Although these tests have not been validated and their reliability has not been established, they provide a useful measure of change in role playing ability. Changes in role test scores achieved in the course of a Role Training Program have been highly correlated with changes in behavior observed in natural groups. Inter-judge correlations of scores on Role Tests have been exceptionally high. We therefore, recommend using these role tests with confidence.

Spontaneity Tests

Role tests, such as the ones we have just described, provide us with some idea of relative spontaneity. The person being tested is presented with stimuli in fairly rapid succession. Failing to respond or responding in a way that is deemed incorrect or incomplete adversely affects his score on the test. He must, if he is to score high, *provide an adequate response*. Furthermore, if he tends to be hesitant, evasive, or repetitious his score is also lowered. Thus, his response must be swift as well as adequate if he is to score high on a role test. For these reasons we consider Role Training as an effective method of increasing spontaneity.

Tests have been designed which provide more direct measures of spontaneity. In a spontaneity test the subject is placed in a situation that he may have found himself in on many previous occasions and faced with stimuli to which he and others customarily respond in a particular manner. However, the situation defined in

Chart IX

RATING SHEET FOR ROLE TEST

NAME OF RATER ______________ NAME OF SUBJECT ______________

Each of the twenty items listed below reflects possible deficiencies in Role Enactment. Will you please score each subject on each item. A suggested guide for scoring is :

No defect noted - Superior (Sup) -- 5
One defect " - Excellent (Exc) - 4
Two defects " - Very Sat. (VS) -- 3
Three defects noted - Sat. -- 2
More than three " - Unsat. - 1

POSSIBLE DEFICIENCY	SUP	EXC	VS	SAT	UNSAT	SCORE
1. Failure to Respond to Other						
2. Incorrect Response						
3. Incomplete Response						
4. Display of Impatience						
5. Display of Indifference						
6. Display of Impoliteness						
7. Hesitancy						
8. Evasiveness						
9. Repetitious Responses						
10. Display of Self-Consciousness						
11. Inflexibility (Failure to adapt to other)						
12. Improper attempts to Dominate (dictate)						
13. Excess of Criticism						
14. Display of Hostility						
15. Display of Irritability						
16. Excess of Excitability						
17. Excess of Fear						
18. Excess of Humility						
19. Lack of Feeling						
20. Falling out of Role						
			TOTAL SCORE			

a Spontaneity Test in some way inhibits the use of the customary solution. If the subject is to solve the problem presented he must come up with a novel solution. The measure of spontaneity generally employed is the length of time it trakes the individual to arrive at a novel solution that is, at the same time, adequate. Persons taking spontaneity tests tend at first to respond to the problem in ways that have been successful for them in the past. Most people persist in their attempts to solve the problem in this way for some time. However, after several unsuccessful attempts a subject begins to realize that his customary solution will not work and offers another with novelty and in many instances adequacy. Persons high in spontaneity move toward new solutions more rapidly than those low in spontaneity.

Chart X illustrates a Spontaneity Test. Before giving the test the director or tester talks for about three minutes on the importance of the goal that is the subject of the test. He does so in general terms without any mention of means to be used. For example, in the test illustrated in Chart X, in his warm-up talk the director goes into the need for punctuality without any mention of transportation facilities available.

CHART X
A TEST OF SPONTANEITY

Instructions to Subject

Everyone knows that it is important to get to work on time. Many people lose their jobs because of frequent tardiness. As a matter of fact, the reason most frequently given by employers for discharging workers is failure to report to work on time. In the test you are about to take we are assuming that you want to keep your job and that you are aware of the need to be punctual.

You are about to take a test in which you are asked to solve a problem which you have solved many times. These are your instructions. It is 7:30 A.M. You are on a corner waiting for a bus to take you to work. The bus generally gets there at 7:30 and gets you to your place of work by 8:00, the time that you are required to start work. You got here at 7:20 and have been waiting about ten minutes. It is now 7:30, the bus has not yet arrived. When I drop this pencil on the floor that means the bus has arrived here. (The director moves off and observes the subject. *He at no time drops the pencil signalling the arrival of the bus.)*

The amount of the time it takes the subject to move from the bus stop to an adequate and novel solution of the problems is his test score. If it takes him five minutes to move toward a solution, his score is ten minutes. If he does not move towards an adequate and novel solution his score is zero. *Note that at no time in the warm-up talk is there any mention of the means of transportation.* In the test instructions the customary mode of transportation (what must be the customary solution) is defined as a bus. That solution is not available because of the action of the tester. The subject must therefore find an alternative solution, in this instance an alternative means of getting to work.

What constitutes an adequate and novel solution?

1. The subject may seek another form of transportation. If he hails a taxi this would be regarded as an adequate and novel solution. Attempting to hitch a ride would also be regarded as an adequate and novel solution.

2. Calling a friend to provide a ride to work might also constitute a novel solution. Its adequacy would depend on the time required. The tester should ask, "How long will it take him to get here?"

3. Calling and explaining the situation to his employer. This solution would be acceptable. However, it indicates a relatively low level of spontaneity. When this sort of solution is offered the director should give the subject another spontaneity test in a few days, if possible.

4. Going to another location to take another bus or another form of transportation would be acceptable. It would also indicate a low level of spontaneity that required further investigation.

5. Giving up and going home would neither be novel or adequate. It would reflect pathological spontaneity. Obtaining help with the transportation problems or selecting a reasonable alternative form of transportation would be considered both novel and adequate.

It has been the experience of persons employing this test that at the beginning of a series of role training or psychodramatic sessions some people score poorly on spontaneity tests. This may reflect a low level of spontaneity in real life. After about ten sessions, their spontaneity level improves significantly. When taking a spontaneity test, they seek new solutions to problems almost immeditely after the old ones fail to produce the desired results. It is assumed that they are also moving more rapidly toward solution of problems arising in their occupational and family roles. Since the focus of Psychodrama and Role Training is on alternative solutions to problems, these may be considered methods to be used where it is desired to increase spontaneity. The spontaneity test provides some measure of the success attained in such programs.

Psychodramatic Projective Tests

Psychologists have invented many projective tests intended to provide an understanding of the personality of an individual including his characteristic ways of behaving, his motivations and the ways in which he sees the world. Among the best known are Sentence Completion Tests, The House Tree Person Tests, the Rorschach Inkblot Test, and the Thematic Apperception Test. In each of these the subject is required to respond verbally, orally or in writing, to unclear incomplete or ambiguous stimuli. The way in which he responds provides clues based upon which an expert may draw conclusions relative to the personality structure of the subject. In none of these is the subject encouraged to interpret the test results. In fact, he is seldom permitted to see them. A psychodrama has also been used as a projective technique particularly by those interested in determining characteristic ways of behaving and perceiving. Psychodramatic Projective Tests are recommended when Role Tests, Spontaneity Tests, or other measures indicate a high degree of social skill and Social Relationship Tests, Sociometric Tests, or information supplied by the subject indicated that he is an isolate or neglectee. Psychodramatic Projective Tests would provide us with clues as to which characteristic patterns of behavior of the subject was influencing others to ignore or reject him. The assumption is that his characteristic behavior patterns are unattractive to others. If we can find out what they are before the subject enters a Psychodramatic or Socioanalytic group, we can provide the subject with some understanding of the problems. He may then examine these behavior patterns and experiment with alternatives in the course of socioanalytic or psychodramatic sessions.

A Psychodrama Projective Test is introduced by a warm-up talk lasting about three minutes. In the course of the warm-up a situation is defined for the subject in unclear, incomplete and ambiguous terms so that he feels that he may express himself in his characteristic way, as free from inhibitions as possible. Three projective tests discussed in this chapter are the Dyad Test, the Triad Test, and the Future Projection Test. There are many variations of each. A Dyad Test is illustrated in Chart XI. A warm-up talk preceding this test would be:

"You will have an opportunity, in the test you are about to take, to examine a relationship with some person you have known in the past or are presently dealing with. This test is not one in which questions are asked and you supply written or oral answers. Rather, you will have an opportunity to act out a scene from real life, one in which you are involved with another person. After you have acted it out we can have a better idea of your relationship. Choose a relationship that is of some importance to you and scene that you consider typical."

CHART XI

THE DYAD TEST
(Time five minutes)

Instructions to Subject:

You are on stage with a person that you are having or have had a relationship with. Describe a situation typical of the relationship. Tell us who the person is, when and where the situation occurred and what it involved. You may choose any person in any situation. *Act out the situation playing both parts.* When you are on the right side of me you are yourself, when on the left side of me you are the other person.

The relationship to other may be scored on a continuum from: Very Friendly, Friendly, Indifferent, Hostile, Very Hostile

The communication with other may be scored on a continuum from: Very much, Much, None, Little, Very Little.

The response to director as evidenced by the action may be scored as:

Very Cooperative, Cooperative, Indifferent, Uncooperative, Very Uncooperative.

After the warm-up the subject is permitted to ask a question or two, if he so wishes. Answers are limited to the same sort of information given in the warm-up. The instructions are then given to the subject and five minutes allowed for action. Each variable on the test is scored on a continuum from 50 to 1. For example, 15 is scored for very friendly, 4 friendly, 3 indifferent, 2 hostile, 1 very hostile. The range on this test is therefore from a possible low of 3 to a maximum score of 15. The director or tester rates the subject on the test and the subject is given a rating sheet on which he may rate himself. The ratings are then discussed with him.

An illustration of this Triad Test is presented in Chart XII. The warm-up talk is similar to the one used for the Dyad Test and the instructions are given in much the same manner. Approximately five minutes are allowed for the test, however, if the subject appears to be involved in a meaningful interaction he is permitted to complete the scene, even if it takes three or four minutes more. The scoring of the test is on a continuum from 5 to 1 for each variable with a range of 6 to 30. After the subject rates himself the scores are discussed with him.

CHART XII

THE TRIAD TEST

Instructions to Subject: You are on stage with two persons both of whom you are having or have had a relationship with. Describe a situation typical of the relationships. Tell us who the persons are, when and where the situation occurred and what it involved. Act out the situation playing all three parts. When you are on the right side of me you are one of the persons, when on the left side of me the other and when directly in front of me you are yourself.

Scoring where subject chose one person of each sex.
The relationship to member of same sex may be described as: Very Friendly, Friendly, Indifferent, Hostile, Very Hostile.

The relationship to member of opposite sex may be described as: Very Friendly, Friendly, Indifferent, Hostile, Very Hostile.

Communication to member of the same sex may be described as: Very Much, Much, None, Little, Very Little.

Communication to member of opposite sex may be described as: Very Much, Much, None, Little, Very Little.

Relationship between two persons is depicted as: Very Friendly, Friendly, Indifferent, Hostile, Very Hostile.

The subject portrays himself in the situation as: Very Satisfied, Satisfied, Indifferent, Dissatisfied, Very Dissatisfied.

Where subject chose two persons of same sex, relationship between the two persons is depicted as: Very Friendly, Friendly, Indifferent, Hostile, Very Hostile.

The subject portrays himself in the situation as: Very Satisfied, Satisfied, Indifferent, Dissatisfied, Very Dissatisfied.

The relationship to the other persons was depicted as:

Friendly to both	Friendly to one indifferent to other	Indifferent to both	Hostile to one indifferent to other	Hostile to both

These tests may be varied to suit the requirements of the subject. For example, in the Dyad Test the subject may be asked to enact a scene involving a typical relationship with a member of the opposite sex, same sex, older person, younger person, policeman, teacher, or any other considered significant by the director or the subject. In the Triad Test the subject may be asked to enact a typical relationship with two persons of the same sex, of the opposite sex, one of each sex, two older persons, younger persons, two members of another ethnic or racial group, or two persons with any other characteristic considered relevant by either the director or the subject. While neither of these tests has been validated, each provides data which may be further investigated by the director and by the subject.

A Future Projection Test

A Future Projection Test may be administered to a subject by a director or tester in much the same manner as the two tests previously discussed. When given to the members of a psychodrama or socioanalytic group it is generally administered with all of the members present. Chart XIII illustrates a future projection test administered to a protagonist at the end of a psychodrama session. It is employed, in this sort of a situation, to afford the protagonist an opportunity to define his goals and aspirations in action. When so used it is evaluated by the director, the group, and the protagonist in relation to the total presentation. It is a descriptive instrument and not a quantitative one. If, for example, the protagonist has enacted scenes portraying an unhappy marital situation, and, in his future projection he places himself in a scene with his wife in a happy relationship, this projection might be considered evidence of a desire for reconciliation. On the other hand, if, after the same original enactment, his future projection shows him happily married to another woman, this might be interpreted as indicative of the desire for a divorce. In some instances, after portraying an unsatisfactory marital relationship the protagonist in his future projection enacts an unsatisfactory marital relationship with his next "wife." This may indicate a growing awareness by the protagonist that some characteristic of his influences the marital relationship adversely.

CHART XIII

A FUTURE PROJECTION TEST

This test is generally administered to a person at the end of the action portion of a Psychodrama in which he is the protagonist.

Instructions to Protagonist: In the course of this evening's presentation you have explored many of your relationships. We have had an opportunity to examine your relationships with people in the past and with some of those in which you are presently involved. It might be useful to us to attempt to look into the future. Let us assume that five years have elapsed. It is now July 10th, 1981. It is 7:00 P.M. Set the stage to show us where you are, what you are doing, and who, if anyone, is with you.

The Action—The Director furnishes auxiliary egos to play the roles required by the protagonist and allows time for interaction. Role reversals are employed so that the protagonist may perform in the role of each person he has placed on the stage. His relationships with each person are explored, and such psychodramatic techniques as the Double, Soliloquy, and Self-Presentation are employed.

If it is desired to examine aspirations the instructions are modified by substituting the following for the last sentence:

"Set the stage to show us *where you would like to be, what you would like to be doing,* and *who, if anyone, you would like to have with you.*"

Future projection tests may be administered and scored in much the same way as are dyad and triad tests. A warm-up talk lasting about three minutes precedes each test. In the warm-up talk the director or tester emphasizes the importance of the future and encourages the subject to think ahead taking into consideration what he would like to accomplish in life, and what the possibilities are for achieving his objectives. Remarks are made in general terms.

After the warm-up talk the following instructions are given: "You will now have an opportunity to examine your relationships with other people at some future time of your choosing. When do you feel that some important change will come into your life?" (The subject is given the opportunity to respond. If he avoids a direct response by saying, "I have no idea," or something to that effect, the director should modify the question as follows:) "When would you like to have an important change come into your life?" Let us assume that the subject replies, "In two years." The director then would say, "Let us assume that two years have elapsed. It is now April 4, 1980. It is 9:00 P.M. Set the stage to show us where you are, what you are doing, and who, if anyone, is with you."

The action then proceeds in exactly the same way as it does in the Triad Test, with the protagonist playing each role as required. Scoring may be based on any criteria selected by the tester and/or the subject. Criteria most frequently scored are friendliness, communication, relative satisfaction, level of aspiration, and optimism. Ratings would be made as in the Triad Test as follows:

The relationship to other persons may be described as: Very Friendly, Friendly, Indifferent, Hostile, Very Hostile, (Breakdowns may be made by sex, age, race, etc.

Communication to other persons may be described as: Very Much, Much, None, Little, Very Little.

The subject portrays himself in the situation as: Very Satisfied, Satisfied, Indifferent, Dissatisfied, Very Dissatisfied.

The subject's level of aspiration as: Very High, High, Average, Low, Very Low.

The subject's view of the future may be described as: Very Optimistic, Optimistic, Indifferent, Pessimistic, Very Pessimistic.

Both the director and the subject score the test in the same way as they do the Triad Test. The results are then discussed with the subject.

Summary

Changes in sociometric status, social perception, social skill, and spontaneity significantly influence the relationships people have with each other. They also play a part in the creation or solution of problems arising out of social relationships. For these reasons the development and use of evaluative measures of change in these characteristics are of continuing interest in Socioanalysis. Measures most frequently employed are: Sociometric Tests, Social Perceptions Tests, Role Tests, Spontaneity Tests, and Psychodrama projection tests.

Sociometric tests provide us with data useful in analyzing the structure of a group and in describing the social relationship each individual member bears to every other member of the group. What we learn about cliques and cleavages in the group is of use in reorganizing and restructuring the group so that it may better perform its functions. Knowledge of existing relationships and changing relationships, particularly the expansion of relationships and the reduction in the extent of isolation, is useful in evaluating the effect of group participation on the members. Awareness of one's sociometric relationships to others in a group, whether a synthetic or natural group, is of value in that one can better determine his impact on others. As one learns which individuals are attracted to him and which reject him, he is better able to evaluate his own behavior with respect to others. He might, for example, come to understand what aspects of his personality or his behavior cause others to reject him. The net result may be that he will either elect to associate with people who are compatible to him (those who reciprocate his choices). Or, he might attempt to modify his behavior patterns which others find objectionable. Either action on his part should reduce his isolation and improve his sociometric position. We are convinced that this sort of learning takes place in such synthetic groups as psychodrama groups, role training groups, and other socioanalytic groups. Furthermore, the learning results in the development of behavior patterns which influence sociometric position in such natural groups as the family, school, occupational and community groups.

Social perception tests provide us with a measure of empathy, the ability of an individual to take the role of other persons.

Increase in this ability must of necessity influence the expansion of social relationships. Also, the experience of making choices in the course of sociometric and social perception tests in itself contributes to an understanding of the basis of such choices. The individual may come to realize, for example, that in choosing A, B and C he is not rejecting D and E. He is simply making choices most compatible with *his needs* at the moment. As he learns to take the role other, he becomes less likely to feel rejected when others fail to choose him. He will be more likely to relate their selections to *their* needs. Thus, with an increase in empathy, should come a lessening of self-centeredness, and an awareness of the needs of others.

Social relationships tests taken at the beginning of a socioanalytic experience provide data relative to the social expansiveness of the individual, the extent of his social atom, as he sees it. Retesting at intervals in the course of socioanalysis helps us to observe changes in relationships in natural groups as perceived by the subject and to evaluate these changes. In so doing, we take into consideration the results of other tests, the observations of the socioanalist, members of the synthetic group with which he has been involved, and the subject himself.

Role tests at the outset of socioanalysis tell us a great deal about the extent to which an individual has learned the social roles and the ways he performs in these roles. A comparison of scores on Role Tests after a period of Socioanalysis, with those obtained at the outset provides us with a measure of the effectiveness of the socioanalytic experience. Similarly, a comparison of spontaneity tests administered before and after a period of socioanalysis helps us to evaluate changes in spontaneity. Changes in scores on Psychodramatic Projective Tests administered at regular intervals in the course of Socioanalysis provide evidence of changes in characteristic behavioral and attitudinal patterns.

No one of these tests is an accurate device for measuring change in relationship patterns, behavior patterns, or personality. With the exception of the Sociometric Tests, none of them have been validated. Nevertheless, improvement on any of the tests indicates some improvement in social skill. The ways in which Sociometric measures are applied in Socioanalysis are described in the next chapter.

Chapter 4

THE SOCIOANALYTIC PROCESS APPLIED

"Would The Gift The Genie Gie Us To See Ourselves As Others See Us." Robert Burns

There is no reason, in my view, that you the reader, cannot successfully accomplish an analysis of your social relationships in the present as well as in the past. Since, in this chapter, I am recommending that you embark on a self-analysis, I am taking the liberty of addressing myself directly to you. If you have read and understood the materials presented in the preceding pages of this book you are probably capable of applying them to a self-analysis. Such an analysis can and should provide you with an increased understanding of others and of yourself. It should also help you deal successfully with such problems as loneliness, helplessness, humiliation, betrayal, and abuse, that are so common in our society. If you feel the need for help with your self-analysis, you may consult a Socioanalist.

How does one begin a self-analysis? I would suggest that you first learn how to use the tools and then start using them. You have nothing to lose but the effort. You have spontaneity and self-direction to gain. Since you are to become your own Socioanalist, you must learn how to apply Sociometry to the study of relationships. This involves learning which people tend to choose each other and why they make the choices that they do. As a corollary you will also learn the choices made by people you like and the reasons for those choices. It is essential that you begin by studying the relationships of others because you may be too emotionally involved in your own to view them with detachment.

A good way to start would be to prepare a simple sociometric test for children and administer it to a small group, no more than fifteen, between the ages of eleven and fourteen. You can probably gain access to such a group at a school. Explain to the teacher that you are studying sociometry and would like to administer a sociometric test. Offer to make the results available to the teacher. Two criteria should be used, one involving an occupational relationship, the other a personal relationship.

An example of a suitable occupational criterion question would be: Who would you like to have study with you? An example of a suitable personal criterion question would be: Who would you like with you when you go on a vacation? After administering the test, arrange to interview the children one at a time. Since the interviews would have to be on a voluntary basis it may be advisable to offer some inducement. Refreshments are usually enough but if necessary some payment, say fifty cents an interview may be necessary. Ten interviews would be enough to satisfy your training needs. The following questions should be asked of each subject. Why did you choose Jim? (Same question for each person chosen.) Why did you not choose Bill? (Same question for each person *not* chosen.)

Having obtained the data, the next step is to prepare a Matrix and then a sociogram. The chapter on sociometry provides sufficient instructions for preparing both. Now that you have the sociogram, you can very easily identify the overchosen, the underchosen, and the isolates. Remember that sociometry operates in much the same way as the capitalist system. For some to be rich in the number of choices received, the overchosen, others must be deprived, the underchosen. You have the reasons for the choices made as well as for choices withheld. It should not take you long to figure out why some of the subjects are greatly underchosen or isolates. These young people are likely to be the ones who experience loneliness, feelings of being helpless and unwanted. Using such information a teacher may provide a great service to these young people. One of the things the teacher can do to improve the situation for the isolate is to assign joint tasks involving the isolate and an overchosen member of the class. His isolation will be greatly reduced. In addition to this worthwhile service to others, however, you will have gained in two respects. You will have learned something about analyzing social relationships and you also will have gotten some ideas as to why young people are isolated by their peers. This knowledge should prepare you for the next step which is to administer a Sociometric Test to a heterosexual group of ten to twenty persons eighteen to twenty-two years of age. You may gain access to such a group in a college classroom, if you are able to arrange it. Other possibilities are young people's groups at churches, or social clubs. While it is desirable to study sociometric choices of young children and young adults, it is not essential. You can learn a great deal by studying any group to which you have access. Just do the best you can to find out the reasons people give for choosing others and withholding their choices.

The occupational criterion question for the college age group would be mluch the same as the one used for the younger people. Who would you like to include in your study group? Who would you like to have with you in an occupational (specify) activity. The personal criterion question might be: Who would you choose as a close friend? Or, who would you choose to spend a summer vacation with?

In warming up the group for this "near" sociometric test, you might point out that, although the choice of friends, or companions on summer vacations will not be determined by the test, everyone taking the test will have an opportunity to consider for himself what sort of person he would prefer as a close friend and also what sort of person he would like to have as a companion for a substantial period.

After the test you should, if possible, arrange to interview as many members of the group as you can. Ask each subject, with respect to each choice made, why he made the choice, and with respect to each choice withheld, why he did not choose that person. When you prepare your matrix be sure to differentiate same sex choices from other sex choices and carefully note the mutual choices in each category. Then make a sociogram of the group. Having organized your data, you are now ready to analyze it. Remember that your primary interest is not in the structure of the group. You are seeking to determine the social status of each member and the reasons for that status.

The data provided by each person in your Sociometric study should then be recorded on a *Socioanalysis Test Card,* a 6 x 9 card with the names of all of the subjects listed on it. The name of the subject whose choices are analyzed is placed at the top of the card. You indicate his choices by preceding the name of the person chosen with an asterisk. List the principal reason for each choice, and also for each choice withheld. It might facilitate matters if you had the cards with you during the interviews and completed them at that time. Chart XIV illustrates a completed Socioanalytic Test Card. On the reverse side of each card note reasons given by others for choosing the subject as well as the reasons given for not choosing him. Also note the number of choices received from members of the *same sex* and from members of the *opposite sex*. A subject may be overchosen by members of the same sex and greatly underchosen by members of the opposite sex. Your data will provide reasons given by others as to why this is so in each case. Also, some subjects may not choose any members of the same sex or of the opposite sex. Your data will provide clues as to why a subject tends to isolate himself from one or the other. You will discover that some people choose members of the opposite sex but are not chosen by any members of the opposite sex and you will have considerable data to explain this phenomenon. You might, if asked by such an individual, tell him the reasons given by members of the opposite sex for withholding choices. I would under no circumstances give the names of the people who commented favorably or otherwise. You may also find that some people make choices of members of the opposite sex and are chosen by members of the opposite sex but choices are not reciprocated. If this happens to a person in ordinary social situations he may conclude that he is not liked by members of the opposite sex. The ones he chooses tend to reject him. He may have no way of knowing how those he does not approach feel about him. If asked by the subject you would help a lot by telling him that the persons of the opposite sex he chose did not choose him. Also give him reasons advanced by *all* members of the opposite sex for withholding choices. Then, and this is most important, give him some information about members of the opposite sex who chose him and their reasons for choosing him. This will give him some idea of what sort of women he appeals to and what sort reject him. This knowledge should help him into positive reciprocal relationships.

CHART XIV

SOCIOANALYSIS TEST CARD

James A.

Reason for Choice

Arnold—Too Conceited

Bernard—Might have picked him - no reason not to.

*Carl—We have a lot in common.

*Charles—We get along very well, I like him.

David—No reason.

*Frank—Is loyal and honest.

George—Too loud, takes advantage of people.

Harold—Too quiet, no interests in common.

James A.—Too quiet, a loner.

William—No reason.

Betty—Hard to get to know her.

*Carol—Friendly, intelligent, pretty.

Cheryl—Too conceited.

Fran—Not much interest in common.

Greta—Hard to talk to.

Jane—Cold, hard.

Joanne—Avoids me, has a boy friend.

*Kathy—A lot of fun, warm, friendly.

Mary—Has a boy friend.

Nancy—Would have picked her if had more choices. She is warm and friendly.

On the reverse side of the card list reasons given by others for choosing *James A* and also reasons given for withholding choices.

Having succeeded in analyzing the social relationships in two groups in which you are not involved you are ready for the next step, the analysis of a heterosexual group in your own age bracket.

You may have difficulty finding such a group, particularly if you are considerably above college age. Nevertheless, there are several possibilities you might consider. Church affiliated groups, charity organizations, political clubs, dance groups, and other social clubs might be willing to cooperate. When you have access to a heterosexual group consisting of twelve to twenty persons, prepare and administer a near sociometric test limited to one criterion question, focused on close relationships. An example of such a question would be: Who would you choose as a close friend? Who would you choose to spend most of your free time with? Before giving the test try to arrange to observe the group for at least one evening. Even a few hours preceding the test would be useful. Observe the people carefully and select a member of the group you consider most like you for detailed study. Note those people who appear to be close to that person and those who are distant. Later on, pay particular attention to the pattern of choices and withholding of choices of that person. Administer the test after a warm-up similar to the one used with the college age group stressing the importance of developing meaningful relationships. After administering the test and preparing the Matrix and Sociogram, prepare a Socioanalysis Test Card similar to the one in Chart *XVI* for each subject. Then try to *predict* the choices, the reason for each choice and the reason for the withholding of choice in each instance. After analyzing the data, interview the subjects asking reasons for choices and reasons for withholding choices. Get as much information as you can about those members of the group who choose or withhold their choice from the person most like you, including the reasons for their choices and the attitudes of others toward them. Enter the data on Socioanalysis Test Cards. You may then proceed in every respect in the same way as you did with the analysis of the college age group. However, this time you will have an opportunity to compare your *predictions* with the actual choices and reasons given by the subjects. If your predictions are fifty percent or more accurate you are ready to undertake your self-analysis. If not repeat the test with another group of about your own age. My suggestion is that you keep on analyzing groups until you can predict in about fifty percent of the cases, what reasons people give for choosing others and what reasons they have for withholding choices. As you learn more about this you will also learn a good deal about why you are choosing and withholding choices from others and also why others are choosing or failing to choose you. Do not be too surprised if your social relationships improve greatly even before you have begun your Socioanalysis.

Having successfully administered sociometric tests, analyzed them, and predicted reasons for choices, you are better qualified to apply sociometry to an analysis of your own social relationships. The essence of the Socioanalytic method is that people can be made to be experts and investigators of the social settings of which they are a part. Now that you have applied Socioanalysis to the study of groups of strangers, you are better prepared to analyze a group of which you are a part. Here you become a participant observer. You follow some of the same procedures you did in analyzing the other groups. You *do not,* however, employ tests or questionnaires. Simply watch the other members of the group in informal activities such as playing cards, bowling, spending time on the beach or at parties. Note on a Matrix who chooses who based on your observations. Then construct an informal sociogram. Also complete Socioanalysis Tests cards for each person indicating the reason for each choice, *as you view it,* and the reason for each withholding of choice or rejection. This effort will provide you with a great deal of insight.

May I suggest that you now obtain the assistance of a Socioanalist as you proceed with your self-analysis. If none is available to assist read the portion of this chapter describing the task of the socioanalist and take the role of socioanalist in your self-analysis. It is difficult, a slow process, but nevertheless possible. View yourself as one anxious enough to change, at least willing to analyze your relationships. If you often have a feeling of being alone and helpless in an unfriendly world, you must find out why you do not have friends who care and for whom you care. This feeling of loneliness can only be overcome by meaningful relationships, by love of others and for others. If you have a feeling of being helpless and confronted by dangers surrounded by people who are indifferent or even hostile to you, you can only overcome this feeling by establishing relationships that negate it. Examine each relationship honestly. Do not pretend that every relationship is satisfying and that this is the best of all possible worlds. Acknowledge freely that you do not like some of the people you are supposed to love. Even admit that you hate them if their behavior toward you warrants such feelings. All of this is a lot more difficult than it seems. But what are our alternatives? If we go on accepting as correct the low evaluations of ourselves presented to us by those who reject us, we must develop feelings of worthlessness, helplessness, and ultimately of rejection of self. In other words we must, when necessary, learn to express our hostility. Before we do this, however, we must honestly determine who we are angry with, who has wronged us, who has diminished our self-image. Participation in a Psychodramatic or Socioanalytic group will provide you with an opportunity of examining your relationships in action. You may even experiment with alternative relationship patterns. You may also learn a good deal about how to express feelings either by watching others express them or by experimenting on your own.

The first step in your Socioanalysis is completed by the end of the third session described in the next section. By that time you will have decided to examine your relationships with several persons; some you have relationships with who do not appear to choose you or whom you do not choose. Others who you do not have relationships with yet choose you or whom you do choose. After attending five Psychodramatic or Socioanalytic sessions try again to answer the questions raised in your first socioanalytic interview (session three). If you feel that you have increased lyour understanding of some of these relationships you are ready for the next step in your self-analysis. Proceed in exactly the same way as you did in the first step except that you examine relationships you had with people when you were sixteen or seventeen years of age. Analyzing the data provided in your Information Sheets and Social Relationship Questionnaires, note the names of those persons with whom you had unsatisfactory relationships and those with whom you did not have the relationships you desired. After participating in five or more Psychodrama sessions go over them again. In the third step of your self-analysis you may proceed in the same manner, but this time as an eleven year old.

Examining your relationships in three stages of your life will afford you an opportunity to discover patterns. What sort of persons are you choosing? What types are you avoiding? Which relationships prove traumatic? How do you get into them? Why do you continue in them? Why does it take so long to terminate them? All of these questions and hundreds more can be answered in Psychodrama sessions. How to change the patterns can best be explored in Role Training sessions or in Role Training Sequences of Psychodramas. Psychodrama sessions may also be used to teach you how to express anger and hostility. Socioanalists have noted that children who are overdependent on parents may fail to express hostility out of fear of losing the parental crutch, others because they have been intimidated by direct or implied threats, still others by love given to them conditionally, and still others because they have been conditioned by their parents to feel guilty. Whatever the reason, there is no doubt that a great many children grow up without being able to express hostility to their parents. The amount of hostility expressed as well as the way in which it is expressed is developed in interaction with other people. Such patterns acquired in childhood may give a person a feeling of helplessness which influences his relationships later in life. In Psychodrama you can learn how you acquired these patterns, how best to express the hostile feelings, and how to get rid of feelings of helplessness. If your self-analysis in the here and now, step one in your self-analysis, indicates loneliness, isolation, feelings of helplessness, difficulty in expressing hostility, or some combination of these, step two, analysis of yourself as an adolescent (at 16) will help you to find out whether these tendencies were present earlier in your life. If they were not you may start looking for the origin of the difficulties in traumatic incidents occurring in your life between age sixteen and the present. Socioanalists do not trace every difficulty to original sin, oedipal conflicts, or primal problems. Trauma can occur at any age and under all sorts of circumstances. However, if the same difficulties existed at age eleven we would hypothesize that the inability to express anger was related to relationships with one or both parents. These hypotheses may be tested psychodramatically in each case and ways dealing with each developed. I have found protagonists unable to express anger coming from all sorts of different family constellations. A boy brought up in a household with five older sisters, another a boy with one older brother, another, the only child in his family, all developed similar emotional patterns despite major differences in early experiences in their respective families.

Psychodramatic and Role Training techniques are described in detail in Part II of this book. One undertaking self-analysis may apply many of these techniques using puppets or dolls to represent people. As one moves behind a doll or puppet representing mother he can try to think and respond as mother would. This action is not too different from that occurring in a Psychodrama, when the techniques of Doubling and Role Reversal are employed. However, participation in a Psychodramatic, Role Training or Socioanalytic Group, directed by a qualified person, is far more effective. Members of such groups are, in a way, representative of the people in the world around us. They provide stimuli, feedback and shared experiences. Not every Socioanalist is qualified to direct group sessions. If he himself does not direct action sessions he will refer you to a qualified director. To be effective, a Socioanalist, preferably a Sociologist, Psychologist, or other professional skilled in the use of Sociometry, should himself have been socioanalized with the assistance of a qualified Socioanalist. At this writing there are such persons trained by the California Institute of Socioanalysis, and very few others. In a very short time it is anticipated that there will be a great many more undergoing training in other parts of the country. You can obtain information regarding the qualifications of a Socioanalist by writing to the California Institute of Socioanalysis.

THE ROLE OF THE SOCIOANALIST

The term therapist in our society includes Psychiatrists, Psychologists, Social Workers, Guidance Counselors, Marriage Counselors, and other professionals to whom people come with social and psychological problems. Many of the professionals we have referred to above are highly trained in their disciplines and are committed to a particular therapeutic or counseling philosophy and methodology. Others are ecclectic and feel free to adopt any methods or techniques which they believe to be effective. They might decide to refer a patient or counselee for socioanalysis as an adjunct to therapy or counseling. The socioanalytic procedures herein recommended are deemed by me to present a model for the application of Socioanalysis by one who has been adequately trained in Socioanalysis.

There are three broad categories of people the Socioanalist may expect to encounter in his practice. The first is the one who comes to him seeking help. Such a person comes because he is dissatisfied with his relationships and seeks some change. Regardless of which category a "therapist" might decide to place him in, the Socioanalist views him as one who is anxious to change, anxious enough to come to him and seek help. An individual who finds himself very lonely and rejected by others would be such a person. A second category includes persons who are referred by therapists or counselors or by persons close to them who are anxious for them to change. An example would be the alcoholic whose wife insists that he go for help. He may not consider himself an alcoholic and, indeed, may be against going to a professional. He comes under duress because his wife threatens to leave him if he does not change. A Socioanalist will assist him with his socioanalysis regardless of any other objectives. A third category, one usually referred to hospitals or encountered in hospital settings includes persons who do not communicate verbally or whose communications are so bizarre as to lead to a diagnosis of psychosis. A Socioanalist can assist such a person if communication can be established.

The procedures outlined in this chapter apply to the first two categories of "patients" or "counselees." With respect to the third category the first task of the professional is to establish verbal communication. Techniques leading to effective verbal communication exist in Psychodrama, dance therapy, music therapy, and other non-verbal forms of communication. Once verbal communication is established socioanalytic techniques may be applied in much the same way as in dealing with persons in the two categories who come prepared to communicate on a verbal level.

Although each subject is viewed as one undertaking his own self-analysis the Socioanalist must, if called upon to do so, be prepared to guide the analysis. Nevertheless, the principal function of the Socioanalist, as I see it, is to provide expertise in the use of the necessary tools. The researcher is always the subject, "patient," or "counselee." The Socioanalist, an expert in the method can, however, contribute greatly to the success of the self-analysis of the subject. Before Socioanalysis begins each subject should, if possible, administer the sociometric tests and conduct the interviews as described in the first portion of this chapter.

To help him accomplish this it may be necessary for the Socioanalist to take an active role. If, for example, a subject is reluctant to administer sociometric tests the Socioanalist must be prepared to have someone administer them for him or do so himself. When doing so he should have the subject accompany the person giving the tests, observe the administration of each test and the interviews that follow. The person administering the tests may introduce the subject to each group being tested as one of his students who is learning how to employ sociometric tests. That is, in fact, a fair description of his role. The Socioanalist may also have to help a subject prepare the matrix and sociogram after each test and go over them with him. Each subject should be encouraged to do these things on his own, however, many people because of lack of experience dealing with groups, may be reluctant to administer sociometric tests. Others may balk at interviewing respondents. The Socioanalist has to do whatever is required in each case. It is important that each subject before he undertakes to analyze his own relationships, understand reasons for choices and reasons for withholding choices, particularly when applied to people like himself. Not until he is able to predict actual choices and reasons given is one considered ready to undertake his Socioanalysis. The Socioanalysis, if guided by a professional, then begins with an initial interview.

The Initial Interview in Socioanalysis.

The following procedures are recommended for conducting the initial interview in Socioanalysis:

1. *Preparation for the Interview*

a. Schedule the subject to arrive at the office of the Socioanalist at least thirty minutes prior to the time of his appointment.

b. Have the office secretary, immediately upon his arrival, give the subject an information sheet to complete. Charts XV and XVI are information sheet forms found useful.

c. Instruct the subject to complete the information sheets while waiting to see the Socioanalist and to hand them to him at the start of the interview.

2. *The Warming Up Process*

a. The warm-up is intended to prepare the subject for what to expect from Socioanalysis. The Socioanalist begins the interview

CHART XV

INFORMATION SHEET PART I

Name______________________________ Address __________

Telephone No. ___________ Occupation _________ Age _____

Please list all of the persons with whom you have family, occupational, or recreational relationships.

Family Relationships (list all of the following)	Age (if living)
Father	
Mother	
Brothers (oldest)	
Brothers	
Brothers	
Brothers	
Sisters (oldest)	
Sisters	
Sisters	
Sisters	
Wives (present wife, if married)	
Wives (former wife, if divorced)	
Children (oldest)	
Children	
Children	

Other family members you associate with:

Occupational Relationships (list only those persons you work with)

Name *Age* *Superior, equal or subordinate to you*

____

____

____

____

____

Recreational Relationships (list only those who participate with you)

Name *Age* *Activity* *Frequency of Participation*

____

____

____

____

____

List those persons you live with. (in same apartment or house)

Name *Age* *Relationship, if any*

____

____

____

____

CHART XVI

INFORMATION SHEET PART II

1. Place in order of frequency the names of persons you most closely associate with. (see most frequently on intimate terms)

Name of person *Relationship*

2. *Date of last physical examination and deficiencies noted.*

3. *Physical problems noted since last physical. List any illness or symptoms no matter how unimportant it may seem to you.*

4. *Please write in order of importance your problems as you see them.*

5. *What do you hope to accomplish in Socioanalysis?*

by discussing with him the problems and goals *he listed* in response to the last question on the Information Sheet. The emphasis is placed on *his* goals, what *he* hopes to accomplish. Socioanalysis is explained to the subject so that he can get a clear picture of what it can do to help him achieve his objectives and also *what it can not do*. The subject should at this time be advised that it will take at least five sessions to arrive at a preliminary analysis and that significant change can not be expected in less than fifteen sessions. The methods are described in general terms and misconceptions of the role of the Socioanalist are cleared up. Also, the subject is encouraged to clearly understand *his* role in Socioanalysis. The more closely the subject can relate Socioanalysis to his objectives the more involved will he become in the process, and the more likely will he be to succeed.

b. The warm-up is directed to the subject of social relationships and their importance to the individual. If possible, some connections are established between the problems and goals listed by the subject and relationship patterns. Remarks should be general in nature. It is well to point out, however, that most people continue some relationships that are unsatisfying to them and even traumatic. The warm-up is concluded with an explanation that Socioanalysis provides the subject with an opportunity to reexamine his relationships and to experiment with possible alternatives.

3. *The Social Relationship Test, Part I*

When the warm-up phase of the interview is completed the testing phase of the initial interview begins. Part I of the Social Relationship Test, the part in which the subject indicates *his* choices, is given first. The subject may be handed the blank form and asked to complete it. However, interrupting an interview in this way tends to inhibit spontaneity. For this reason, I prefer to ask the questions and to write down the responses. I move from the warm-up through the test without any break in the verbal communication.

The Second Session—Testing

It is suggested that action tests such as: Role Tests, Spontaneity Tests, and/or Psychodramatic Projective Tests be administered at the beginning of the second session. An auxiliary ego, a trained assistant, may be employed to play the roles required by the action tests. If, for example, the test is in an occupational role and the subject is involved in an interaction with an employer, an auxiliary ego plays the part of the employer while the subject plays the role of the worker. The test invariably includes a role reversal. When this technique is applied the auxiliary ego assumes the role of worker and the subject plays the part of the employer. In this way the subject is tested in both roles. When giving action tests, I prefer to play the complementary roles myself. By limiting the number of persons present at the initial interview to two, myself and the subject, I find that I am better able to establish rapport with the subject. Furthermore, the subject faces the same stimulus person in all of the tests and retests. To secure the same results using auxiliary egos would require me to have the one who assists in the first testing available for all future tests. This is often difficult to achieve.

Part II of the Social Relationship Test is usually administered after the action tests are completed. In this part of the test the subject names those persons who he believes would choose him. I give Part II of the test in the same manner as I give Part I, by asking the questions and writing down the answers.

The Third Session—First Socioanalytic Interview

It is recommended that the Socioanalist, having obtained enough data to prepare an initial sociogram, conduct this interview by relating the data provided in the Information Sheet to the data provided in the Social Relationship Test.

The Socioanalist has before him completed information sheets with a description of the *actual* relationships of the subject, Part I of a Social Relationship Questionnaire which indicates the names of persons the subject *would like to have* in these relationships, and Part II of the Social Relationship Questionnaire which contains the names of those persons the subject believes *would choose him* for those relationships. The interview should proceed in three stages.

Stage I—The attention of the subject is invited to the names listed on the Information Sheets and Part I of the Questionnaire. With respect to the latter, he is asked why there is *not the actual* relationship, if the Information Sheets so indicate.

With respect to those people whose names appear on the Information Sheet as sharing *actual* relationships with the subject but have not been chosen for those relationships, he is asked:

1. Why he did not choose them.
2. Why, if he does not choose them, he associates with them.

and,

3. Whether or not he would like to change his relationship with them.

Stage II—Invite the subject's attention to the names listed on the Information Sheet and Part II of the Questionnaire. With respect to the latter, ask him why the person indicated would choose him, what he does, how old he is, and why there is *not the actual* relationship, if the Information Sheet so indicates. With respect to those people whose names appear on the Information Sheet as sharing actual relationships with the subject, but *would not,* according to his prediction on the Questionnaire, *choose him* for those relationships, ask him why they would not choose him, and what he could do to influence their choice. Then ask him whether or not he desired relationships with those people he predicted would choose him. If he answers in the affirmative, ask whether he wanted to have them *in addition to those he now associated with* or *as substitutes* for some of his present associates.

Stage III—Invite the subject's attention to the names listed on Parts I and II of the Questionnaire. For each person he has chosen in Part I who he predicted *would not choose* him in Part II, he is asked why they would not choose him, whether or not he expected them to choose him in the future, and why. For each person he predicted would choose him in Part II, that he did *not choose* for the indicated relationship in Part I, he is asked why he did not choose that person, what that person would have to do to influence him to choose that person, and whether or not this was likely.

The interview should not be hurried. The subject should be given adequate time to consider each person named, *one at a time.* Hesitancy and avoidance in answering should be noted, but *not* discussed with the subject. This interview provides valuable clues for relationships to be explored in future sessions. Problems and goals indicated by the subject on the Information Sheet *should not be discussed* with the subject in this interview but should be considered for exploration in Psychodrama. Ideally, this interview should be taped. Pen and paper interviews of this type tend to inhibit communication and fail to reflect emphasis and emotional tone as accurately as sound and voice. The director may excerpt relevant portions and transcribe them for his files. This interview greatly influences the choices of sessions to follow.

The Socioanalist then prepares a Social Behavior Chart similar to Chart XVII for each subject. After discussing with the subject the results of any Role Tests, Spontaneity Tests, or other Action Tests he may have given, he should score each problem area listed on the chart giving his reasons for each score. In using the chart, I score each of the ten areas on a continuum from 1 to 5. Subsequent scoring may be based on observations made at sessions of a Socioanalytic group if the subject participates in such a group, or after each Socioanalytic interview.

At the conclusion of the initial interview the Socioanalist explains to the subject that his Socioanalysis is essentially a self-analysis, and instructs him on what he ought to do before he begins it. First and foremost one must learn how to apply Sociometry to the study of relationships, and learn as much as he can about why people make the choices they make. Such knowledge is useful to any person who is lonely, feels alienated, or is dissatisfied with any of his relationships. It is particularly important to the individual who has a low self-image.

Many people when they see others favored and themselves neglected feel that there is something wrong with them. Psychologists and Psychiatrists in searching for causes within the individual, reinforce this belief. Psychoanalytically oriented therapists contribute to despair as they seek to attribute difficulties one is experiencing to patterns developed in the first few years of life in one's family. This type of analysis may have been meaningful for persons socialized in an 18th Century Viennese family in which Freud's neurotic patients grew up. It is largely inapplicable to persons brought up in the urban industrial society that predominates in modern America and Western Europe. No matter how supportive or rejecting a nuclear family experience may be a person is now likely to develop his self-image as he experiences acceptance and rejection in his peer groups throughout life, first as a child, then as an adolescent, and later on as an adult. In applying Sociometry, one can learn why children choose others.

Chart XVII

SOCIAL BEHAVIOR CHART

____
(name of subject)

0 = Initial Interview

SESSIONS

(Score each ; 1,2,3,4, or 5.)

	0	1	2	3	4	5	6	7	8	9	10
1.) Interaction with others (isolate -- star)											
2.) Isolate - Satisfaction (depressed -- very satisfied)											
3.) Isolate - Voluntariness (withdraws -- seeks interaction)											
4.) Isolate - Behavior (negative -- positive)											
5.) Initiation of Interaction (none -- great deal)											
6.) Response of others (none -- great deal)											
7.) Response to others (none -- great deal)											
8.) Interaction with opposite sex (none -- great deal)											
9.) Understanding of Relationships (none -- great deal)											
10.) Desire to change Relationships (none -- great deal)											

He will learn that each child chooses others who he believes will best serve his purposes. Choices and rejections have little to do with the qualities of the person chosen or rejected. This is why we often find a person clearly attractive to the opposite sex closely associated with two or three unattractive individuals. The attractive girl or boy *chooses* the unattractive ones so that he or she will stand out, get more attention, be the star. The unattractive *chooses* the attractive so that he or she may bask in the glory of the attractive one, or be part of an attractive group. The tough muscular leader of a gang may closely associate with physically weaker individuals to reinforce his feeling of power. They associate with him to be part of an important group. This gives them a feeling of importance. An intelligent, strong individual may be rejected by the gang leader because he is perceived as a potential rival. His qualities may then be unrecognized by the satellites because they need to be close to the leader. The gang leader may fasten a belittling nickname on a potential rival. The gang members will then call him by that nickname. He must accept lowly status if he is to remain in the gang. If a boy, rejected in this way, remains in the gang, he is likely to develop a low self-image. In some neighborhoods he has little choice. I have known many potentially able young men who developed a low self-image in gangs in which they were nicknamed "stinky," "dopey," "dumbo," etc.

Similar processes may operate in adolescence, particularly in heterosocial relationships.[1] They may also operate in occupational and social groups of adults. It is not unusual in a business organization for the son or son-in-law of the boss to be groomed for the top job while the contributions of the most capable are ignored or attributed to the chosen relative. Once the subject understands that the choices people make in relationships *are based on their needs* and have little to do with the characteristics of the persons chosen or rejected, he may reappraise his self-image. As he works with Sociometry he will also learn which people choose people like him, and which reject people like him, and the reasons for these choices and rejections. Each subject should be asked to administer Sociometric Tests to one or more groups of children, adolescents, and adults in the manner described at the beginning of this chapter. Following each test, the subject should interview as

[1] I use the term heterosocial relationships to involve all sorts of relationships involving men and women not necessarily including heterosexual behavior.

many of the persons involved as he can and record the reasons given for making and withholding choices. The Socioanalist can help the subject obtain access to groups to be tested. He must also be available to help prepare the matrix and sociogram of each group tested, and assist in evaluating the data.

The subject will correctly predict reasons for choices of some persons and will also make many incorrect predictions. The Socioanalist, as he goes over the incorrect predictions with the subject tries to find reasons for them. It is likely that patterns will emerge. For example, one may be able to correctly predict choices of men and not of women, of older people, and not of younger, etc. When in the course of analyzing groups a subject develops the ability to predict reasons for choices in about fifty percent of the cases he is ready for the first step in his own Socioanalysis.

While he is learning how to use Sociometry in his Socioanalysis, the subject may also be encouraged to attend a Socioanalytic Group, a Psychodrama Group or a Role Training Group. However, it is best that he avoid becoming a protagonist in an action session until he begins his first step in Socioanalysis. Participation in Psychodramatic Growth Groups, Sensitivity Training Groups, or Encounter Groups should be postponed until a later stage in Socioanalysis.

The First Step in Socioanalysis

In the course of the first Socioanalytic interview clues are provided to both the subject and the Socioanalist as to which relationships require examination. Certainly relationships which the subject continues to maintain despite the fact that he did not choose the persons involved in social relationship tests need to be explained. So, too, do relationships with persons who do not appear, according to these tests, to choose the subject. These relationships may be examined by the Socioanalist and subject in the course of Socioanalytic Sesions; one-to-one, and in groups, as described in the next chapter. The subject may also be encouraged to participate in group sessions in Psychodrama, Role Playing or Role Training directed by the Socioanalist or other qualified persons. These are described in Part II. The number of such sessions required varies according to the needs of each subject. When the subject feels he has explored all his current questionable relationships, usually after four or five sessions with a

Socioanalist, he is ready for a second Socioanalytic interview. In this interview he again answers the questions raised in his first Socioanalytic interview and notes all changes in relationships that have occurred during his Socioanalysis. If he is satisfied that he has adequately increased his understanding of his existing relationships he is ready for the next step in Socioanalysis.

The Second Step in Socioanalysis

The first step in Socioanalysis deals with the current relationships of a subject. For patterns to be established it is useful to go into past relationships, particularly those in adolescence and childhood. The second step in Socioanalysis focuses on relationships in adolescence. The subject takes his own role as a sixteen year old and completes information sheets and Social Relationship tests. The analysis proceeds in much the same manner as the first step in the course of his third Socioanalytic interview. The ensuing sessions are devoted to an examination of relationships with persons close to him whom the subject did not choose or who did not appear to choose him. This step is concluded when in a fourth Socioanalytic interview the subject indicates that he is satisfied with his understanding of his relationships in adolescence.

The Third Step in Socioanalysis

The analysis proceeds in much the same manner as in the previous two steps except that the focus is on relationships of the subject at age eleven or less. The subject plays himself at ten or eleven in the course of the sessions examining the relationships of his childhood and during the fifth and sixth Socioanalytic interviews. The latter interviews follow the patterns employed in the third and fourth Socioanalytic interviews discussed in our description of the second step.

The three steps in Socioanalysis focus on the relationships of an individual in three important stages of his life. At age ten or eleven he begins to contribute to rules regulating his behavior. Up to then virtually all rules governing his actions had been prescribed by parents and other adults. At age ten if a member of peer groups with rules established by reciprocal cooperation, he begins to develop a new morality. How he develops this may be explored in Socioanalysis. At age sixteen or thereabouts his new morality is developed and his "right ways" may be different from those of the "old morality" prescribed by his parents. The nature of his relationships during this period of his life are important and should be examined in Socioanalysis. Certainly any conflicts with authority and the ways in which they are resolved should provide valuable clues toward an explanation of adult behavior and relationships.

The three steps in Socioanalysis which deal with relationships in three important portions of one's life may be explored in approximately fifteen sessions. It has been my experience that participation in fifteen Psychodramatic Role Training sessions results in significant changes in spontaneity and social skill as measured by Role Playing Ability. At the conclusion of fifteen such sessions a subject should have a clear understanding of his relationship patterns, what sort of persons he chooses to associate with and why. He should also have some ideas as to which associations are constructive and which are destructive.

I found that Role Training sessions limited to family roles resulted in an increase in spontaneity in occupational roles, and all sorts of community roles not touched upon in the Role Training sessions. It has been observed that behind every successful man one is likely to find a supporting and helping wife. My way of explaining this is that a man who is secure in his family roles tends to be more spontaneous and creative in his occupational and community roles. This spontaneity and creativity contributes to his success. In years of college teaching I have noticed that those students who are happily married or are involved in apparently stable heterosexual associations tend to achieve at a higher level than those who are playing the field in unstable relationships.

When considered appropriate, sessions in Socioanalysis may be devoted to experimenting with changes in relationships, consideration given to consequences and alternatives. If the subject indicates an interest his potentials may be examined as well as his aspirations for the future. The subject, at the completion of Socioanalysis should be able to associate himself with those persons who encourage his spontaneity and avoid those who inhibit his spontaneity unless association with some of the latter are considered valuable by him. Association with such persons should continue only if the subject consciously desires them to continue after examining the consequences of breaking them and alternatives available to him. When these objectives are attained, a subject may be said to have completed his Socioanalysis.

Even before your Socioanalysis is completed you will know whether or not you are part of a Personal Reference Group, (PRG) a face to face group in which you receive recognition, appreciation and approval for just being yourself. One in which you do not have to "achieve" to be important. One in which you are not continually evaluated, criticized for deficiencies or put down for failures. In such a group you can develop spontaneity, achieve a measure of self-direction and enhance your personal growth. To direct the course of your life you need the support and assistance of others. In the PRG, with people you like and who like you, you are likely to find the necessary support.

In a Therapy Group, Sensitivity Training Group, Encounter Group, and even a Self-Help Group the principal emphasis is on what is wrong with you. The social and political thrust is essentially conservative and in support of the status quo. The sessions focus on getting *you* to become aware of *your* deficiencies, getting *you* to change or to accept your fate. In the PRG where everyone is accepted and appreciated as a person the emphasis can shift to examining the deficiencies and failures of our society. We can shift the focus from "what is wrong with us" to what is wrong with our social and political systems. We can explore ways of changing *them*. We can also ask ourselves to what extent psychologists and psychiatrists are serving the establishment against our interests in their efforts to change us in the direction of conformity to the attitudes and values of the dominant forces of our society.

What if you find that you are not part of a PRG? You can use what you have learned in Socioanalysis to form one around you and people you like. Start by finding one person whom you like and who likes you. Meet with him at least once a week to rap about the things you would like to change around you; at work, in your community, in the nation, or in the world. You can then expand the group to include others until your group has six to ten members. Numbers are not important. What is most important is that the members like each other. As they develop appreciation and give recognition to each other, they become a PRG. It may take time but, in my opinion, it will greatly increase your spontaneity, growth, and self-direction toward more meaningful life experiences.

Chapter 5

SOCIOANALYTIC SESSIONS DESCRIBED

No man can reveal to you aught but that which already lies half asleep in the dawning of your knowledge.

The teacher who walks in the shadow of the temple, among his followers, gives not of his wisdom but rather of his faith and his lovingness.

If he is indeed wise he does not bid you enter the house of his wisdom, but rather leads you to the threshold of your own mind.

Kahlil Gibran

In the course of each step of his Socioanalysis the subject examines relationships with persons with whom he was closely associated whom he did not choose, or who did not appear to choose him. This analytic process is pursued through at least three important periods of his life; during his childhood, his adolescence, and at the time of his Socioanalysis. The Socioanalist may have the subject explore these relationships in a Socioanalytic, Psychodramatic, or Role Training Group or in One-to-One Psychodrama or Role Training sessions directed by him.

Psychodrama as a group method is well established in the professional world. What is not well known is that Psychodrama is also used by psychiatrists and others in private practice with individuals. It may also be used in Socioanalysis with an individual who desires to explore his social relationships with the aid of a Socioanalist. A Role Training or Psychodramatic session including a Socioanalist and one subject usually takes place in the office of the Socioanalist who directs the session. There are no auxiliary egos, no audience, or group,and usually no stage. The three phases that make up a Psychodramatic group session are equally a part of the Psychodramatic session with only two people present. The director starts such a session with a warm-up, a five or ten minute discussion of the problem area raised by the subject. He may in the course of the warm-up ask a few questions of the subject not for the purpose of eliciting information, so much as for the purpose of focusing the attention of the subject on the relationships to be explored. The warm-up portion of the session is completed when the director recommends to the subject that he enact or reenact a specific situation. Most of the techniques available for Psychodramatic groups are available in the dyadic session. Since there are no auxiliary egos the director plays the roles required by the subject. When he does so the technique of role reversal is employed in exactly the same manner as it is in a group session. The director takes the role of the subject and the subject moves into the role of the person in interaction with him. If the director wishes to employ the double technique he must act as the double, since there are no other persons present to serve as doubles. Several of the other techniques; self-presentation, soliloquy, and future projection do not require a person other than the director and the subject.

One technique that is frequently used in the dyadic Psychodrama is the auxiliary chair technique. In this technique there is an empty chair opposite the one in which the protagonist sits. The protagonist is instructed that when sitting in chair A, he plays himself and when he moves to chair B, he plays the other person. The director may interview him as himself; he may also interview him when he is on the other chair as the other person. For example, if the subject is enacting a situation in which he is discussing a matter with his father, he is told that when he is in chair A he is himself, when he is in chair B, he is the father, and he is told to move from chair to chair as the dialogue progresses. The director may question him in either role, may double with him in either role, and may have him soliloquize in either role. The result is that, aside from the benefits derived from group discussions and from interaction on a stage, the same general learning experience can take place in the dyadic situation as takes place in the group situation. In my opinion this leaves a great deal to be desired. The support of a group, catharsis derived in a group setting, and the experience of facing problems in a group situation are very important to an understanding and facing up to social relationships and problems. Nevertheless, there are some people who are afraid of groups. They are embarrassed in front of a group and are reluctant to go into experiences of their personal life before a great many people. This may result from the fact that in our culture there are practices and activities that are so strongly rejected that a public identification with them might result in serious repercussions for a protagonist. An example of this is homosexuality. The latent homosexual should not be encouraged nor even permitted to present his problems on the psychodramatic stage in front of a group. His career might be seriously affected and his relationships with other people in the society severely limited. For persons with unusual problems or problems which are strongly stigmatized by our society, psychodrama may best be employed in a dyadic session. Where, however, an individual desires a dyadic psychodrama because he is shy, or is afraid to appear before a group, one goal of the one-to-one sessions should be to prepare him to enter a group. The experiences in a Socioanalytic, Psychodramatic, or other synthetic group, will better prepare him to function in his natural groups.

The three phases of a one-to-one session differ somewhat from the phases of a group session. Nevertheless, they follow each other in the same sequence. The director starts each session with a warm-up. There are three basic types of warm-ups used in a dyadic session. These are:

1. *The General Warm-Up:* In this type of warm-up the Socioanalist, in his opening statement, discusses relationships in general with no emphasis on any one in particular. In the interview part of the warm-up he asks general questions leaving to the subject the relationship area to be explored. In the course of the warm-up objectives for the session are determined. When the action starts he leaves to the subject the specific situations to be examined.

2. *The Directed Warm-Up:* This type of warm-up is identical with the one of the same name described for use in warming up a group. The opening statement of the director is limited to a specific relationship or problem. The interview focuses on the same relationship or problem and the warm-up for action presents the protagonist with a choice of scenes involving the relationship discussed by the director in his opening statement.

3. *Warm-Up for an Encounter:* Using this type of warm-up the director makes an opening statement on the importance of prepar-

ing for the particular encounter and interviews the subject on the anticipated nature of the encounter. He then warms up the subject for action by suggesting a time and place for the encounter and asking him to enter the scene.

The warm-up portion of the session is completed when the subject begins to enact a situation. Many of the techniques described in the chapters on Psychodrama and Role Training may be used in dyadic sessions. Where a technique requires the services of an auxiliary ego the director functions in that capacity. Scenes selected for enactment follow the same sequence as for Group Psychodramas, moving from the peripheral to the serious or traumatic. The discussion phase too resembles that of a group session, the difference being the size of the group. Presented below, for illustrative purposes, are excerpts from a one-to-one session directed by the author, and reconstructed from memory a few hours after the session. Although not accurate in every detail, the techniques were employed as indicated. Mr. Howard, the subject, who had a Master of Arts degree in psychology, expressed a desire to apply for a psychological internship in a state hospital. He had contemplated taking this action on several previous occasions but in each instance had postponed action. He was disturbed by the fact that he could not go through with the steps necessary to further his career as a psychologist.

Preparation for an Encounter

Warm-up: I talked for about five minutes on the importance of being prepared for an interview, pointing out that, using the Psychodramatic Method, one could experiment with several approaches and could prepare one's self to answer all sorts of questions in advance of the interview. We could, in short, anticipate many of the problems that might arise in the course of the encounter. In the interview, part of the warm-up, I asked Howard why he had not arranged for the interview. He replied that he was afraid of rejection by the hospital at this time and the effect of such rejection on future applications. After discussing the possibility of acceptance at various hospitals, I completed the warm-up by suggesting that he enact an interview with Dr. Burns, Chief Psychologist at hospital A to take place two weeks from the time of the session. Total time: 10 minutes.

The Action Portion

Director: Howard, I will play Dr. Burns, and you play yourself.

Director: (As Burns) Have a seat, Mr. Howard. I have read your application and resume. Is there anything you would like to add?

Howard: No, I don't believe so. I am prepared to answer any questions you may have.

Director: (as Burns) One thing I don't quite understand. You have been out of school two years. Why did you delay applying for the interneship until now?

Howard: Well, as you know from my application, I am married and have two children. It was essential that I earn more money than I could get as an intern.

Director: (as Burns) Has the situation changed now?

Howard: Yes. I have saved enough to get along for a year on intern's pay.

Director: Let us reverse roles. You be Dr. Burns for a while and present some difficult questions.

Howard: (as Burns) Are you continuing your studies?

Director: (as Howard) I intend to next year.

Howard: (as Burns) Have you applied for admission to a Ph.D. program?

Director: Let us reverse back. You play yourself. (They change place each time they reverse roles.)

Howard: No. Not as yet.

Director: (as Burns) When do you intend to apply?

Howard: Next year.

Director: (as Burns) Do you think you will be accepted?

Howard: Yes. Friends of mine with similar grade averages have been accepted at U.S.C.

Director: You have been playing yourself and Dr. Burns at different times through the application role reversal. Now will you play both roles so that I can perform other functions. When you are seated on the left side of the desk, you are Howard, when on the right side, you are Burns. (Director moves aside [1]

Howard: (as Burns) I notice that you have given Dr. Smith as a reference. How well does he know you?

[1]After a few role reversals the protagonist is accustomed to moving from one role to the other. At this point the auxiliary chair technique is introduced to free the director for other functions.

Howard: I was a student of his for two years. He was my advisor.
Howard: (as Burns) I will consider his opinion of you and the opinions of the other persons you gave as references and will let you know my decision.
Director: Dr. Burns, I would like you to think out loud about Howard, reflecting on what you consider his strong points and weak points and your decision. I will double with you. We will both think as Burns.[1]
Howard: (as Burns) He seems like a good man, but why has not he applied for a Ph. D. program?
Director: (as double) Most interns are Ph. D. candidates.
Howard: (as Burns) He says he will apply next year.
Director: (as Burns) Not all who apply are accepted.
Howard: (as Burns) Two years is long time to be out of school. I wonder if he has kept up with his reading.
Director: Dr. Burns, are you going to act favorably on Howard's application?
Howard: (as Burns) Not if I have any application from Ph. D. candidates.
Director: Howard, I am going to employ the mirror technique to give you an opportunity to see how you appeared to me while in action. I shall try to play your part as you did to the best of my ability. (The director then reenacted the previous scene as Howard had done it.)
Director: Do you think that I portrayed you fairly and accurately?
Howard: Yes. That is about the way I acted.
Director: Are you satisfied with the performance?
Howard: No. I think I was too insecure. I should show more confidence.
Director: Let's do it again showing more confidence. (Howard reenacted the scene. This time he took the offensive asking questions about working conditions, facilities, opportunity for advancement to residency and offering information about his present guidance job and the relationship it bore to psychological practice. He expressed satisfaction with the way he played the part, but as Burns, was doubtful on the subject of hiring Howard. The action portion lasted a total of forty minutes.)

[1] Note the use of the Soliloquy and double techniques. The director is free to double.

The Discussion Phase

Director: You seem to think that the fact that you have not applied for admission to a Ph. D. program is an insurmountable obstacle. Is that so?

Howard: I am afraid that it may be.

Director: Is there some way that you could overcome that?

Howard: I suppose I can apply. But I couldn't afford to pursue it right now.

Director: Could you apply and take only one or two courses a semester for a year?

Howard: I could do that. But do you think that would influence Burns?

Director: I don't know. We can assume you have done it and try a future projection to help you evaluate its effect. Do you think it would help if you carried letters from your references, particularly Dr. Smith?

Howard: It is not a good idea. They like to correspond directly with the references.

Director: Is Smith a friend of Burns?

Howard: Yes. Smith mentioned him often.

Director: Is there some way you could get Smith to write or call Burns about you before your interview?

Howard: I think he would do it if I asked him to.

Director: At this point we can do a future projection. You have applied for admission to the U.S.C. doctoral program and Dr. Smith has written to Dr. Burns on your behalf. Now act out the interview with Burns.[1] In the enactment Howard, performed very much as he did after the mirror except that when asked about the Ph.D. he replied that he had applied at U.S.C., and because of his grade point average was confident that he would be accepted.

Dolls or puppets may be used by a Socioanalist and subject to examine relationships with two or more persons. I have used this technique in the course of exploring family relationships and other aspects of the social atom. Chairs and dolls are employed to represent the people with whom relationships are being examined. For example, if the subject decides to reenact a scene involving his father, mother, and sister, I have him designate

[1] In a sense every enactment in this psychodrama was a future projection.

a chair to represent each person in the scene at approximately the same distance they were from him and from each other. In the chair representing his father, I place a male doll. In the chair representing his mother and sister, I place female dolls representing different ages. The subject moves behind each chair and speaks and acts for the person represented. When playing his own role he directs his comments to the appropriate doll and moves behind the doll representing the person responding when appropriate. I employ the double technique whenever I consider it useful, moving along with the subject and stimulating the action. The subject, through the use of soliloquy, doubles, and role reversals gains considerable insight into his relationships with the absent persons and also increases in empathy.

Using Psychodrama or Role Training One-to-One with a subject, it is possible for the Socioanalist to assist him in completing a self-analysis without the aid of any other persons. It is preferable, however, for the subject to participate in Psychodrama or Role Training sessions with others in a group setting. Another possibility, is to form a Socioanalytic group consisting of persons each involved in his own Socioanalysis.

A Socioanalytic Group

A professional who applies Socioanalysis in his practice might consider it desirable to form a Socioanalytic group, consisting of people in Socioanalysis. In the Socioanalytic group each counselee could, with the assistance of others in the group, experiment with the modification of relationship patterns, particularly if his Socionalysis indicated a need for change. The director of a Socionalytic group then directs sessions most useful in the Socioanalysis of members of his group. Memebers of the group are encouraged to participate in examining their own relationships and to cooperate with each other as each examines his relationship patterns and the possibilities for change.

In the Socioanalytic group a democratic permissive atmosphere is provided so that each participant feels free to communicate honestly without fear of ridicule or rejection. The director encourages each individual to explore all possibilities of increasing communication with other members of his nuclear and extended family. It is in these groups that one must first achieve a measure of security as insecurity in family relationships is often reflected in poor relationships in other groups. As the individual learns to communicate effectively in his family and other intimate groups, if any, he becomes more likely to risk communication in other groups. Therefore, it is good practice to begin Socioanalytic group sessions with the exploration of the social atom of each member of the group. Each participant reenacts scenes depicting his present relationships with members of his immediate family; particularly those residing with him, as well as others who play an important part in his present social atom. Once relationships with others in his social atom are thoroughly examined each participant should be encouraged to examine his relationships with all those people who choose him on the sociometric tests. With the help of the group, he may examine the possibilities of building significant relationships with some of these people. Because it is easier to communicate with people who choose us and because reciprocal relationships potentially provide the greatest amount of security, communication with those who choose us is more likely to be rewarding and more likely to help us improve in social skill. Having acquired, in the Socioanalytic group, effective techniques of communication with members of his social atom and with others who choose him, each individual should be encouraged to experiment with relationships in groups in which he is most likely to gain acceptance, approval, and recognition. He may in the Socioanalytic group, experiment to prepare himself for successful participation in the activities of such groups. With the aid of each individual sociogram, the director and each member of the group can assist each other member in these examinations and experiments.

A Socioanalytic group session begins when the group, led by the Socioanalist, selects a protagonist for the session. He may speak to the group briefly, suggesting that those ready to examine relationships so indicate. After a vote is taken the member receiving a plurality becomes the protagonist. Once a protagonist is selected, the Socioanalist warms up the *protagonist and the group* by briefly describing his individual sociogram. Mutual choices, other choices, and failures to choose are discussed. The protagonist is then encouraged to reenact scenes depicting his relationship with one member of his social atom; preferably a relationship he would like to improve. Other members of the group play the parts of those persons not present. Following the enactment the protagonist is placed in the role of the other person, the one with whom he has the relationship, and each member of the group illustrates how he would handle the situation portrayed. This procedure is called a "Role Training Sequence." Following the Role Training Sequence there is a group discussion and a final enactment by the protagonist in which he shows how he might deal with a similar situation in the future.

To illustrate: Bill a member of the group, is selected as protagonist. He undertakes to reenact scenes with his wife, Sally. He chooses a member of the group, Emily, to play the role of Sally. Bill reenacts one scene in which he and Sally quarrel over money, another in which they disagree over recreational activity, and another over the distribution of labor around the house. Following the enactments Bill is placed in the role of Sally (the wife). Each member of the group, in turn, comes forward to play the role of Bill and illustrates how he or she would deal with the situation. In each instance, Bill responds as Sally, the wife. In the course of this Role Training Sequence he learns several alternative ways of dealing with Sally in the situations portrayed. After the Role Training Sequence the group discusses the relationship of Bill and Sally and the alternatives available to Bill. Bill then shows the group how he would handle the same situations should they arise in the future. When there is a conflict between two people, Bill and Sally, there are several alternatives available to Bill.

1. He may surrender and do as Sally wants him to. This may be because he agrees that her position is correct or that not conceding might result in a greater loss. She might leave him, for example.

2. He may insist that Sally surrender and do as he wants her to. This may be because he is convinced that he is right and that she will yield or that failure to insist might result in a greater loss. She might, for example, lose respect for him if he did not maintain his position.

3. Recognize that both positions have merit and find some means of satisfying both. Recognize, for example, that Sally needs new clothes and Bill needs a new set of golf clubs and satisfy both by borrowing the money. Both Bill and Sally are too tired to clean the house, hence, they should hire someone to do it.

4. Arrive at a compromise, each yielding on some points.

5. Bill might leave Sally, this would represent a break in the relationship.

The Role Training Sequence helps the protagonist by presenting him with many approaches involving several alternatives. In the role of Sally he has an opportunity to respond to them. This should help him to predict her response, and evaluate its effect on him. The objective of the session is to increase awareness of alternatives. As Bill becomes more aware of the effect of his behavior on Sally, and as he experiments with alternative courses of action he is likely to develop new attitudes toward his behavior and toward Sally. His perception of himself in the situation may change as others exhibit different behavior in playing his role.

Even though Bill may be the sole protagonist at a Socioanalytic group session every other member of the group may learn from his experiences and from each other as alternatives are presented and discussed. Each, as he plays the role of another, gains experiences which may be applicable to his own life situations. Furthermore, through participation in the action and discussion portion of a session each member gains a measure of acceptance and later on approval. Some members of the group learn most when they can offer advice, and persuade or influence others.

The Socioanalist should prepare a protocol of each Socioanalytic group session as soon after it as possible, while it is still fresh in his memory. Even if the session is recorded on tape it is important that the protocol be prepared immediately after the session, because tape does not adequately record expressions of the persons involved, movement of the persons involved, and other forms of communication such as grimaces, facial expressions, and unexplained silences. These may be of great importance and may be noticed by the director. With a lapse of time, however, they are likely to be lost. Chart XVIII contains recommendations for information to be included in a protocol.

CHART XVIII

PROTOCOL OF A SOCIOANALYTIC GROUP SESSION

Those Present at the Session. If we have an ongoing session with twelve of fifteen people all that is necessary is to record the names of those absent. The director and any of his assistants present should be recorded as should the date.

Type of Warm-up. Here we have not only the answer to the question whether the warm-up is directed warm-up, a group centered warm-up, or an indirect warm-up, but also a brief description of the warm-up.

The Names of the Protagonist or Protagonists. There may be two, three, or more protagonists. In each instance the roles enacted should be described as should the degree of involvement of the protagonist and others.

Auxiliary Egos. It is important to list the auxiliary egos and the degree of participation of each. The auxiliary egos are drawn from the group and, therefore, the training given to auxiliary egos in the session closely approximates the training given to the protagonist. In addition to the participation of the individuals we should also have some appraisal of the degree of involvement of each.

Discussion. Those involved in a discussion should be mentioned as should the degree of involvement. Salient points in the discussion should be presented in the protocol. Persons who do not participate in the discussion or in the enactment should be mentioned at this time. The significance of this failure to participate may be important for structuring later sessions. For example, if it becomes apparent upon examination of several protocols that a particular individual has not participated the director may take steps to involve that particular person.

Remarks. This portion of the protocol is reserved for the director. In this way he may evaluate the progress of the group, of any individual in the group, and the progress of the program as a whole.

Where the session is not on tape a protocol is indispensible. Along with the protocol the director might wish to complete a Rating Sheet in which he indicates for each participant of the session his degree of participation as protagonist, as auxiliary ego, and discussant. Ratings are based on the protocols of each session, providing a log of the nature and degree of participation of each member of the Socioanalytic group. In this way, comparison of scores attained at successive sessions is greatly facilitated. Chart XIX presents a Director's Rating Sheet recording the scores of members of a Socioanalytic Group, over a period of five sessions. A copy of the Rating Sheet is maintained in the file of each member of the group or that portion of the Rating Sheet applicable to a member is extracted for his file. A person doing his self-analysis without the aid of a Socioanalist should prepare a protocol of every session in which he participates and on it record and rate the nature of his participation.

The protocol and the director's rating sheet together with the results of Sociometric Tests, Role Tests and Spontaneity Tests, serve to measure the progress of individuals participating in the Socioanalytic group. Ideally, the director should evaluate each member of the group based on the above, every five weeks. In that way, the director will have some idea of the progress made by individual members of the group. The assumption is that all members of the group should make progress. If some do not make progress in five weeks, that is they do not indicate any improvement in their sociometric status, and they do not indicate any change in degree of participation, these facts should serve as a signal to the Socioanalist that such persons require additional attention. He can give them additional attention by moving them into auxiliary ego roles in the course of a session in which another person is the protagonist or by involving them in the discussions by addressing questions to them. If he considers it important enough he may direct an entire session around the person by employing an indirect warm-up. Improvement in role playing ability as measured by Role Tests or improvement in sociometric status as measured by Sociometric Tests are considered evidence of improvement in social skill. Persons showing marked improvement in these areas should be encouraged to experiment in expanding their relationships in natural groups. The assumption is that those who achieve success in the socioanalytic group are better prepared to succeed in the natural groups in which they par-

CHART XIX

DIRECTOR'S RATING SHEET

Session No's.	1	2	3	4	5	No. of Part.
Activity	P A D	P A D	P A D	P A D	P A D	P A D
Bernard	- - -	- - 2	- - 4	- - 4	- 2 4	0 1 4
Charles	- - -	- - -	- - -	- - -	- - -	0 0 0
Frank	- 2 3	- 3 3	- 3 3	- 2 3	- [illegible] 3	0 4 5
Henry	- - -	- - -	- - 3	- - -	- - -	0 0 1
John T.	- 3 3	- 4 3	4 - 3	a a a	- 3 3	1 3 5
John W.	- 2 3	5 - 4	- 3 4	- 3 4	- 3 4	1 4 5
Robert	- 4 3	- 3 4	- 3 3	4 - 5	- 3 4	1 4 5
William	- - -	- - -	- - -	- - -	- - 2	0 0 1
Betty	- - -	- - 2	- 3 2	- - -	- - -	0 1 2
Clara	- 3 3	- 3 3	- 2 3	- - 4	4 - 4	1 3 5
Joan	4 - 4	- - 3	- [illegible] 4	- 4 3	- 3 3	1 2 5
Kathy	- - -	- - -	- - 3	a a a	- - 3	0 0 2
Lillian	- - -	- - -	- - -	- - -	- - -	0 0 0
Mary B.	- - -	- - -	- - 4	- 5 3	- 3 3	0 2 2
Mary T.	- - -	- - -	- - -	- - -	- - 3	0 0 1
Total No's.	1 5 6	1 4 8	1 5 11	1 4 9	1 6 10	

a= absence
P= Protagonist
A=Auxiliary Ego
D=Discussant

Score reported in Protocol of Session 4 Chart XVIII are entered in Director Rating Scale.

ticipate. Where a member of the socioanalytic group raises questions about his experiences in a natural group of which he is a member he should be encouraged to reenact the experience before the group. If he reenacts it before the socioanalytic group, a synthetic group which provides him with security, safety and support, he may increase his understanding of the experience and the relationship. If he experienced failure in the natural group he may also learn how to improve his chances for success in subsequent experiences.

If the Socioanalysis has been conducted in dyadic sessions involving the subject and a director, it is recommended that the relationship tests, role tests, and spontaneity tests be administered by someone other than the director. The close contact between the director and subject over a period of time might influence his scoring of such tests. Nevertheless, a measure of change is necessary and the testing provides this measurement. Furthermore, the results of these tests will provide clues for the subject and the Socioanalist as to what areas require further exploration. Although a Socioanalysis may begin with a dyadic relationship (subject and socioanalist) it should be expanded to include others as soon as practicable. While it is possible to complete a Socioanalysis in a dyadic examination of relationships the participation of others in a group setting provides greater opportunity for exploration. In a Socioanalytic group, a synthetic group which provides a protected environment, an individual may experiment with all sorts of relationships. He may also observe others examining their relationships and participate in providing them with alternative courses of action. As he learns new ways of relating to people he can experiment with modified patterns of behavior in his natural groups. The subject and the Socioanalist may, from time to time, review the material examined in past sessions by reviewing protocols of these sessions. Chart XVIII sets forth the requirements of a protocol of a Socioanalytic Group Session. The same form, appropriately modified, may be used to record the relationships considered in a dyadic session or even in a self-analysis.

Self-Help Groups and Socioanalysis

During the 1930's a few people with serious problems resulting from or accompanying excessive consumption of alcohol formed

Alcoholics Anonymous. In the 1940's the activities of this organization, having become national and to an extent international in scope, were widely publicized. The principal objective of Alcoholics Anonymous was then and is to this day, to help other alcoholics to recover from their "illness." In this endeavor working with other alcoholics was to play a vital part in keeping each participant sober. Thus, alcoholics anonymous is the prototype of a self-help group organized by people who have a problem in common and attempt to solve it together without the intervention or direction of outsiders regardless of their professional qualifications. The leaders of Alcoholics Anonymous borrow freely from science, religion, medicine and other sources considered relevant by them. They recognize, for example, that abnormal drinking is a symptom of personal maladjustment to life. Nevertheless, they feel that they are more effective than professional practitioners because they are able to capitalize on one great advantage, their personal experiences as drinkers who have recovered. The Alcoholics Anonymous model was used in forming narcotics anonymous, gamblers anonymous, TOPS (take off pounds sensibly), and other self-help groups formed by former prisoners, mental patients, and others with problems in common.

Can such self-help groups apply socioanalysis without the assistance of professionals and if so how? It would appear that there are at least two ways in which the necessary skills could be made available to small self-help groups. The group might have one of its members obtain training in socioanalysis and then apply the method and techniques. The trained member acts in the role of socioanalist and performs the functions prescribed for the socioanalist. He, as the expert in the group, would have to do the necessary reading, gain as much experience as he could, and, at times consult with a professional when confronted with an unusual problem.

Another, and perhaps more effective way of applying Socioanalysis in a self-help group, would be to have each member embark on his own self-analysis. The group could then operate in much the same way as a Socioanalytic group directed by a Socioanalist. Each member would have the advantage of knowing that every other one was coping with a similar effort to gain an understanding of his own relationships. Obstacles encountered by one could be observed by others less emotionally involved.

Furthermore, each member of the Socioanalytic self-help group would still be free to participate in a Psychodrama directed by an expert and thus gain insights from others not associated with his self-help group.

Whenever possible it is recommended that Socioanalysis with a self-help group be directed by a Socioanalist. The recovered alcoholic, for example, must develop satisfying occupational relationships, social relationships, not involving the consumption of alcohol, and activities or hobbies to take the place of alcohol. Alcoholics Anonymous groups help him to remain sober but do not do enough to equip the individual to enter into meaningful social relationships. In may instances it was precisely the deficiency in such relationships which led to the abnormal consumption of alcohol. If we substitute drugs for alcohol, we must reach the same conclusion about Narcotics Anonymous.

PART II

THE PSYCHODRAMATIC METHOD

The next four chapters provide a rather detailed description of the Psychodramatic Method including techniques and ways of employing them. It may appear to you, the reader, that they are intended solely for professionals. Certainly the material presented should be of use to psychodramatists. It provides techniques which they can integrate with those they now employ and descriptive material that will help them train others. It is my belief, however, that any person participating in a Psychodrama session can benefit greatly by an understanding of the method, its objectives, its instruments and the techniques employed. The more he knows about the method the more effectively he can apply the process to his own Socioanalysis. As we noted in Part I, each person must participate actively in his Socioanalysis. To sit by as a passive recipient of data relying upon interpretations and analyses of an expert obstructs the Socioanalytic process and ultimately defeats it. The more you know about the method the more you will get out of each session. You will be better able to apply Psychodrama to an understanding of your natural groups.

A person coming to a Psychodrama session for the first time is likely to be uneasy, even anxious, if he does not know what to expect. He may sit in his seat immobilized because he is fearful of having to participate. Unless he has some idea of what participation involves, a high level of anxiety is to be anticipated. For this reason, I recommend that before going to a Psychodrama one learns as much as he can about the Psychodramatic Method and the techniques employed. The more a person knows about the method the less anxious and the more spontaneous he is likely to be and the more capable he is of participating to his advantage. Furthermore, the more he knows about the techniques the better able he is to judge the competence of the director. Psychodrama directors are not licensed and there is no legal requirement that they complete any course of training. The result is that many persons attempt to direct Psychodrama sessions without having acquired the necessary skills. The fact that one is licensed to practice Psychiatry, Psychology, Social Work, or some other profession does not of itself guarantee that he is qualified in Psychodrama. Few academic departments of Medicine, Psychology or Social Work provide such training. Moreno Institute at Beacon, New York and affiliated institutes in other parts of the country train directors of Psychodrama and certify those who they consider qualified. Also, the American Society of Group Psychotherapy and Psychodrama has established standards for accreditation of directors. However, even among formally trained directors some are more experienced and better qualified than others. A participant who has some idea of what a director should be doing to increase his awareness or otherwise help him define his goals is better able to evaluate the competence of the director. Secure in the knowledge that the director can effectively utilize psychodramatic techniques he may become sufficiently spontaneous to risk involvement in the session. Your director may be introducing a psychoanalytic bias into the sessions he directs. The psychoanalytic view of a group may be summarized as follows— The therapist or analyst is seen as parent substitute. The "patient" is seen as one who directs the emotions and attitudes which he has for his parents to the therapists. This process is referred to as "transference". The members of the groups are seen as sybling substitutes. According to this view, each "patient" responds to other members of the group as if they were his brothers or sisters. The entire group then is seen as a substitute family. Socioanalysis is not related to Psychoanalysis and does not share its preconceptions.

In over twenty years work with Psychodramatic and Role Training groups I have found no evidence to support this view of group behavior. I have found that group members have perceived me in a variety of ways. Some protagonists start out by seeing me as an expert who will advise them on how to improve their behavior or what courses of action to follow. They raise such questions as; Should I divorce my husband? Should I marry Bill? and expect me to answer them. They soon learn that I reject that role as demeaning to the protagonist and other group members. Most then begin to see me as an expert in method seeking to have them use my tools. Eventually they see me as one who is constantly examining alternatives and encouraging them to do so. In the course of several sessions they begin to see other members of the group as fellow sufferers and fellow researchers all looking for alternatives. The Psychodramatic group soon becomes a laboratory in which one can freely experiment with alternatives. It may be true that a person will first react to a male authority figure in much the same way that he reacted to his father. However, this tendency, when it exists, is evidenced not only in interaction with the director but also with other male authority types in the group. We do not need the concept of transference to explain this phenomenon. A far more logical explanation is that the individual in the course of his life experiences has developed certain attitudes and patterns of behavior toward authority figures. Some may have been acquired in childhood and continued over time. Others may have been acquired at school, work, or in social interaction in other situations. In Psychodrama one may experiment with new patterns of behavior and, decide for himself whether or not he wishes to change them and what changes he would like to introduce.

It has been noted that ours is a society which fosters the development of a neurotic personality. Many people are more or less emotionally disturbed because they are brought up to believe and then to internalize values and attitudes which lead them to become ineffective and unhappy. They accept goals others have selected as appropriate for them and then brainwashed them to accept in the socialization process. They accept standards of behavior for themselves which perpetuate failure and lack of satisfaction. One objective of Psychodrama is to expose values and attitudes that cause the conflicts the individual is experiencing and trace them to their sources. Once this is accomplished the individual is ready to examine alternative attitudes and values—attitudes toward himself and toward his behavior as well. In this way he may learn either to accdpt himself as he is, or modify his behavior patterns to make him acceptable to himself and others.

As I see it, the process of dealing with emotional problems includes dealing with, understanding, and improving interpersonal relationships. An important requirement of all "therapy" would therefore be to increase self-esteem and self-acceptance. With increased self-esteem the individual is better able to overcome his feelings of inadequacy. To the extent that such feelings are overcome, spontaneity may be expected to increase. The individual will be able to take more risks because he will realize that he is "adequate" and that he can win.

Chapter 6

PSYCHODRAMA IN SOCIOANALYSIS

Dr. J. L. Moreno, the originator of Psychodrama, defines it as the science which explores the "truth" by dramatic methods. An examination of articles published in Group Psychotherapy, Sociometry, and other professional journals indicates that Psychodrama has been employed in the following contexts:

1. As a diagnostic technique by psychologists, psychiatrists, and others engaged in counseling or psychotherapy.
2. As a therapeutic method by Psychologists, Psychiatrists, and Social Workers; psychodramatic techniques are used by many who do not fully accept the psychodramatic method. Psychoanalysts, Rogerians, Adlerians, and psychotherapists committed to other schools of psychotherapy report the use of psychodramatic techniques and procedures in their work.
3. As a training technique in education and in industry.
4. As a technique in pastoral counseling.
5. In Socioanalysis, as a method of exploring *in action* the social relationships of a person to other people and the problems arising from such relationships.

Although in this book our interest is in Socioanalysis, the Psychodramatic method and the techniques described herein are essentially the same when used in the other contexts referred to above. Although they are the ones most frequently used and most essential to socioanalysis, they constitute a small fraction of the two hundred or more discussed in the literature.

Psychodrama, as an action method, makes available to people a laboratory setting in which they can examine relationships in the here and now, reexamine those past relationships which they consider relevant in the present, and experiment with possible changes for the future. In providing the individual an opportunity to examine his social atom with the assistance of a skilled director and a group, Psychodrama serves as a form of preventive psychiatry. Each increase in the ability to consider alternative courses of action and choose between them tends to liberate the individual from limitations on his spontaneity.

Psychodrama is used in the treatment of those stigmatized as "mentally ill". It is also used by marriage counselors, guidance counselors, social workers, psychologists, and others who deal with people seeking to imporve their relationships. *What is most important to me, however, is that it provides a method by which people may examine relationships in which they are involved and experiment with alternative patterns of interaction.* The Protagonist, the person who examines his relationships on the psychodramatic stage, as I see it, is the *researcher.* The professionial, whatever his status may be in other settings, is, when directing a psychodrama session, an *expert in method and no more than that.* Each person who employs the Psychodramatic Method, as a protagonist, is responsible for examining his own life experiences on the psychodramatic stage, in past, present and future situations and choose between alternative courses of action open to him.

Psychodrama originated in the Theater of Spontaneity which Moreno started in Vienna in 1921. The Theater of Spontaneity did not employ professional actors. Persons who performed were not given a script and only the most rudimentary props were required. Moreno, the director, would appear on the stage and, as part of the warming up process, would invite attention to items in the news likely to be considered important by his Viennese audience. As members of the audience became involved in discussion with him, he invited them on to the stage, and, under his direction, encouraged them to reenact an event reported in the newspaper of that day. Following an enactment, people in the audience were asked to engage in a discussion based on it. Moreno found that the personal problems of the people in the audience not only influenced the choice of topic, but also the way in which participants played their parts. Their perceptions of important happenings were influenced by their own needs and experiences. He also discovered that the enactments and ensuing discussions resulted in catharsis, that is to say, those who were part of the audience as well as those who performed on the stage appeared relieved as they left the theater. Moreno concluded that in the course of the enactment and the discussion that followed people discovered that the doubts and fears that troubled them also disturbed others. He believed that it was the involvement in the problems of others and the sharing of experiences with many other people that produced the cathartic effect.

The Living Newspaper, produced in the United States in the 1930's was partially inspired by Moreno's Theater of Spontaneity. In the Living Newspaper the production was also based on important events of the day. Events of the day were reenacted by performers employing a script based on these events. The major difference was in spontaneity. The script used in the Living Newspaper limited the spontaneity and creativity of the actors. Performances in the Theater of Spontaneity were impromptu, created on the stage by members of the audience in the 'here and now'. Nevertheless, performances of the Living Newspaper produced a cathartic effect on the audience.

Moreno had derived the idea for a Theater of Spontaneity from the Greek Tragedians who recognized that drama, when it presented incidents arousing pity and fear to a large audience, produced catharsis of these emotions. Spectators, after watching the enactment of such dramas seemed to be free from fear, and the theatrical performance in which the tragedy was presented was credited with freeing them. Tragedy, as Aristotle had defined it, was an *imitation* of action and of life. Moreno endeavored to produce an *extension* of action and of life. He sought to accomplish this in the Theater of Spontaneity by having people act out the events and then discuss them. The person in the audience who came on to the stage of the Theater of Spontaneity and acted out an event was involved only as a part of the collectivity that produced the event. He was not acting out an event from his own life experience.

In order for an individual to produce an extension of his own experiences, it was necessary that he reenact situations in which *he had participated in the past, act himself in the present, or experiment with actions he might have to take in the future.* He had to enact or reenact *important events in his own life,* past, present, and anticipated. To provide people with an opportunity to achieve this sort of extension of life is the essence of the Psychodramatic Method. In no respect is Psychodrama an imitation of life.

In the classic version of Psychodrama, the one which Dr. Moreno started with and the one which he considered to be best suited to his temperament, the spontaneity of the group was important, just as important as was the spontaneity of the director. Each session was in the here and now, unrehearsed, and entirely unplanned. Moreno stated that he wanted to start free of any bias and therefore did not want to see or know anything about the people in the group in advance of his encounters with them. He later developed three additional versions. The first, which he referred to as the emergent Psychodrama, *in situ,* was developed when he became a medical doctor. In a session he would deal with all of the people present who were intimately involved with each other. The entire family, for example, was the "patient." He also developed a group-centered Psychodrama in which the entire group was involved with no predetermined director or protagonist. In such a session all were technically equal and anyone might emerge as director. In this sort of session spontaneity was maximized. The third type of Psychodrama he developed he called *leader-centered.* One person is accepted in advance of the session as the director. Throughout the session the director remains entirely neutral, does not impose his values on protagonists or group members, and limits his role to that of catalyst. This version of Psychodrama is the one most widely used by Psychodramatists who are not Psychiatrists. I employ a modified version of this model in my style of direction which I refer to as *protagonist-centered.* I am a leader-centered director who encourages the protagonist to choose relationships to be examined and situations to be enacted or reenacted.

The actors and the acts in the 'here and now' are the primary data. The reenactment of experiences from one's past are intended to provide an opportunity for close examination and experimentation with courses of action different from those pursued in the past. The psychodramatic stage provides a laboratory in which alternative solutions to unsolved problems may be sought within a free and flexible social setting. The Psychodramatist is convinced that events of the past, present, or those anticipated for the future can be better communicated in the course of enactments or reenactments than in verbal forms of communication, written, or oral. He deals with the total situation involving an individual or group and encourages communication within it. Members of the psychodrama group can examine alternatives and choose between them.

Moreno, the psychiatrist, introduced Psychodrama into the world of psychotherapy. Although primarily a group method, Moreno and others have employed it in private practice with individual patients. Used in this way, the two persons, patient and therapist, are viewed as a group, a dyad. The therapist is in the interaction with the "patient," involved with him. He does not remain aloof and detached. When used as group treatment, the psychodrama provides members with an opportunity to present and solve their problems with the assistance of the Director, a staff of assistants called auxiliary egos, a stage, and other members serving as both a "Therapeutic" group or audience. It is employed as both a diagnostic and "therapeutic" method. Over the years, techniques have been developed to deal with every conceivable type of emotional or relationship problem. Persons are observed in interaction with others representing any persons the protagonist or the director places on the stage, for whatever purpose. They may explore relationships with friends, enemies, employers, members of their families, and any other persons with whom they have interacted in the past, would have liked to interact with in the past, or present, or would like to in the future. Increased understanding is the goal and the exploration of all significant relationships is encouraged, particularly of those believed to have produced trauma. When applicable, persons are encourged to reenact scenes from their dreams, fantasies, or hallucinations.

When psychodrama is employed in socioanalysis, the choice of scenes to be enacted or reenacted is always left to the protagonist. The director may make suggestions, but the decision of the protagonist that he does or does not desire to enact or reenact an experience is regarded as final. I categorically reject the label "patient" and refuse to apply it to a fellow human being. Furthermore, I refuse to recognize the caste relationship which the term "patient" implies. To a socioanalist, as a Psychodrama director, the protagonist is not only his own researcher, he is also his own master. If we do not trust an individual to decide what he wants to do on the psychodramatic stage how can we honestly expect him to assume responsibility for his actions in other life situations?

The action portion of a Psychodrama may produce an enormous amount of data. How this is interpreted or used depends largely on the philosophy and experience of the Director. There are, for example, two Psychoanalytic schools in France employing Psychodrama. Obviously, a Psychoanalyst would interpret the data produced in an enactment in psychoanalytic terms. Individual psychologists, a title used by followers of Alfred Adler also employ Psychodrama and interpret the data obtained according to Adlerian Hypotheses. Socioanalists apply Spontaneity Theory and Sociometric Theory but avoid interpretation. No matter who uses Psychodrama however, the data is obtained in much the same way.

Psychiatrists have reported the successful treatment of many types of "emotionally disturbed" people through the application of Psychodrama. In most instances the reports relate to the effects of the treatment on a "patient" rather than on members of a Psychodrama group. Where the result of the treatment of groups are described, several members of the group have participated as protagonists, and it is impossible to evaluate the effect of membership in a Psychodramatic group without such participation. The effect of Psychodrama on "patients", according to psychiatrists using it, is beneficial because:

1. It produces *catharsis.* "Patients" show substantial reduction in anxiety. Catharsis, as a concept, was introduced by Aristotle. He used the term to express the strange effects Greek drama had on its audience. He maintained that drama tended to purify the spectators by exciting certain emotions which provided some relief for them. The concept as used in Psychodrama is neither a passive mental catharsis nor solely a reaction of an audience. It may be experienced by both the protagonist on the stage and members of the audience who identify with portions of his presentation.

2. "Patients" gain *insight.* They develop new understanding of their problems. When an individual sees the connection between his present behavior and a pattern of repetitive behavior learned in the past he is said to have developed *insight.* However, insight does not guarantee a solution to a problem. In the Psychodramatic or Role Training session alternative courses of action are explored so that the protagonist and other members of the group may discover solutions that are novel for them.

3. "Patients" develop *spontaneity.* They are better able to develop new approaches to problems and provide more adequate solutions.

Group Psychodrama does not arouse the anxiety that individual therapies do. The awareness that others have difficulties in their relationships, and are also hesitant and lacking in spontaneity helps to dissipate anxiety. As the group continues to function the support one receives from other members of the group contributes to his acceptance of himself and creates an atmosphere in which one can risk some spontaneity.

4. "Patients" improve in *Sociometric Status*. They tend to choose associations with more people and they are chosen more often by others.

The important thing for an individual deficient in spontaneity is to change the patterns of his interaction with people. He must transform failure in relationships to success and this must occur in his natural groups. He may be suffering from the effects of unsuccessful experiences. In the Psychodramatic group he can learn a great deal about his relationships, those which diminish and ddiscourage him, and those which inhibit his spontaneity. He can examine the possibility of change in relationship, and alternative courses of action. As he learns in the synthetic group which relationships are detrimental to him and which encourage his spontaneity, he can begin to make changes in his natural groups.

I am convinced that the Psychodramatic experiences should not be limited to those persons stigmatized as "patients" and see no reason why any person participating in a Psychodrama group would not benefit in similar ways.

In Socioanalysis we are primarily interested in applying Psychodrama to the exploration of relationships. We would, therefore, apply it to Marriage Counseling, Guidance Counseling, Industrial Counseling, Education, the Field of Corrections, and in any other area where an understanding of social relationships is an important objective. A method that is effective in facilitating changes in behavior patterns and associations is invaluable, if persons are to increase their spontaneity. I am convinced that Psychodrama is such a method. It can be employed most effectively in conjunction with Sociometric Techniques, and Role Training. Many of the instruments and techniques used in the Psychodrama groups may also be used in Role Training and Socioanalytic groups. Some of them may be applied in Sensitivity Training groups, Encounter groups, Therapy groups, and discussion groups. The method, as described in this book, will focus primarily on the examination of social relationships and related problems. In Socioanalysis, Psychodrama is the principal method used to achieve change because it provides a laboratory in which people can explore the possibilities of change.

Instruments Used in Psychodrama

The Psychodramatic Method, applied in a group setting, involves the use of five basic instruments in combination. These are: a *stage,* a *director, one or more protagonists, auxiliary egos,* and a *group or audience.* The stage used is generally circular or oval and is constructed on three levels, if practicable. Each level of the stage represents a degree of committment or involvement in the problem of an individual.

When the individual moves from the group on to the first level of the stage he starts his presentation of a problem to the director and to the group. His movement to the second level symbolizes an intent to present his problem *in action.* The director and the group, by implication, become committed to exploring it with him. When he moves to the third level, the individual becomes the protagonist, in action. The entire session, from that point on, is focused *on his relationships* and on his problems to the extent that he desires to present them. The stage should be large enough to allow for movement and action. An upper level fourteen feet in diameter is considered sufficiently large for most purposes. The space represents an extension of the life space of the protagonist and on it he should be able to act out any situation important to him. Few props are required. Often a table and few chairs suffice. There should be an attempt, however, to simulate at least symbolically, every object in the space or situation recalled by the protagonist. If the protagonist says he is lying in a bed, a few chairs may be designated to simulate the bed. However, this must be done in an overt manner so that he can symbolically lie on the bed. A lighting system is employed to focus the attention of the group on the action. The degree of light and the coloring may be manipulated for many purposes. Lights are employed to reflect the mood of a protagonist. Brightly colored lights are used to represent gayer scenes while dim lighting is used to represent sad scenes. Lights may also be dimmed in an effort to move the protagonist further from the group. If the protagonist seems depressed, lights may be brightened to create a more cheerful atmosphere.

Whenever one is available, a stage is employed in a psychodramatic presentation, particularly if the psychodrama is conducted in a group setting. If a stage is not available a portion of the room is designated as an action area, and all action is concentrated in that area as if it were a stage. It is in this area that the props are placed at the beginning of a session and it is from this area that the director addresses the group. The protagonist is moved into it and the action takes place there.

Psychodrama may also be conducted "in situ," that is, in a classroom, a home, an office or any other place in which a relationship is explored. Furthermore, psychodrama may be conducted in a dyadic relationship in which the director and the protagonist are the only persons present. Where Socioanalysis involves a dyadic relationship, the action usually takes place in an office, and the director and the protagonist act out whatever parts are considered necessary. However, in a group setting, a portion of the room is designated the action area: It should be so situated that all members of the group can focus their attention on it. It is important that individuals participating in an enactment move from their chairs to the action area. Unless this is done the protagonist may become involved only in a peripheral sense, and other members of the group may not become involved in the action.

The second instrument of the psychodrama is the *director*. He is the producer of the psychodrama and the expert on whom we rely to focus the production on the problems of the protagonist and at the same time maintain rapport with the group. He is the expert in the method and it is he who makes available to the protagonist the various techniques of psychodrama intended to increase his understanding of his relationships with the people he is portraying. The director is also the catalyst, the person who stimulates action through the use of appropriate techniques. A director interested in socioanalysis avoids analysis of the action and emphasizes group discussion of all relationships and problems. The functions of the director are the following:

1. *To plan each session considering the needs and interests of the members of the psychodramatic group as he perceives them.* Prior to the session the director should review all available data, including protocols (summary outlines) of previous sessions, test results, and

material derived from interviews. Sessions should be so planned that each member of the group has an opportunity to be a protagonist at least once in every ten sessions.

2. *To further a warm, permissive atmosphere in which group members will feel free to express themselves.* In two portions of the psychodramatic production the director has an opportunity to involve every member in interaction with him. One is at the beginning of a session, in the warming up process, the other, the discussion following the action portion of the session. In warming up the group, he may and should address each member of the group, individually, and communicate with him briefly in a friendly and warm manner. Even if a member responds with verbal hostility he must avoid remarks which might be considered rejection of the person. It is this friendly exchange of views which occurs in the good warm up that helps to create a functioning psychodrama group out of the disparate individuals who came to the session. Success in the establishment of cooperation will carry over to the group discussion that follows the action.

3. *To warm-up the group in such a way as to enable it to decide on goals and proceed toward them.* As problems are raised by members of the group he helps the persons involved to define them for the group and summarizes all those presented so that the group may consider them one at a time.

4. *To assist the group in the selection of protagonists at each session.* In doing this he takes into consideration the needs of each member to participate and encourages people to offer to examine relationships they hope to improve. The decision on who is to be the protagonist is usually left to the group. A protagonist selected by a majority vote of a group is more likely to obtain the support of the group.

5. *To do what he can to make the members of the group feel at ease in interaction.* Although he concentrates his efforts on the protagonist, he must make every effort to involve all of the members in the interaction and discussion wherever practicable. Members of the group may gain valuable insights when performing in auxiliary ego roles. What is desired is *involvement* of the protagonists in the interaction on the stage and *involvement* of all other members of the group, either in the interaction or the discussion. Superficial participation on a verbal level is not enough. The goal is *involvement*.

6. *To assist the protagonist to set up each scene and act in it.* In doing so he calls upon his training and experience for suggestions as to relationships to be explored, scenes to be enacted, and experiments to be undertaken. If he notices symptoms of extreme depression, isolation, or self-rejection, he must be careful to suggest enactments that tend to alleviate these symptoms. He should make every effort to avoid enactments that might tend to aggravate them. However, the choice as to whether or not to enact or reenact a scene rests with the protagonist.

7. *To provide the protagonist with techniques which have been found to be effective* in dealing with problems and relationships he is attempting to explore. It is in the performance of this function that his expertise is most relevant. If he employs any of these techniques without consulting the protagonist or the group, the responsibility for their use is exclusively his. He must, therefore, exercise great care in their application. While it is true that the focus of a particular session may be on the relationships of one protagonist, the director has a responsibility to every member of the group and should avoid the use of a presentation or technique which might result in some embarrassment to the protagonist or to some other member of the group.

8. *To protect the protagonist from attack by other members of the group.* When, in the course of the group discussion, or at any other time during a session, a member of the group criticizes or otherwise demeans the protagonist, the director must intercede on his behalf. His response may take the form of challenging the basis for the attack or defending the position of the protagonist. Where neither of these courses of action is suitable, the director may invite attention to the relative universality of the deficiency referred to by the critic. My method of dealing with an attack on a protagonist is to divert it to me as director. For example, I may ask the attacker why he is dissatisfied with me as director or what I have done to arouse his hostility. I do not permit the attack on the protagonist to go unchallenged.

9. *To lead a group discussion after the action portion of each session.* While the director, at his descretion, may involve the group in discussion at any point in the session, the period generally allotted comes after the enactments of the protagonist are over. The director should try to involve as many members of the group as possible. He may do so by addressing questions to the group as a whole,

or he may address members of the group individually. His obligation to protect the protagonist from attack has already been discussed. He also has a duty to protect any member of the group who is treated harshly or unfairly by others.

10. *To summarize the action and discussion based upon the feedback obtained in the group discussion.* In doing so he may refer to summaries of previous sessions, areas of interest still unexplored, and the relationship of the session just completed to the goals of the group. A good summary should lead directly into the area to be examined at the next session. In a sense it provides the prelude to the warm up of the next session and should, at least in part, be referred to in the warm up talk of the next session. It is in this way that continuity between sessions is maintained.

When working with an ongoing group, one which is scheduled to meet ten times or more, a director employs sociometric techniques to measure changes in group structure and in the sociometric status of each member. Improvement in sociometric status is highly correlated with improvement in occupational, family, and community roles and with general social adjustment. It is, therefore, considered evidence of progress. Social relationships tests, role tests and psychodramatic projection tests may be administered after every fifth session. This practice is strongly recommended for use with any group participating in a series of Psychodrama sessions. The use of these tests provides clues to the progress of members, the relative isolation of some and the role areas requiring emphasis, and the cliquing or subgroupings, if any. The results of these tests should be discussed with each member in private conferences.

While each Psychodrama director tends to develop a style to suit his personality and talents, there are four styles most frequently employed. These four basic styles of Psychodrama director are: Psychiatric, Protagonist-Centered, Group-Centered, and Democratic. Although an experienced director can employ any of them, each Psychodrama director selects a style most compatible with his philosophy and personality. A brief description of each of these four styles of directing follows:

1. *The Psychiatric Director:* Not all persons employing this style are psychiatrists, however, those employing it generally work with people who identify themselves as patients. Dr. Moreno, as a psy-

chiatrist, frequently employed this style when in a hospital setting. He has, however, innovated in many other styles, and directed in whichever style he considered appropriate. The Psychiatric Director simply selects the protagonist, invites him up to the stage, and, after a warm-up, procedes into action. The assumption is that the members of the group rely on the director to decide who shall be the protagonist.

2. *The Protagonist-Centered Director:* The protagonist is selected by the group. Once on the stage the protagonist is asked to select a scene he wishes to enact or reenact. He is also asked to select persons from the group to play in auxiliary roles (his wife, mother, employer, or whosoever are the "others" with whom he is interacting). While the director may make suggestions, all decisions on scenes or sequences are left to the protagonist. I am committed to this style of direction and am generally identified with it. Most of my work has been with persons stigmatized as juvenile delinquents, criminals, drug addicts, alcoholics. I have also directed thousands of sessions with groups of professionals, students, and persons drawn from the general public. None of these people define themselves as "patients." Hence, the style of Protagonist-Centered Director is not only suitable to me as director but to the persons in the groups I work with. This style is strongly recommended for Socioanalysis.

3. *The Group-Centered Director:* One or more protagonists emerge from the group in the course of a session. While the director may focus for a time on a relationship or experience of one protagonist, others in the group are not excluded from participation. Using this method, a man who is examining his relationship with a son may find himself in interaction with young men examining relationships with their respective fathers. Each may be considered a protagonist, and the director concerns himself with all of them as well as others in the group. This style of direction has been used effectively with persons who do not define themselves as patients, including all those enumerated above. However, highly sensitive individuals seem to prefer to examine their relationships in protagonist-centered sessions.

4. *The Democratic Director:* This style of direction involves the establishment of a warm relationship between the director and members of the group. The director exchanges banter with members of the group, introduces humor and tries to create an at-

mosphere of free exchange. A protagonist may emerge from the group as a result of some exchange between members of the group or the director and any one of them. Even after the protagonist is in action the director frequently refers to the group for comment and suggestions. This style of psychodramatic direction is peculiarly suitable to the session open to the general public. People coming to such sessions do not define themselves as "patients" and most do not acknowledge that they have any "problems" in relationships. The democratic director accepts the assumptions of the group and leads it wherever it wants to go.

The third instrument of a psychodrama is the *protagonist*. He is the individual who moves into action on the stage to present the problems he encounters in the course of his social relationship. He is asked to be himself on the stage, and to portray actual situations from his past or in his present. He may, if he wishes, act out situations he expects to face in the future. The director instructs him to be himself and not perform as an actor. He is afforded an opportunity to reenact any scene that *he* considers important and is given freedom of expression in that scene. Spontaneity is encouraged. Although the protagonist may tend to communicate on a verbal level for some time, he is encouraged to move into action as much as possible. Our concern is with the *here and now* of the protagonist. If we begin with the reenactment of scenes out of the past, it is because the protagonist is more familiar with these scenes and can act them out with greater security. It is not important that the protagonist repeat every word that happened in the course of a dialogue or reenact a scene exactly as it occured. His perceptions of it, to the best of his recollection, are adequate. An attempt to secure absolute fidelity of recollection would result in loss of spontaneity. In the psychodramatic session an important goal is involvement with others in interaction and this is encouragedd to the maximum extent. The protagonist is encouraged to encounter, on the psychodramatic stage, persons with whom he has experienced difficulties or with whom he has unsatisfying relationships. Psychodramatic techniques are employed to give him new understandings of his present relationships and patterns of behavior, what they were like in the past, and how they could be modified in the future. He is also afforded the opportunity of experimenting with other patterns of behavior and changed relationships.

In selecting a protagonist, the protagonist-centered director accepts the decision of the group. Once the group has made its selection and a protagonist has moved into action, the scenes enacted are selected *by him* and the discussion revolves around his *relationships* and *his problems*. The entire session may then be devoted to his social world. Members of the group may be called upon to participate in the enactments if required by him, and to contribute to a discussion of the problems he presents. In a sense, however, the protagonist is an instrument of the group. Members of the group, as they identify with portions of his production, relate them to similar experiences of their own. They may gain valuable insights as they apply what is enacted to their own relationships.

When a protagonist moves into action, the stage becomes his laboratory. The director may suggest that he examine one or another relationship but the decision on whether or not to do so is always left to the protagonist. It is he who *examines, explores,* and *experiments.* He, not the director, is the researcher. His autonomy and authority are respected at all times. The director may encourage him to reenact a situation or prepare, in action, for a possible future encounter. He may, in a scene, advise him to experiment with a different pattern of behavior. At no time, however, will he insist on an enactment if the protagonist decides against it. The director frequently introduces techniques without consulting the protagonist. He does so because he is the expert in techniques and the protagonist may not even be aware of them. However, if the protagonist rejects a particular technique, the director discontinues it's use. Techniques employed to encourage the expression of feelings and attitudes are successful only if the protagonist cooperates. The same may be said for techniques used to facilitate the expression of the unexpressed. When any other technique is employed, however, whether at the suggestion of the director or an auxiliary ego, the protagonist is afforded an opportunity of expressing his objections, if any. The ways in which this may be done will be explained when the various techniques are described and discussed.

The group-centered director, as we have noted, does not limit himself to the needs of one protagonist. Working with more than one protagonist at a time he encourages interaction between them and also between each of them and members of the group. The relationships to be examined, the scenes to be enacted, and the techniques to be employed are determined to a great extent by the director. The same is true when a session is directed by a Psychiatric director. In a sense, everyone in the group is considered a protagonist by the democratic director.

A fourth instrument employed in psychodrama is the *auxiliary ego*. The auxiliary ego may be a member of the director's staff trained to perform in roles and to play a part in applying various psychodramatic techniques. He may also be a person selected from the group by the protagonist or the director to play some role. Auxiliary egos may come on to the stage as agents of the protagonist, as agents of the director, or as persons acting on their own.

1. *The auxiliary ego as agent of the protagonist:* In exploring a relationship with a person or persons in his social world, the protagonist may decide to reenact a situation in which he interacted with that person or persons. Unless they are members of the psychodramatic group they are not likely to be present at the time and place of the enactment. The psychodramatic method requires that they be represented on the stage by other persons. For example, a protagonist who wishes to reenact a quarrel he had with his wife, needs someone to portray his wife on the stage. An auxiliary ego is selected from the staff of the director or from the group to play the wife. Through the use of such Psychodramatic techniques as self-presentation and role-reversal, the auxiliary ego learns enough about the wife to portray her on the stage. It should be noted, however, that the wife is not present and since the role of the wife is performed solely in accordance with the instructions of the protagonist, the role of the wife may be distorted by his perceptions and/or by his intentional misrepresentations. The auxiliary ego representing an absent person in the social world of the protagonist actually functions as *his* agent and presents *his perceptions* of that person.

2. *The auxiliary ego as agent of the director:* Some of the techniques used in psychodrama involve action by a person assisting the director. Two of the most important, the *double* and the *mirror*, will be described in a subsequent chapter. Auxiliary egos who employ these techniques under the instructions of the director must be highly skilled in their application. They must be thoroughly familiar with the psychodramatic method and the roles

assigned to them. The mirror techniques, for example, requires an auxiliary ego to duplicate a performance of the protagonist in a previous enactment so that he and others may review his patterns of behavior. The double technique requires that an auxiliary ego assist a protagonist to express his hitherto unexpressed feelings and attitudes and to help him define and redefine his relationships. For an auxiliary ego to do so effectively he should have some training. Since he goes into action at the request of the director and is required to follow his instructions, he is considered an agent of the director. The hypotheses he helps explore are those of the director and his effectiveness is measured by the extent to which he carries out instructions. He enters on to the scene when told to, performs in accordance with instructions, and leaves the stage when the director orders him to do so.

3. *The auxiliary ego as his own agent:* Some of the psychodramatic techniques, future projection, for example, place the protagonist in a situation he may never have been in before. Since the scene is not a reenactment, the auxiliary ego has much wider latitude in the role of the other. Where, for example, the protagonist is being interviewed by a prospective employer, neither the protagonist nor the director can accurately predict the behavior of the 'possible' employer. The protagonist is being prepared to face him. The auxiliary ego, in such an enactment, is generally permitted to ask any questions he deems appropriate, to react to the protagonist in any way he considers advisable, and to provide as many problems and stimuli as he believes to be useful. He is, in a sense, a social investigator, whose task it is to raise as many problems as he can so that the protagonist can prepare to deal with them in the 'safe' laboratory situation provided by the psychodramatic stage. Similar latitude is given the auxiliary ego in most applications of the future projection technique, a technique which will be discussed in the next chapter. It is when the auxiliary ego functions as participant in an experimental situation that he exercises greatest autonomy and independence and acts as his own agent.

It is largely in interaction with auxiliary egos that the protagonist provides clues to the nature of his relationships and to the patterns of social behavior he characteristically exhibits. These clues may be valuable to the director, the other members of the group, and most of all to himself, the principal investigator.

Problems he experiences in his natural groups become more clearly defined as he interacts with others on the psychodramatic stage. For these reasons it is important to the protagonist that auxiliary egos present him with a great many alternative reactions to the behavior. The more accurate his perceptions of others becomes, the more appropriate his responses are likely to be. To a considerable extent the value of the psychodramatic experience to a protagonist is dependent on the auxiliary egos, who not only provide stimuli in the forms of 'others' in the interactions with him, but also, as agents and social investigators help him to examine his own attitudes, feelings, and behavior patterns. One of the most important contributions of the director to the success of a psychodrama, both from the point of view of the protagonist and the group is his choice and use of auxiliary egos.

A fifth instrument of psychodrama is the group or audience. This includes all persons present at the session who did not directly participate in the action. The members of the group represent, to the protagonist, persons in the natural groups to which he belongs. Collectively, the audience may represent the world at large and the opinions expressed, 'public opinion'. When he presents himself, his relationships, and his problems on the stage before a psychodramatic group he is, in effect, seeking either approval of his present patterns or clues to desirable change in behavior patterns, relationships, or both. If the group approves he is likely to perceive this approval as rewarding. If his enactment of changed behavior patterns wins the reward and approval of the group he may experiment with the new patterns in his natural groups. Thus, the synthetic group, the psychodramatic group, can help the protagonist experiment with new forms of behavior and provide him with approximations of the responses these forms of behavior will elicit in actual situations in natural groups. He can then decide to discard those patterns of behavior likely to fail and adopt others more likely to provide success. If, for example, he has been isolated and withdrawn in his natural groups, and has won approval for more outgoing behavior in the psychodramatic group, he may be better able to warm up to others in natural groups and achieve warmth and acceptance in return. Insights and understandings may come to the protagonist while engaged in interaction on the stage or in the discussion period which follows the action. It is in the course of the discussions that group members do most to assist the protagonist. This process will be discussed in the next chapter.

In addition to assisting the protagonist to better understand his relationship problems, members of the group may learn a great deal about their own relationships and problems. Each is a *learner* who may benefit by an enactment. If the protagonist enacts experiences with members of his family, for example, each member of the group may apply the knowledge gained to *his own relationships* with members of his own family. The same may be said for other life situations explored by the protagonist. We share a common humanity and most of us are members of family constellations, occupational groups, community organizations and other natural groups which resemble those of most others in many significant respects. Our basic relationship patterns tend to be similar and our characteristic behavior patterns if not similar, at least familiar to most of us.

The members of the group, in the discussion portion of a psychodrama, are encouraged by the director to call upon *their own* experiences for examples of solutions to problems similar to those reflected in the enactments of the protagonist. As a member of the group expresses indentification with a problem presented by the protagonist he may gain a better understanding of one of his problems. Where several members of a group identify with portions of an enactment, group morale and solidarity tends to develop. As members of the group condemn or support *actions of teir own* similar to those portrayed by the protagonist, *he and other members* increase their understanding of their problems in social relationships and alternative solutions to those problems.

Members of a psychodramatic group are encouraged to be as spontaneous as possible in discussion but are urged not to '*analyze*' the protagonist. The presence of a group which accepts him and offers him understanding may be important to a protagonist, particularly if he has been somewhat isolated prior to the session. A willingness on the part of others to identify with him and to support him may increase his ability to develop meaningful relationships, first in the psychodramatic group, and later in his natural groups. A good director does not permit a psychodramatic group to become a plurel of spectators if he can prevent this from happening, nor does he countenance any attack on a protagonist by a member of the group. He makes every effort to encourage members of the group to *share* their experiences with the group.

The five instruments of psychodrama described above are calculated to assist a protagonist to examine any of his relationships past, present, or future. The goal of psychodrama is to help him to understand the relationships he shares in his natural groups so that he can be satisfied with them as they are, improve them, or abandon them. In the process he might decide to modify his behavior patterns to bring about improvement in his relationships. He might also decide to abandon some present relationship in favor of an alternative as he increases his awareness of available alternatives. The stage and the auxiliary egos provide a laboratory setting in which he can experiment with alternatives. The director, an expert in method and a catalyst, recommends techniques for use in his explorations. The audience or group constitutes a public which can offer understanding and support to him as a person, while approving or disapproving patterns of behavior. As he increases his awareness of alternatives and in his ability to choose between them he increases in spontaneity. Furthermore, in the course of a Psychodrama session he may become aware of factors and relationships that inhibit his spontaneity. He can be encouraged in action, to deal with these inhibiting or limiting factors.

Chapter 7

THE PSYCHODRAMA SESSION

While there is considerable variation in directorial style and in problems enacted there are certain characteristics that Psychodrama sessions have in common. These will be described and illustrated in this chapter.

There are three phases, each more or less clearly defined, through which each Psychodramatic session passes. These are: *a warm-up, an action portion,* and a *group or audience discussion.* A Psychodramatic group is, in a sense, a synthetic group. Each member of the group comes to it for what is essentially a *private* purpose, to get help in solving his own problems, to arrive at a better understanding of *his* relationships, and to experiment with modifications of *his behavior* while examining the possibilities of alternative relationships. The focus of a Psychodrama session is not on relationships of one member of a group to other members of the group. Group goals, if any, are subordinated to individual goals. The principal benefit a person can obtain in the course of participating in a synthetic group are knowledge, insights and skills for use in his natural groups. The goal of the director is to provide experiences which will prepare each participant to derive greater satisfactions in daily life in natural groups. A warming up process is required to get the disparate individuals who come to a Psychodrama session to develop some group goals and to become involved in the problems of each other. As members of a Psychodrama group begin to take an interest in the relationship problems similar to their own, the synthetic group may come to resemble a natural group. It is in the course of the warming up process that the awareness of the relationship problems of others in the group begins.

In the action portion of a psychodramatic session the protagonist, a member of the group, enacts with the assistance of others, situations taken from his present or past experiences or those anticipated in the future. He explores *his problems and relationships* on the stage for his own benefit but the learning experience is shared by others in the group. One of the most important functions of the warming up process is to help the group select a protagonist. The more closely the problems and relationships presented in action are related to those of others in the group, the more complete will be the involvement of others in the action and in the ensuing discussion.

The discussion phase of a psychodrama which follows the action portion performs two important functions. It provides an opportunity for each member of the group to offer assistance to the protagonist in arriving at an understanding of his relationships. Having witnessed the enactment, each may, *based on his own experience;* suggest ways of dealing with problems similar to those presented by the protagonist. As he relates his own experiences to those enacted by the protagonist, each member of the group that participates in the discussion may arrive at a better understanding of *his own problems and relationships.* The action portion of the psychodrama serves as a warm up for the discussion that follows it. Thus, each member of a group may arrive at valuable insights in the course of an enactment, in the group discussion or in both. He should also learn ways of using these insights to produce change in his own behavior patterns or in his relationships.

The Warming-Up Process

The director begins every psychodramatic session, from the very first to the last of a series, by warming up the group. Whether the session involves only two persons, (a dyad consisting of a director and one subject) a psychodramatic group comprised of eight to fifteen members, or a hundred or more persons assembled in an auditorium for a lecture-demonstration of psychodrama, the warm up starts with the opening remarks of the director and it ends when a protagonist emerges and moves into action. The choice of protagonist and the relationships explored in action are greatly influenced by what the director emphasizes in the course of the warm-up. There are many approaches to warming up a group and considerable variation in style and content. Poetry, music, dance, non-verbal techniques have been employed when deemed appropriate by directors. In Socioanalysis verbal warm-ups are most frequently used. These may be divided into four general categories: *initial warm-ups, group-centered warm-ups, directed warm-ups,* and *indirect warm-ups.* Each type is employed for a different purpose or purposes. The decision as to which to employ at a particular session rests with the director.

The first of a series of sessions: The Initial Warm-up

Individuals coming together for the first meeting of a psychodrama group may not be acquainted with each other and may have little in common. Each person, when he arrives is involved in his own problems and relationships and is interested primarily in his own needs and goals. The director is frequently the only person at the session who bears some relationship to all of the others present. It is up to him, therefore, to furnish the leadership required to stimulate the evolution of group goals and the participation of members in achieving them. The entire first session of an ongoing group is generally devoted to orientating the group toward these objectives and is in a sense an initial warm-up to a series of psychodramas. Nevertheless, as in all psychodrama, the first session passes through three phases: a warm-up, an action portion and a group discussion.

As director I begin my warm-up with a ten minute talk in which I describe the Psychodramatic Method and discuss it's applicability to problems in social relationships. In the course of this talk I introduce myself and explain my role as director. There is nothing magical in the ten minute time period alloted to the warm-up talk. I generally limit my initial talk to about ten minutes because it has been my experience that it takes about that long for people to focus on what is happening in the new situation in which they find themselves. If I talk much longer in my warm-up some members of the group tend to tune me out. They begin to day dream or become involved in private thoughts not related to the Psychodrama session.

I then address each member of the group, I extend my hand to him and, if he takes my hand, we clasp hands for a moment as I speak to him. This practice is interpreted by some as a handshake, a form of greeting. I regard it as a reaching out by the director to each member of the group. To initiate a relationship between two people it is often useful for one to reach out to the other. In my view, the director should be the one to reach out, and I do so by extending my hand to him. This action notifies each member of the group that I am interested in him and affords each member an opportunity to express himself. in some way prior to the action portion of the session. Furthermore, the response of a member to my extended hand and greeting provides me with some clues as to his level of spontaneity at the moment of our encounter.

At the initial meeting I address some general questions to each member of the group in almost identical terms. I avoid any element of surprise in order to minimize the amount of anxiety experienced by each individual as he awaits his first public encounter at a session. Typical questions are:

Have you ever been a member of a Psychodrama group before?
When did you first learn about Psychodrama?
What have you heard about Psychodrama?
What would you like to achieve at Psychodrama sessions?

In the course of these encounters each member of the group has an opportunity to respond to me as director and to express himself without being challenged or criticized. As he does so he warms-up to me as the director and I warm-up to him. In addition, each member of the group learns that others have interests and goals and that some of those expressed resemble his own. Each begins to warm-up to other persons and their goals, and in this way group goals begin to evolve. *The 'interview' part of the warm-up described above I use only in the initial session of a group.* After that is completed I proceed to warm-up the group for action, an activity I engage in at the beginning of every Psychodrama session. I do not consider it advisable at the first meeting of an ongoing group to explore the social relationships or problems of one of the members. Instead, each member of the group is encouraged to participate in an enactment so that his subsequent movement into action on the stage will be less inhibited. My principle objective as director is to make an individual's first experience on the stage as interesting and free from trauma as possible.

In groups consisting of adults I frequently begin by inviting a member of the group to the stage or action area to *ask me* questions. He may make his questions as personal as he wishes. I then suggest that he present himself, that is, tell the group the things he would like them to know about him. I then suggest that he invite someone from the group to ask him two or three questions and then present himself. This process is continued until every member of the group has had the opportunity of coming before the group, ask some questions, and present himself to the group.

In adolescent groups, I describe a simple scene and invite two members of the group to enact it for illustrative purposes only. I usually select for enactment a temporary encounter which I consider uncomplicated and unlikely to stimulate emotional involvement. Situations I most often use are; ordering a meal at a restaurant, making a purchase at a store, or asking for directions while on a trip. I make it clear that every member of the group is going to play a part in the same scene and that the purpose of the enactments is to give everyone the 'feel' of being in interaction on the stage. If possible, I have a volunteer go through the first enactment and I continue with volunteers as long as I can.

In the action portion of the initial session outlined above, each group member is asked to perform in a role while another member of the group performs in the complementary role. In the 'ordering a meal' situation, for example, each subject starts by playing the customer while another member of the group plays the waiter. I explain to the group that the person playing a complementary role like the role of waiter in this scene is called an auxiliary ego, and that the auxiliary ego is following my instructions. The waiter takes the customer's order and delivers the wrong food. If challenged by the customer he apologizes and brings another 'wrong' item. If challenged again he apologizes and brings the correct item, and attempts to charge for three items. The technique of *role reversal* is then introduced. The subject plays the part of the waiter, and the part of the customer is played by the auxiliary ego. With the auxiliary ego in the role of customer, the technique of the *mirror* is introduced. This requires the auxiliary ego to mirror the subject, that is, to play the part exactly in the same way as the subject did.

After the enactments are completed, the group is asked to discuss the situation enacted and the techniques employed; role reversal and mirror. The discussion is limited to the relationship, waiter—customer. I discourage any comments relating to deficiencies noted in particular enactments and urge group members to limit contributions to the discussion to their own experiences in the role, present or past, asking them to refrain from analyzing the presentations of others in the group. The group discussion at the first session is intended primarily to set the pattern for future discussions by acquainting the members of the group with the functions of group discussions in psychodrama and the ground rules to be followed. One ground rule that I emphasize is to limit the discussion phase of a psychodrama to a sharing of experiences and to refrain from analyzing or criticizing persons who participate in action. A successful first session serves as preparation for future sessions by familiarizing the members of the group with the psychodramatic method, and the functions of the director, auxiliary egos, and group members.

The Group-Centered Warm-up

From the second session to the completion of a series of sessions the warm-up I most frequently use is the group-centered warm-up. In employing this warm-up I have three objectives. These are:

1. To elicit from members of the group sufficient information to help the group determine the problem areas and relationships of greatest significance to its members at a particular time.

2. To help the group decide upon a protagonist for the psychodramatic session.

3. To move the person selected as protagonist into action confident in the knowledge that he has been selected by the group and that the other members of the group are interested in him and in his relationships.

The group-centered warm-up, consists of three portions; an opening statement, interviews, and a warm-up to action. In my opening statement which lasts about ten minutes, I talk in a general way about problems people have in relationships with employers, parents, members of their families, friends, and acquaintances of the same sex and opposite sex. I refrain from emphasizing any type of relationship or problem area, pointing out that most people experience difficulties in some of their relationships and find others rewarding. This portion of the warm-up, as I see it, performs two functions. First, it directs attention to the general purpose of the session, the exploration of social relationships. Secondly, it affords each member of the group an opportunity to relate his own problems to the one's memtioned by the director. Having come to the group meeting from his other activities and interests, the group member needs some time to redirect his attention to the goals of the group. The few minutes spent in listening to the opening statement of the director provide both time to reflect and an opportunity for each group member to direct his interests to the Psychodrama session.

After completing my opening statement, which I generally make from the center of the stage or action area, I move to the interview part of the warm-up. I approach each member of the group, greet him by name, and ask a question or two. This affords each person an opportunity to influence the choice of topical area and protagonist. I start at one end of the room and proceed to interview each person in turn, moving clock-wise or counter-clockwise. In the first few sessions of an ongoing group I ask identical questions of each member of the group. Typical questions are: "Is there some relationship you would like to understand better or improve?" "Who would it be with?" Once I begin the interview part of the warm-up each member of the group should be able to predict accurately when he will be approached and what he will be asked. This procedure minimizes tension and anxiety by giving each person time to prepare his response. The following illustrates the interview portion of a group-centered warm-up which I began after talking to the group for about ten minutes on the subject of problems. in social relationships.[1] In the course of the warm-up talk I referred to relationships with employers, wives, husbands, and friends which could be examined in a psychodrama.

Director: Good evening, Joe. How are you this evening?

Joe: O.K., I guess.

Director: Is there some relationship you would like to understand better or improve?

Joe: None that I couldn't handle.

Director: You may think of some later on.

—to Bill): (Same greeting and first question).

Bill: I had trouble with my boss last week, but it's nothing new. I always have trouble keeping a job. That's why I'm here.

Director: We may go into that later. Did you think of any problems you may have had in getting along with anyone else?

[1]Portions of a session in which Helen was protagonist are presented for illustrative purposes. They were reconstructed from protocols and the memory of the author and are not accurate in every detail. They are, however, useful as a model. The session from which portions have been excerpted was the third in a series of fifteen. Henry was the protagonist at the second session. Other members of the group were: Joe, Bill, Betty, Joan, John, Dora, and Helen.

Bill: I seem to do all right with everyone except people who push me around.
Director: (to Betty) Greeting and first question.
Betty: I've always gotten along fine with my employers and supervisors. The only one I have any trouble with is my mother.
Director: Is she the only one you can't get along with?
Betty: No. But the others don't bother me too much.
Director: We may go into your relationship with your mother.
Director: (To Henry) (Same greeting) After thinking over the last session did you feel that there were some other relationships we should have examined?
Henry: I still don't understaand why I can't get along with my brother.
Director: Is that the only relationship that gives you trouble now?
Henry: No. But it seems like most of the people I can't stand are a lot like my brother. They listen to me but don't pay attention to what I have to say.
Director: Think about it some more and maybe we'll go into it at another time.
Director: (to John) Greeting and first question.
John: I've had trouble with bosses a few times but I manage all right now. It's my brother I can't get along with. He's a lot like Henry's brother only he doesn't seem to want me around.
Director: We may go into that.
(To Joan): Greeting and first question.
Joan: I never really had a job. I worked part-time while going to college but never had any dealings with supervisors.
Director: Did you think of any problems you had in getting along with anyone?
Joan: Some fellows take advantage of me. I would like to know more about why I am so easily fooled.
Director: Has this happened often?
Joan: Every time I get interested in a man it turns out bad for me.
Director: We may go into that tonight or surely at some later time.
Director: (To Dora) Greeting and first question.
Dora: I never have trouble with employers until they try to become boyfriends. I feel a lot like Joan. Fellows always seem to be taking advantage of me.
Director: We may go into that with either you or Joan, if the group decides to.
Director: (To Helen) Greeting and first question.

Helen: I have never had any difficulty getting along with employers or supervisors.
Director: Did you think of any problems you had in getting along with anyone?
Helen: I'm having a great deal of trouble right now. I'm in love with a fellow and he lies to me. He says he wants to marry me but he's not honest with me. This is always happening to me and I would like to know how to handle it. I could use some help right now.
Director: We may go into that this evening if the group decides to.

At this point, having completed the interviews, the director returns to the front of the stage and proceeds to the third part of the warm-up, the selection of a protagonist.

Director: (To group)—What are we going into this evening? We have a few members of the group who have had problems with employers and we have three women who have problems with boy friends. Which area interests you most right now? Will you raise your right hand if you prefer relationships with employers. (No hands were raised). Will you raise your right hand if you prefer relationships with boyfriends. (Six members of the group raise their hands). We have three women, Joan, Dora, and Helen who have relationships with boyfriends, they would like to examine. Which do you want to go into this evening?
Joan: My problem is not as urgent as Helen's. Why don't we take her's this evening?
Director: Will you raise your right hand if you would like Helen as the protagonist. (Six hands are raised).
Director: (To Helen)—The group has decided to have you as protagonist. Will you step over here (to stage) please.

At this point the warm up is completed and the action phase of the session begins. The choice of protagonist was an excellent one. The group centered warm up had succeeded in helping the group select as protagonist someone with a relationship problem common to three members and of interest to at least three more. A high degree of interest and involvement in the enactment was assured. Furthermore, Helen could enter into the protagonist role with the knowledge that others were interested enough to want to help her. It is important at early sessions of a series that the psychodrama deal with problems common to several members. An early session which is irrelevant to the needs and interests of most of the group members might result in indifference on the part of the members and lack of support for the protagonist. As director, in employing the group centered warm up I observed the following rules or principles:

1. I addressed the same questions in identical language to every member of the group except Henry who had been protagonist at the preceeding session. The idea is to have every member of the group prepared to respond to the questions asked without being surprised.

2. I did not reject a proposal by any member of the group to go into a relationship area of interest to him. Note that in every instance I as director remarked, after a suggestion was made by a member, that 'we' meaning the group, might decide to go into it.

3. I did not indicate preference for a particular relationship or protagonist regardless of the urgency with which the problem was presented. To give preference to one may be experienced as rejection by others. Furthermore, if the director indicates a preference for a particular relationship area, the attention getters in the group may stimulate difficulties in that area.

4. I put to a vote a group choice of relationship areas. In the example above I suggested a choice between problems with employers and relationships with boyfriends. I omitted a reference to relationships with a brother because that was the subject matter of the previous psychodrama. Only one person had indicated difficulty with a mother and she did not object to the choice offered.

5. I left the choice of protagonist to the group. This process helped make it clear to Helen, the protagonist, why she was chosen. More people in the group were interested in her problem than in that of any other member. Those not chosen knew why Helen was chosen. Furthermore, the members of the group in selecting the protagonist were in a sense responsible to her

The Directed Warm-Up

The group-centered warm-up is considered to be the most effective way of helping a group to focus on a relationship problem common to a significant number of it's members. It is also most likely to result in the selection of a protagonist whose problems are relevant to others in the group. However, if a majority of the members tend to avoid the examination of a particular kind of relationship, the democratic process characteristic of this kind of warm-up makes it possible for them to do so indefinitely. The director may employ a directed warm-up, one which emphasizes a relationship or problem area, if he considers this to be in the best interest of the group. If, for example, after four or five meetings of a group, the director observes that the group rejects as protagonists those members who mention problems in relationship with parents, he may decide to encourage an examination of such relationships.

The structure of a directed warm-up is similar in most respects to that of a group-centered warm-up. The director begins it with an opening statement lasting about ten minutes: he then proceeds to interview each member, and to assist the group in selecting a protagonist. The principal difference is that in the directed warm-up his introductory ten minutes talk deals with a relationship or problem which he has decided upon prior to the session. The entire warm-up is centered around the preselected relationship.

The warm-up intended to produce a protagonist who will explore relationships with parents would proceed as follows:

1. In his opening statement the director would talk about the importance of understanding relationships with parents. He would then, giving examples drawn from his past experiences, discuss problems arising in the course of such relationships.

2. In his interviews with each member of the group he would inquire *only* about problems experienced in the course of such relationships. He would ask each member of the group the following questions:

Is there a relationship with a parent you would like to understand better?

Is there a relationship with a parent you would like to improve?

No other relationship would be mentioned by the director. Since some members of the group had previously indicated difficulties arising out of such relationships two or three would be expected to respond in the affirmative. If this had not been the case there would have been no need for a directed warm-up.

3. In helping the group select a protagonist he would ask the members to choose between those who answered one of the above questions in the affirmative. If only one member of the group acknowledged having such a problem the director would move the person to the stage as the protagonist for that session.

I have had many occasions to use the directed warm-up in the manner discribed above. It has been my experience that even when most members of a group deny having relationship problems with parents, once a protagonist emerged from the group and reenacted experiences with parents, most of the other members of the group became involved in the enactment, the discussion or both. The directed warm-up affords an individual the opportunity to explore his relationship with a parent even though a majority of the group members might voice a preference for some other relationship and protagonist if the warm-up had not focused on that relationship. When family realtionships are explored in a psychodrama the discussion involves most members of the group and frequently stimulates others to reexamine their own family relationships at subsequent sessions. The directed warm-up is therefore recommended when a group avoids choosing as protagonists those persons who present difficulties in particular relationships in response to questions asked in group-centered warm-ups.

The Indirect Warm-Up

After a group has been together for several sessions the director may notice that one member of the group has not participated as protagonist. A review of the protocols of the sessions may indicate that the member in question avoided involvement by denying any relationship problems or, having stated that he had a problem, was not selected as protagonist by the group. Whether I employ a group-centered warm-up or a directed-warm-up, I am committed to leaving the choice of protagonist to the group. To help such a person become the protagonist, another type of warm-up is required. The same is true for a person who does not present a relationship problem and does not afford the group an opportunity to choose him. If as director I decide in advance of a session that a particular individual should have an opportunity to be the protagonist. I employ an indirect warm-up, one in which the choice of protagonist is influenced by pre-determined techniques.

I have developed two forms of indirect warm-up. For the unselected member, the one who has indicated a willingness to participate as protagonist by acknowledging relationship problems, I use a simple role playing situation as an indirect warm-up to a psychodrama. For the reluctant member, the one who avoids moving into action by denying the existence of problems, I employ Sociodrama as an indirect warm-up.

Role Playing as Indirect Warm-Up for Psychodrama

The director sets up a role playing situation similar to the one described in our section on the Initial Warm-Up. Each member of the group is asked to play the role of customer ordering food at a restaurant, for example. After a role reversal each plays the role of the waitress. Let us assume that I as director have decided to select Dora, a member of the group who has mentioned problems in relationships with other women but has never been chosen by the group. I instruct a trained auxiliary ego, in advance of the session, to portray Dora in an unfair, unflattering manner when she 'mirrors' her in the role playing situation. Immediately following the role playing situation in which she was unfairly portrayed, I would then question her about it. The following dialogue will serve to illustrate.

Director: (To Dora) Do you feel that Sylvia (the auxiliary ego) has portrayed you accurately?

Dora: No. I don't. She made me out to be mean and rude. I was very pleasant to the waitress.

Director: Have you often found other women to be unfair to you?

Dora: There have been some who have.

Director: (To group) Do you have any objections to Dora becoming the protagonist? (Group objection is rare if the perspective protagonist is on stage and wants to proceed.)

Director: Think of a situation when such a thing happened before. Set up the scene and show us what happened.

In the event that Dora had responded differently and accepted her portrayal by the auxiliary ego, we might have had the following dialogue:

Director: In imitating you in the role of customer she presented you as being rude and unreasonable. There did not appear to be anything unusual in the way you treated the waitress. Do you often permit people to accuse you unfairly without challenging them?

Dora: I guess so. (or I don't think so)

Director: (to group) Do you have any objections to Dora becoming the protagonist?

Director: Choose any situation where someone treated you unfairly in the past and let us see how you handled it.

In either instance the session changes from the role playing enactment by each of the members of the group, in turn, to a psychodrama with Dora as protagonist. The transition is usually accomplished without comment from anyone and the session proceeds in much the same manner as any other psychodrama.

Sociodrama as an Indirect Warm-Up

Sociodrama is an action method which focuses on problems in relationships people have as members of a class, group or category. Techniques employed are much the same as those used in psychodrama. The emphasis, however, is on a particular social role or relationship, one common to several persons participating in a session. The role of mother, son, student, negro, employee, and nurse are examples. The director of a Sociodrama usually starts the session with a ten minute warm-up talk, moves the group into action and then leads it in a discussion.

When using Sociodrama as an indirect warm-up for a Psychodrama, I speak, in the opening portion of my warm-up, for about ten minutes on some controversial topic, one which is likely to reflect a division in the group. Let us assume that the purpose of the indirect warm-up was to get Bill, a reluctant member of the group, on to the stage and give him an opportunity to become the protagonist. The topic selected for the Sociodrama need *not* be in any way related to Bill or his relationship problems. For example, if the group includes several married people who disagree on the advisability of married women working outside the home, I might choose the role of 'working wife' as the topic of the Sociodrama. This despite the fact that Bill, the intended protagonist is single and not interested in the topic.

After an opening warm-up talk I ask for comments from members of the group. This portion of the Sociodramatic warm-up is analogous to the 'interview' part of the Psychodramatic warm-up. I then complete the Sociodramatic warm-up by inviting two or three volunteers on each side of the question to come to the stage. The action portion of the Sociodrama takes the form of a panel discussion with members of the group being moved forward to substitute for the original panelists. When Bill is reached he is invited to come to the stage on one side or the other. The following dialogue illustrates how Bill would be moved to the stage.

Director: (To Bill) Do you favor or oppose the idea of married women working outside the home?
Bill: I don't have any opinion. I'm not married and I have never given it any thought.
Director: That's fine. We need someone who is really neutral. Will you please come to the stage as chairman of the panel and try to get the two sides to reach some common understanding of the problems involved.

A few minutes after Bill assumes the role of chairman the number of persons on each side of the panel is reduced to one to facilitate communication. A woman, uusually the most vocal, is selected by the director to represent one side, and a man the other. Bill remains the chairman. After several exchanges the director invites Bill's attention to a relationship problem which he may wish to explore. The following dialogue illustrates the way in which this is done.
Director: (To Bill) You seem to be having trouble getting Mrs. Jones to listen to you. Has this sort of thing happened to you before?
Bill: It's hard to get a woman to listen when she has her mind made up.
Director: Would you like to examine this as a protagonist?
Bill: Yes.
Director: (to Group) Is there any objection to Bill becoming the protagonist? (Usually no comment from anyone in group)
Director: Choose a situation in which you had trouble getting someone to listen to you or see your side of something. Show us how you handled it.

As Bill enacts such a situation the session changes from a Sociodrama ot a Psychodrama with Bill as protagonist. I first developed this type of warm-up for use with adolescent boys who seemed to be reluctant to become protagonists. I found the warm-up to be invariably successful in stimulating them into action. I have since employed the method with adults in psychodrama groups and with professionals in demonstration sessions. Each time I used the Indirect Warm-up it not only produced the protagonist selected in advance, but also an excellent Psychodrama. The length of the warm-up was justified by the results.

Choosing the Appropriate Warm-Up

The importance of the warm-up in developing the goals and interests of a group and maintaining a high degree of involvement cannot be over-estimated. The success of a series of psychodramas in serving the needs of the group members depends largely on the director's choice of warm-ups and the effectiveness with which he carries them out. In his initial warm-up the director must acquaint the participants with the Psychodramatic Method and do so as much as he can to reduce inhibitions which limit movement into action. He may use the directed warm-up when he wishes to influence the choice of problems area. He may use the indirect warm-up in an effort to influence the choice of protagonist. It is the group-centered warm-up, however, which is most often used with an adult group. By means of this type of warm up the director, if successful, helps the group to select relationship problems most relevant to it's members and protagonists most representative of these problems.

As much of the following data as are available to him are considered by a director in arriving at a decision as to which type of warm-up to employ.

1. Information obtained in the course of initial interviews preceding the first psychodrama session. A person is assigned to a psychodrama group pursuant to such an initial interview. The information sheet which he brings to that interview includes data relating to his family constellation, relationship problems as he sees them, and his goals in socioanalysis.

2. Test results, if any. At his initial interview each person may be given Social Relationship Tests, Role Tests, and if deemed useful, Psychodramatic Projective Tests. At the second or third meeting of an ongoing group, Sociometric Tests and Social Perception Tests are usually administered. Data provided in all of these tests are considered.

3. Protocols of previous sessions. Immediately following such sessions the director prepares a protocol in which he summarizes the events of the session including such information as: type of warm-up, problems raised by each member in the course of the warm-up, summary of the action, scene by scene, and discussion including significant comments of each member. The names of protagonists and others participating in the action portion are listed with the nature and extent of participation indicated, Chart XX contains a protocol of a psychodrama session.

Reviewing the information obtained in initial interviews, the director takes note of those problem areas common to several members of his group. If, when he examines the protocols of the first five sessions, he finds that one such area has not been touched upon, he may decide to focus attention on it by means of a directed warm-up. If a review of the protocols of eight or nine sessions indicated that one of the members of the group has not made himself available as protagonist or has been ignored by the group, he may decide to employ an indirect warm-up.

An important factor influencing the choice of warm-up is the nature of the group itself. If the group is a heterogeneous one, consisting of from eight to fifteen people with a variety of relationship problems, the warm-ups will be selected in accordance with the criteria discussed above. In general, heterogeneity of membership is considered desirable because a diversity of experiences and relationship increases the likelihood that alternative solutions to problems will be presented. However, when groups are established to deal with a specific relationship the warming up process centers around the choice of protagonist rather than choice of relationship to be explored. For example, if a group is specifically organized to deal with problems arising in husband and wife relationships the problem area is defined at the outset. In a group-centered warm-up with such a group the director, in his opening statement would discuss problems arising in *this one relationship,* such as; disputes over money, jealousy, infidelity, and the like. The interviews would relate to these problems and the choice of protagonist would be made from those voicing them. A directed warm up would be focused on one of the problems arising in the course of a husband-wife relationship, jealousy, for example.

Regardless of the type of warm up the director elects to employ, he must, in his opening statement focus the interests of the group on the examination of some relationships and assist the group in the development of goals for the session. In the interview part of his warm-up he must stimulate communication to him and to the group. It is this portion of the warm-up that gives each member an opportunity to express himself and to feel part of the group. In the final portion of the warm-up, the part in which he leads the group toward the selection of a relationship problem, he must do what he can to encourage the emergence of a protagonist who will involve as many members of the group as possible. The degree of success of the warming up process. Expertise in this area may be acquired

CHART XX

PROTOCOL OF A PSYCHODRAMA SESSION

Session 4 Date

Attendance (a) Indicates absence

Bernard	John T. (a)	Betty	Lillian
Charles	John W.	Claire	Mary B.
Frank	Robert	Joan	Mary T.
Henry	William	Kathy (a)	

Warm-up—Group centered—25 minutes

Joan, Frank and Robert raised problems and sought to be protagonists. Robert was selected by the group. Several members of the group reported having difficulties with employers, the problem Robert raised.

Action—Several scenes involving discussions with present employers. Performance on job and absences were main issues. Three scenes with previous employers involved disagreements over attitude toward work. Two scenes each with father and mother showed that Robert resented being ordered to do anything. In future projection Robert portrayed himself as his own "boss" in a retail business. When faced with a "bossy" customer he reacted with hostility and verbal aggression.

Discussion—Joan W., Bernard and Claire each revealed identifying experiences. Joan, Mary B. and Frank discussed their inabilities to control anger. By implication they attributed Robert's difficulties to his verbal aggressions and "lack of tact."

in training and experience. I do not agree with those who maintain that certain 'personality' characteristics predetermine success or failure in the role of Psychodrama Director. In my view, any professionally qualified person can be trained to be an excellent director and one can begin to acquire skill in directing by learning how to best warm up a group. Directors are trained. No one is born a director. The training of a director should begin with developing his skills in warming up a group.

The Action Phase of Psychodrama

The warm-up is completed when a member of the group moves to the stage or action area to enact or reenact a situation involving a relationship problem he has had in the past or is having in the present. As he comes forward, whether subsequent to a group-centered or directed warm-up, the director interviews him briefly on the first level of the stage. At this point the status of the individual changes from that of group member to that of protagonist. If the person selected as protagonist is performing in that role for the first time the technique of *self-presentation* is employed to introduce him to the group. Otherwise, the interview takes the form of a few questions about the relationship to be explored. The director then suggests a situation for enactment and asks the protagonist to describe the place in which the encounter occurred and the person or persons involved in interaction with him in the scene selected by him. The director and the protagonist then move to the next level at which time the protagonist is asked to describe the action space in detail and to designate props to symbolize each important item he designates as part of the scene. He is also asked to select other members of the group to represent absent persons required in the scene. The action then begins.

It is unusual for a person to refuse to participate as protagonist in a psychodrama if the warming up process is effectively employed. The director should if he has not done so in the warm-up, make it clear to the protagonist and others in the group that the protagonist is the researcher and that the relationships he explores are for his benefit and the enactment he produces are of his own creation. Once a member of the group becomes the protagonist the director holds the interference with the action by other members of the group to a minimum. So far as practicable, he himself intervenes only to assist in the application of techniques and to suggest changes in scene. If the protagonist chooses to reenact a scene involving a friend, relative, associate or other person with whom he has interacted in a natural group or relationship, he is asked to pick someone in the group to play the part of that other person. Permitting him to make this selection gives him greater control of the production and enables him to select someone who may stimulate him or affect him in much the same way as the person represented. Only when the director employs techniques requiring specialized skills need he call upon a trained auxiliary ego to assist in the action. The following suggestions are offered as guidelines to directors of the action of a Psychodrama:

1. Encourage the protagonist *to enact* scenes involving problems in relationships. If he starts out by talking about his problems allow him to continue for a while. However, as soon as possible have him recall a situation in which the problem arose, set up the scene, and reenact it.

2. Action on the stage takes place in the present, in the 'here and now'. If the protagonist, in reenacting a scene from his past, persists in using terms indicating that the action happened in the past he is reminded to speak in the present. Thus, if, in the interaction, the protagonist says, "I told him"., move him into the present by saying; "You are telling him now".

3. Permit the protagonist to select each scene he desires to examine. Even if the scene seems unimportant to the director, the protagonist should not be inhibited from enacting it. As he reenacts what may appear to be unimportant situations he may gain awareness of what the psychodramatic method can do for him and then move into more significant relationships. It is important, however, that we allow him to pick each situation including the time, place, and persons involved in the interaction.

4. The protagonist will usually select for his first enactment a situation involving a superficial encounter. As his involvement in the psychodrama increases he tends to move into more significant ones, particularly if the director suggests them. A director should discourage the reenactment of traumatic events early in the psychodrama. If the protagonist selects such a situation in the early stage of the psychodrama suggest that he reenact other scenes before going into it.

5. Although the protagonist is instructed to perform in each situation as nearly as possible as he did in the original event, he is told not to try to recall every word that was said in the way it was said. To do so would greatly inhibit the spontaneity of the protagonist and in some instances distort the action. Encourage him to communicate *the substance* of the exchange or interaction as he recalls it. If he is reenacting one of a sequence of scenes with another person, his wife, for example, he is encouraged to telescope several substantially related encounters into one scene.

6. Encourage the protagonist to express himself as completely as possible in action. To reduce the possibility of injury to the persons in interaction he should be given a symbolic way of expressing violence. For example, he may be instructed to strike a table with a newspaper if the scene involves a physical blow. "Each time you hit the table with the newspaper you are hitting the other person", would be an appropriate instruction.

7. Using the technique of role reversal, give the protagonist an opportunity to play the role of each person with whom he interacts on the stage. When in the role of other, interview him briefly to increase his perception of other.

The following scenes are drawn from the action phase of the psychodrama involving Helen, the warm-up phase of which was presented in abbreviated form in our section entitled: The Group-Centered Warm-Up. The dialogues and sequences have been reconstructed from a protocol of the session and the memory of the author. They are intended primarily to indicate ways of which techniques are applied in the action phase of a psychodrama. Some of the sequences are presented in considerable detail in order to illustrate the application of techniques while many others scenes are summarized. The approximate time taken by each scene is presented to minimize the effect of this distortion. The action phase of the session began when Helen, at the request of the director, moved to the front of the stage.

Director: Tell us something about yourself, Helen, anything you consider important.?[1]

[1]Since this was Helen's first session as protagonist the technique of self-presentation was used to introduce her to the group. The entire sequence leading up to the first scene lasted six minutes.

Helen: I am thirty years old and have never been married. I was graduated from Hunter College when I was twenty-one and began teaching the same year. I have been teaching ever since. That's all I can think of except that I enjoy teaching.
Director: Do you live by yourself?
Helen: Yes. I have had my own apartment ever since I started teaching.
Director: Are your father and mother living?
Helen: Yes. They are divorced. My father left home when I was nine years old.
Director: Helen, will you move over to my right and play the part of your mother for a few minutes. (Helen moves to place indicated) What is your name?
Helen: (as mother) Margaret.
Director: Tell us something about yourself, Margaret. Anything you consider important. How old you are, what you do, what sort of place you live in, who lives with you — that sort of thing.
Helen: (as Mother) I am fifty-two years old. I work as a legal secretary. I have been doing this kind of work all my life. I never liked it but that is the only way I can earn money enough to get by. I have a four-room apartment which I share with my sister, Virginia.
Director: Is Helen your only child?
Helen: (as mother) No. I have another daughter, Patricia, who is married and a son who is in the army.
Director: Tell me, Margaret, which one of your children do you like the most?
Helen: (as Mother) I love them all. I suppose that Patricia is more considerate of me than the other two, but then, she lived with me for a longer time. I have no favorites.
Director: What do you think about Helen?
Helen: (as Mother) She's good but she doesn't listen to me. She should get married and have a family but she always picks the wrong sort of men.
Director: Have you told her this?
Helen: (as Mother) Many times.
Director: Now, Helen, will you step to the left side and play the part of your father. (Helen moves to place indicated) What is your name?[1]

[1]Before each time a protagonist is asked to perform in a different role it is recommended that he or she move to a different position. Movement of this sort serves to reduce possible confusion of role.

Helen: (as Father) Stephen.
Director: Stephen, will you tell me something about yourself—where you live, what you do—things like that.
Helen: (as Father) I live in Philadelphia. I am married and have two children. My first wife divorced me twenty years ago. I'm a salesman. Right now I sell cars. I don't make a lot of money but we get by.
Director: You say you have two children. How about the children you had with Margaret? Don't you consider them your children?
Helen: (as Father) I haven't seen them more than two or three times in the last fifteen years. After I left Margaret I visited the children a few times but she didn't want to let me see them. They are my children but I guess they are not interested in me.
Director: Do you care what happens to Helen?
Helen: (as Father) I guess so. I don't know much about her. I wouldn't recognize her if I met her.
Director: Well, Helen, that gives us some idea of your present relationship with your mother and father. Come over here and play Helen again.(Helen moves center front) Before coming up here you mentioned that men were not honest with you. You said you were having this sort of problem right now. Is that right?
Helen: Yes. My present boyfriend, Tom, has not been entirely honest with me.
Director: How long has Tom been your boyfriend?
Helen: About three months.
Director: How did you first meet him?
Helen: I met him at a dance. I was introduced to him by my friend, Mabel.
Director: Who suggested going to the dance?
Helen: Mabel did.
Director: Can you reenact the scene in which you discussed going out together?
Helen: Yes, we were having lunch in the school cafeteria when she suggested it. Mabel teaches in the same school that I do.
Director: (Moving up to the action level of the stage) Here is the school cafeteria. Show us where you were sitting and how it happened.[1]

[1]Before dealing with the problem relationship and risking the possibility of a traumatic scene the director leads the protagonist into a preliminary scene with a friend.

Helen: There are about twenty-five or thirty tables in the cafeteria. Each can seat four people but most of them seat two. There is plenty of room. Mabel and I were sitting at a table on that side (pointing to the right) and the counter was on the opposite side of the room. Mabel and I had served ourselves and were seated and eating our lunch.
Director: (to Helen) Pick some one in the group to play Mabel and show us what happened.
Helen: Joan can play Mabel. (Joan moves to the stage and both girls sit at the table) How is Dave?
Director: Joan would not know how Mabel answered. You, Helen, were the only person with Mabel at the time. Why don't you reverse roles so that you can play Mabel for a while. (the girls change seats)
Director: (to Helen as Mabel) Mabel, How long have you known Helen?
Helen: (as Mabel) About nine years. She is my best friend. We both started teaching at this school nine years ago and have been friends ever since.
Director: Do you have a steady boyfriend?
Helen: (as Mabel) Yes. Dave and I expect to be married in a few months. We have been going out with each other for six months.
Director: Does Helen go along with you when you go out?
Helen: (as Mabel) That's a problem. We used to go out together a lot but since she broke off with her boyfriend I don't see her often except at work.[1]
Director: (to both girls) Now you can reverse back. Helen, you play yourself and Joan, you play Mabel.
Joan: (as Mabel) Dave is fine. Would you like to go to a dance with us tomorrow night?
Helen: I don't have a date.
Joan: (as Mabel) Dave can get someone for you.
Helen: You know that I don't like blind dates. You become sort of obligated to spend the evening with a fellow whether you like him or not.
Joan: (as Mabel) Do you feel like going to a dance?
Helen: Why don't I just go with you and Dave. There will be

[1]When the protagonist reverses roles with someone for the first time, she is interviewed in the role. The brief interview is intended to give her a better perception of the other, and also to prepare the auxiliary ego to start playing the part.

plenty of stags at the dance. One of us might even know some of them.

Joan: (as Mabel) Fine. We'll call for you at about eight o'clock tomorrow.

Director: (to Helen) Is that how this conversation ended?

Helen: That is about right. Actually, I agreed to go to Mabel's apartment and wait for Dave with her.

Director: (to Helen) Suppose you show us how you met Tom.

Helen: Dave knew three of the fellows at the dance. He introduced me to them and I danced with all three of them at one time or another. Tom was one of them.

Director: Pick someone in the group to play Tom and show us how you met him or what happened at the dance.

Helen: (Helen selects John to play Tom and he joins her on the stage.).

Director: (to Helen) Why don't you reverse roles and play Tom for a while until John learns the part. (they change places) (to Helen as Tom) Tom, what do you do for a living?

Helen: (as Tom) I am an investment counselor.

Director: How is it that you came to this dance without a date.

Helen: (as Tom) I am from Cleveland. I arrived in New York a few days ago and wanted to meet some people. An acquaintance at my hotel recommended this dance.

Director: You have just met Helen. What do you think of her?

Helen: (as Tom) She is a good dancer. She'll do.

Director: Let us see you dance with her. (The two dance around the stage a few times) You are not holding her very close. Don't you want to get closer?

Helen: (as Tom) We're close enough. I want to make a good impression on her.

Director: Do you think that you will try to date her?

Helen: (as Tom) Yes. I'll ask to take her home.

Director: (to both) Reverse back to your original roles. You, John, now know how Tom behaved.

John: (as Tom) Would you like me to take you home?

Helen: If you like.

John: (as Tom) (Calls taxi and both leave stage)

Director: (to Helen) What happened when you both got to your apartment? Did you invite him in?

Helen: No. I'm very careful about getting too well acquainted with strangers. He was a perfect gentleman. He didn't make any passes at me or offend me in any way. Before saying good night he asked if he could call me.

Director: Did he call you the next day?

Helen: Yes. He invited me to dinner.[1]

Director: The telephone is ringing, Helen, but before you answer it, tell us who you think is calling you.

Helen: I'm sleepy. I have no idea who could be calling at 10 o'clock on Sunday morning. I just picked up the phone.

Director: This time you are thinking about it. Think out loud.[2] Who could it be?

Helen: Well. It could be Mabel calling to find out how well I enjoyed the evening. But she would never call this early. It might be my mother. She may have had an accident or sickness and is calling for help of some kind. She wouldn't call me unless something unusual happened. Besides, I spoke to her on the telephone yesterday. It can't be mother. It's probably Sam, a former boyfriend. We broke up a month ago but he keeps calling me to patch things up.

Director: Would Sam telephone on a Sunday morning?

Helen: He often calls early if he wants me to spend the day with him. If I had to guess who it was I would pick Sam as the most likely call at that time.

Director: Answer the phone now, Helen. (to John) Go ahead Tom, you are calling Helen. Let us hear the conversation.

John: (as Tom) Good morning, Helen. Did I awaken you?

Helen: Who is this?

John: (as Tom) It's Tom. Don't tell me that you have already forgotten me.

Helen: I didn't expect a call this morning. The ring of the telephone sort of woke me from a sound sleep.

John: (as Tom) I'm sorry. I didn't mean to disturb you.

Director: Reverse roles. You play Tom, Helen; we have no other way of knowing what Tom said.

Helen: That's about what he said. (as Tom) You said I could call you for a date and I thought I ought to take you up on it before you changed your mind.

[1]The two scenes, the one with Mabel and the first meeting with Tom took six minutes to reenact.

[2]The technique the director is introducing is called "soliloquy". The soliloquy is contained in Helen's next response.

John: (as Helen) I didn't expect you to call so soon. What did you have in mind?

Helen: (as Tom) We might have dinner together this evening and go to a show after dinner, if you'd like.

John: (as Helen) That sounds great to me.

Helen: That is not what I said.

Director: Reverse back. Helen you are now playing yourself and John will play Tom.

Helen: I never go out on Sunday evening. I have to be at work early on Monday. As for this afternoon, I already have an appointment.

John: (as Tom) Why don't you break it and go to a movie with me this afternoon. Wouldn't you rather spend the afternoon with me? We could still have dinner together.

Helen: I never break appointments. Besides, I don't like to be rushed into anything.

John: (as Tom) You said I could call for a date and I'm inviting you to dinner. I can't see how that is rushing you into anything.

Helen: I'm sorry. I didn't mean it that way. It is nice of you to invite me but I shall be busy until next Friday. Why don't you call me on Wednesday evening.

John: (as Tom) Fine. I'll call you on Wednesday at about ten. Is that o.k.?

Helen: Yes. I should be home by then. Thank you for calling and good bye for now.

John: (as Tom) Good bye.

Director: (to Helen) Did you really have an appointment?

Helen: No. I just wanted time to think. All I knew about Tom is that he was in the investment business in Cleveland and was visiting New York. Going out with him was sort of like going out with a tourist or a traveling salesman. I couldn't make up my mind.

Director: If the call had been from Sam instead of Tom, would you have gone out with him?

Helen: I was pretty lonesome at the time. I might have but I don't think so.

Director: You mentioned breaking up with Sam. When was that?

Helen: About four months ago, just before Easter. It was about a month before I met Tom. But Sam and I were still on speaking terms. We are still friends.

Director: Let us see how the break up came about. Set the scene.[1]

Helen: We had just returned from dinner where we had been quarreling all evening. We were sitting in the living room of my apartment. I was sitting her, in an easy chair and Sam was sitting on the sofa. We each had a drink on the coffee table between us.

Director: Pick some one in the group to play Sam and show us how it went.

Helen: Henry could play Sam. He looks like him. (Henry advanced to the stage and sat down on the sofa.)

Helen: That is all there is to it, Sam, we must stop going out together. It's no good for me. It leads me nowhere.

Henry: (as Sam) Helen, you know I love you. What can I do to prove it to you?

Helen: You keep saying that but you stay with your wife. I used to believe you but you have lied to me so many times.

Henry: (as Sam) When have I ever lied to you?

Helen: You know very well that you have failed to keep any of the promises you made to me. Our entire relationship is based on lies.

Director: Henry does not know enough about Sam to go any further. Reverse roles. Helen, you play Sam while Henry plays your part. (They change places)

Director: (to Helen as Sam) Tell us something about yourself, Sam. How old are you? What do you do for a living? How long have you known Helen? What is your family like? Things like that.

Helen:[2] (as Sam) I am forty-three years old. I have been married for twenty-two years and have two children. Ruth who is twenty and going to college and Ben who is eighteen and about to enter college. I have not had any sort of relationship with my wife since I left her three years ago. I returned home because of the children but there is nothing between us.

Director: How long have you known Helen?

Helen: (as Sam) Nine years. I was teaching in the school when Helen began teaching. About five years ago I became assistant principal.

Director: Then you are Helen's boss.

[1]The telephone conversation and the interview leading up to the scene with Sam took about five minutes. The fact that Helen was anticipating a telephone call from Sam despite the 'break up' indicated to the director that her relationship with him was unclear to her and worthy of examination.

[2]Helen is now doing a soliloquy in the role of Sam. This technique encourages her to think as another person, Sam.

Helen: (as Sam) Not directly. I am an administrator. All the teachers I deal with are friends of mine.
Director: When did you first go out with Helen?
Helen: (as Sam) I left my wife about three years ago. At that time I moved in with Helen. We had been dating seriously for a few months before that.
Director: Have you remained with her since that time?
Helen: (as Sam) No. I returned home about six months later. I couldn't continue to sponge on Helen. It took almost all the money I earned to support my family. Besides, the children missed me. It was unfair to them.
Director: Even after your return home did you continue your relationship with Helen?
Helen: (as Sam) We broke off for a month and then made up. Every year or so she breaks off with me but she misses me and we get together again.
Director: Do you love Helen?
Helen: (as Sam) Very much. She knows that.
Director: Then what are you quarrelling about?
Helen: (as Sam) She is always pressuring me to leave my wife. I promised to leave my wife and marry her as soon as Ruth graduates from college. Its only one year more but she is impatient.
Director: Let us see the way you broke up.
Helen: (as Sam) You know that I can have a divorce anytime I want it. Still, I can't marry you now. It takes all I earn to support the children at college. I owe that to them. Next year when Ruth graduates Ben will only have two and a half years to go. I'll be able to make it then.
Henry: (as Helen) I want a home and family of my own. I'll just have to find another man.
Helen: (as Sam) Is that why you are breaking up with me? Do you have someone else in mind now?
Henry: (as Helen) No. You monopolize most of my time. If I don't see you I might meet someone who can give me what I need.
Helen: That is not what I said to him.
Director: Reverse back. Helen, play yourself again.
Helen: In a year Ruth will graduate. Then there will be something else. You know I have plenty of money. I have over $20,000 in savings. If money is the obstacle, get a divorce and I'll take care of all our expenses until both children graduate.

Henry: (as Sam) We tried that three years ago. It didn't work. If I live on your savings, you can't respect me and I lose my self-respect.

Helen: What about my self-respect? What about my life? You have your family and me. Now you must make a choice. Become my husband or forget about me.

Henry: (as Sam) There is nothing I can do about my situation for another year. You know that. I'll call you in a few days. You are too upset to discuss it now.

Helen: I am upset. This time I mean it. I don't want to discuss the matter again because it is obvious to me that you have made your choice.

Director: Is that the way it ended?

Helen: There was a lot more but that was the idea. He finally left. (Henry leaves the stage)

Director: Sam has left. You are alone and thinking about what happened. Think out loud. Sylvia (a trained auxiliary ego) will be your double. (Sylvia moves to the stage, sits alongside of Helen and assumes a position similar to hers) The lights are dimmed.[1]

Helen: This is the last time I will go out with Sam. He doesn't love me. I'm just convenient.

Sylvia: (to Helen) I am your double. We are both Helen. If this Helen says something you disagree with, contradict her.

Helen: His promises are all lies.

Sylvia: I've been kidding myself.

Helen: I don't believe I love him anymore.

Sylvia: I still need him, though.

Helen: I can get along without him. I got along without him before.

Sylvia: I got along without him, but I missed him.

Helen: I missed him for a while.

Sylvia: I was awfully lonesome without him.

Helen: I'll have to find someone else.

Sylvia: I can always go back to Sam.

[1]The technique employed here is called soliloquy with a double. When Helen 'thinks out loud' she is soliloquizing. Sylvia, the double, attempts to extend the expression of feeling and stimulate the protagonist into a more accurate perception of the relationship. If there is no trained assistant available to double, the director may double himself. The technique of doubling is important and adds a great deal to the understanding a protagonist gains while playing a role.

Helen: Yes. That is what I have always done, go back to Sam. Not again. I'll look for someone else this time.
Sylvia: I'll have to find someone. I can't stand being alone.
Helen: No one wants to be alone. I'll find someone.
Sylvia: It won't be anyone as good as Sam.
Helen: It doesn't matter if he is not as good so long as he is all mine. Sam's home and family are far more important to him than I am.
Sylvia: I'm just nothing to him.
Helen: A convenient friend or mistress.
Sylvia: I can be very important to the right man.
Helen: All I have to do is find him.
Sylvia: I'll wait until he finds me.
Helen: No more waiting for the right man to come along. This time I'll look for him.
Director: Is that the conclusion you reached after Sam left?
Helen: Pretty much, I guess.[1]
Director: A month later you found Tom. Can you think of a situation which best reveals the nature of your relationship?
Helen: We went places every Saturday and Sunday for about a month. He took me to dinner, then a show, and then home. The dates were very similar. He kept telling me how rich his father was and how beautiful his house in Cleveland was. A month ago we became engaged.
Director: Where did he propose to you?
Helen: In a restaurant. We were having dinner.
Director: Set up the scene and show us how he proposed.
Helen: We were sitting at a corner table in this very high class restaurant. There was a violinist moving from table to table playing Hungarian music. It was very romantic. (John comes to the stage to play Tom.)
Helen: This is the most romantic restaurant I have ever eaten in.
John: (as Tom) I'm glad you like it. Did you enjoy your food?
Director: Let us reverse roles so that Helen can show us how Tom proposed. (They change places.)
Helen: (as Tom) You know, Helen, that I have to return to

[1]The scene with Sam and the soliloquy lasted fourteen minutes.

Cleveland soon. There is something I must ask you before I leave and there is no time like the present.

John: (as Helen) What is it?

Helen: (as Tom) I know we have only known each other for a short time but I'm going to ask you what I have never asked a girl before. I'm going to ask you to marry me.

Director: Helen, you will have to play both parts. John can't possibly guess the answers. (John leaves the stage) When you are sitting where you are now you are Helen, when you move to the opposite side of the table, you are Tom. Is that clear?[1]

Helen: Yes. I think so. (moves to other side.)

Helen: Yes, I believe I love you, but this proposal is so sudden. I haven't met any of your friends or family. Will I fit in with them? Do you think that they will like me?

Helen: (as Tom) My parents will love you. They were always afraid that I'd bring home some showgirl or tramp. You will be a most pleasant surprise. Besides, it wouldn't matter what they said or thought. I'm twenty-eight years old now. I'm old enough to make up my mind.

Helen: You must have many glamorous girl friends. I wonder what you see in me.

Helen: (as Tom) I have been too busy to bother much with running around. All of the girls in my social set are parasites, you know, the bridge and golf set. I can't imagine myself going through life with any of them. A weekend seems like an eternity.

Helen: I know so little about you.

Helen: (as Tom) What would you like to know? I'm Tom Baker, Jr., vice-president of Thomas Baker and Co., Incorporated, Cleveland, Ohio. I have an M. A. in Business Administration from Ohio State. I make enough to support a wife and I love you. What else is important to you?

Helen: We've known each other for so short a time.

Helen: (as Tom) We've been going out three or four times a week for over a month. We're not children. I knew from the first time we met that you were the girl for me. Don't you know yet whether you love me or not?

Helen: I like you a whole lot. I suppose I do love you. But marrying you means giving up my teaching and moving to Cleveland.

Helen: (as Tom) Helen, I want you to give up teaching and come

[1]This technique is called 'the auxiliary chair'.

to Cleveland with me. You know what I earn a year. We can get along on that but if I need more my father will increase my salary. There's no need for you to work.
Helen: I like teaching. I also like my independence.
Helen: (as Tom) As soon as the first child comes you would have to quit anyway. However, I'm sure you can get a job teaching in Cleveland, if it's that important to you. They are short of teachers everywhere.
Helen: I have seniority rights, pension rights, all these things would be lost if I quit here.
Helen: (as Tom) You said that you have no one here but your mother. I have a large family and many friends in Cleveland. You don't object to having the wedding there?
Helen: I haven't said I was going to marry you yet.
Helen: (as Tom) Teaching does give you a feeling of financial security. I understand. And then, there is the pension. I have an idea. Between us we have about sixty thousand dollars in savings. We can place it all in a trust fund for you, in your name alone. That way if something happens to me or you are not satisfied with me as a husband, you can be secure.
Helen: You make it sound like I am marrying you for your money.
Helen: (as Tom) Then you are saying you will marry me.
Helen: You seem so sure of yourself.
Helen: (as Tom) Well, I am a good catch. You know I love you, Helen, and I've known for some time that you loved me. All we have to do is set the date.
Helen: I can't leave here until the end of June. Any date after that will be fine.
Helen: (as Tom) I'll leave for Cleveland next week and make all the arrangements. How about the first Sunday in July?
Helen: I would like to meet your family before the wedding.
Helen: (as Tom) I'm sure that can be arranged. I'm not forgetting about that trust fund either. Meet me at the Chase-Manhattan Trust department on Tuesday and we can set it up.
Helen: Do you think it wise to put all of your $40,000 in a trust fund for me? Won't we need some money to get started?
Helen: (as Tom) Our wedding presents should more than off set the trust fund money. Dad alone will probably give us that much. You worry about every little detail. Perhaps this trust fund will make you more secure.
Director: Is that how it ended?

Helen: We spent the whole evening planning. We talked for hours, about the type of house we were going to buy, the way we were going to furnish it, who we would invite to the wedding, things like that. Finally, Tom took me home and left.

Director: Is that all? Didn't he make love to you?

Helen: We kissed and petted. Tom never suggested sleeping with me. He said he wanted us to share in our first sexual experience on our honeymoon. He seemed so honest and sincere. (Helen was in tears.)[1]

Director: Did you invite him to spend the night at your apartment?

Helen: I never did. If he had asked I would have agreed. However, I like the fact that he respected me and did not ask.

Director: Helen, you are back home after the proposal and thinking about it. Think out loud. Sylvia will be your double. (Sylvia mounts the stage and sits down alongside Helen.)[2]

Helen: Well, at last I have found a man who loves me.

Sylvia: He says he loves me.

Helen: He seems to mean it.

Sylvia: Sam said he loved me.

Helen: But Sam stalled when it came to marriage.

Sylvia: Sam never had enough money to marry me.

Helen: Money was never important to me.

Sylvia: But it's good to know that Tom has lots of money.

Helen: I wouldn't care if he didn't have a dime, as long as he loved me and wanted me.

Sylvia: I want someone who will marry me.

Helen: A marriage proposal proves that a man loves you.

Sylvia: And can afford to marry you. Not like Sam.

Helen: I offered to help Sam financially. Money was not the obstacle to our marriage.

Sylvia: I was willing to supply the money to Sam if he would only marry me.

Helen: He didn't love me enough.

Sylvia: Do I still love him or is it Tom?

Helen: Sam never would marry me. Tom will.

Sylvia: I'm thirty and alone. I need a husband.

Helen: A woman needs some sense of security.

[1]The action was not interrupted. The director dimmed the lights but otherwise ignored the tears. The expression of emotion is viewed as a sign of strength.

[2]Soliloquy with double. The double, at the outset, reminds the protagonist that she is a double and that the protagonist may reject any comment made by the double.

Sylvia: Tom thinks of my security.
Helen: I know I shall be happy with Tom.
Sylvia: I hate to leave New York.
Helen: I'm sick of New York. I'm so alone here. I don't know if Cleveland will be any better, but at least Tom has people there. I have no one anywhere.
Sylvia: I'll be happy in Cleveland.
Director: So, Helen, you were eager to go ahead with the marriage. Did Tom keep his promise and establish the trust fund?
Helen: We went to the trust department of the bank on Tuesday and I signed the necessary papers. I gave Tom the Savings Bank check for $20,000 the next day to complete the arrangements. He left for Cleveland on Thursday evening. I saw him off at the airport.
Director: When did you next hear from him?
Helen: He called me on Sunday night and told me that he would be back for me in a week. He said that there might be some change in plans. He asked me if I had quit my job. I told him that I had another ten days to go to finish the semester. The girls were planning a shower for me and I intended to leave for Cleveland right after that. He told me not to do anything until he spoke to me again.
Director: What happened then?
Helen: Tom had seemed upset on the phone. I thought something had gone wrong. The next day I called him in Cleveland. I placed a person to person call to Mr. Thomas Baker, Jr. I finally got him. (Helen burst into tears—the lights were blacked out)[1]
Director: I know that this is very painful for you, Helen, but it happened almost a month ago, before you joined this group. It will help you to face it. Tell us what happened. (long pause, Helen crying.)
Helen: He said he didn't know me, that he hadn't been in New York in over a year, and that someone must have been impersonating him. I then called the bank and learned that the trust fund had never been set up.
Director: What action did you take? Did you notify the police?
Helen: The police found out later on. That night I tried to kill myself.

[1]The 'black out' technique is frequently used to help a protagonist regain composure. In this instance it was obvious that the experience was traumatic.

Director: Helen, we are going to relive that Monday night. You have learned about the impersonation, the loss of the money, and you are thinking out loud. Sylvia will be your double. We are not interested in exactly what you thought that night, what went through your mind. What is important is that, with the help of your double you rethink the whole relationship and then decide what to do. (Sylvia sits beside Helen)

Helen: I was in bed.

Director: The couch will be your bed. Sylvia will be alongside you in bed. (Three chairs were used to simulate a bed.)

Helen: How could I have been so blind?

Sylvia: Love blinds one.

Helen: Why would anyone fall in love with me. Why was I stupid enough to believe it?

Sylvia: I'm not worthy of love.

Helen: A millionaire falling in love with an old maid school teacher. I must have seen too many films.

Sylvia: It couldn't be real.

Helen: How can I face my friends?

Sylvia: They would laugh at me if they knew.

Helen: They'll know the marriage is off.

Sylvia: They will laugh at my misfortune.

Helen: They will consider me an idiot.

Sylvia: Real good friends.

Helen: I can't live with myself. To hand all of my savings over to a stranger.

Helen: I was going to marry him.

Sylvia: I was going to marry a stranger.

Helen: He never meant to marry me.

Sylvia: If he married me and took my savings it would have been all right.

Helen: If he loved me and married me he could have my savings. It's not the money that is important.

Sylvia: The money is not important. I'll kill myself because he won't marry me.

Helen: I'll kill myself because life is not worth living.

Sylvia: Life is not worth living without Tom.

Helen: To hell with Tom. He is just a thief.

Sylvia: To hell with Tom. Life is not worth living without my savings.

Helen: I don't need the money. It's just that I don't want to live anymore.
Sylvia: I'd rather go to another world.
Helen: I can't face my friends or myself.
Sylvia: I may as well be dead.
Helen: Yes. I may as well be dead.
Sylvia: Than all my friends will be sorry.
Helen: I don't care if they are sorry or not.
Sylvia: Sam will be sorry.
Helen: I'm not trying to hurt Sam.
Sylvia: Mother will be sorry.
Helen: Mother will be sorry but I'm not trying to hurt her.
Sylvia: Who am I trying to hurt? Tom?
Helen: He wouldn't care.
Sylvia: Maybe he would. He would feel guilty.
Helen: Is that why I want to kill myself? To make Tom feel guilty?
Sylvia: Sam might feel guilty too.
Helen: I'm not trying to make anyone feel guilty.
Sylvia: Why am I trying to kill myself? Aside from the loss of money, I'm no worse off than before I met Tom.
Helen: That was over three weeks ago. Now that I have thought it over, I would not harm myself.
Director: Well, Helen, I am pleased to see that you are much better now. (lights are brightened.) The trauma and the shock you experienced a month ago led you to extreme despair. You appear to have recovered considerably. At the beginning of the session you indicated that you had a problem now. Has Tom returned?
Helen: No. I am ashamed of myself when I think of what a fool I have been. Ever since Tom left I have been away from school on sick leave. Everyone knows I was jilted. The police interviewed everyone of my friends with questions about Tom. My friends all know about the loss of the money. I just can't face them anymore. Sam keeps trying to see me and I need someone, but I am ashamed to face him. After what happened I don't think I can trust anyone or face anyone.
Director: Helen, you have bravely and honestly presented your problem to the group. At this point we shall turn to the group and ask for assistance from the others. (To group) In discussing the problems and relationships presented by Helen, I must ask you not to analyze her but to call upon your own experience for in-

sights that may be of assistance to her and to others in the group.[1]

Helen had been crying during the latter portion of the session. The lights had been out or dimmed ever since her outburst. As the director moved from action to discussion the lights were brightened and both he and the protagonist sat down on the middle level of the stage. Both faced the group. In this way, what had been, in a very real sense, exclusively Helen's psychodrama, became a group psychodrama. All of the members of the group were now called upon to participate. To emphasize his support of Helen, the director held her hand in his as they both faced the group. Holding the hand of the protagonist symbolizes the unity of the director and the protagonist as they face the group together. The director explains that any attack on the protagonist is considered an attack on the director and *he will respond.*

Analysis of the Action:[2] The director was aware of the trauma experienced by Helen in her relationship with Tom and her attempted suicide. So was Sylvia, the therapeutic assistant. He, therefore, suggested beginning the session with a scene involving her in a discussion with Mabel, her friend. Had she started with a presentation of the traumatic events she would have been to emotionally involved to examine her relationships. Beginning with the scene with Mabel, she had an opportunity to place her relationship with Tom in it's proper context. She was lonesome. She had broken with Sam and as a result was lonesome. She was isolated from 'couples' as friends. She observed in the soliloquy sequence that she was actively 'looking' for a man. The director recommended, at this point, a reexamination of her relationship with Sam. This would have been extremely difficult, if not impossible, after the traumatic scene was enacted. The only scene in which Helen was placed in interaction with Tom was the proposal scene and in it she was asked to play both roles. In this way she could examine the relationship carefully. The invitation to part with her savings came in a logical effort to provide her with security. Helen had an opportunity to reexamine the offer and, as she presented it, one could see that she had no reason to be suspicious. The interview with the director in which she told of the deception was not nearly as traumatic as a reenactment of the conversation would

[1]These remarks indicate the movement of the session from action to discussion.

[2]The action phase of the session lasted about fifty-five minutes.

have been and just as productive. It was important that she honestly acknowledge the fraud to the group. She did so. In so doing she was able to face the world or public and, in the discussion phase of the session, experience a reaction. The final soliloquy with Sylvia as double enabled her to reexamine her decision to commit suicide. She regained her composure as she was clearly able to reject it.

The Discussion Phase of a Psychodrama Session

The discussion phase of a psychodrama ordinarily begins after the action portion is completed. However, it is not limited to the last part of the session. The director may invite the members of the group to discuss any sequence and, in some cases, encourage a general discussion if he considers it appropriate. It is the director who initiates and leads the discussion. He tries to involve as many of the members of the group as he can in order to maximize feedback and the exchange of ideas, whether they are directly participating in the action or temporarily seated in the audience; members of the group are not regarded as spectators. They are participants and may be called upon to assist in an enactment or engage in a discussion at any time that a director deems it in the best interests of the protagonist or others in the group.

The director starts the discussion by asking the members of the group to identify with some aspect of the problem presented in the action portion. He urges them to relate their own experiences to those of the protagonist and to discuss problems presented on the stage in terms of their own experiences. The contribution that is considered the most desirable is one in which a member of the group shares with the group problems that *he* encountered in relationships similar to the ones portrayed in action by the protagonist. The action portion of the psychodrama with Helen as protagonist ended when the director invited comments from the other members of the group. A reconstruction of the discussion follows:

Director: Sylvia, in doubling with Helen you seemed to identify very closely with her problems. Were any of your experiences similar to those she enacted?

Sylvia: I had one experience in which a man I had been going out for a long time suddenly, without any explanation, started taking out a close friend of mine. He simply stopped dating me. This was very traumatic to me. I felt that all of my friends knew that I was jilted. It was a very uncomfortable feeling. I was embarrassed no end. Prior to that time it was I who terminated a relationship. Even if a fellow wanted to break off he permitted me to save face. On this one occasion I was not allowed to maintain my public image as a desirable woman. It hurt. Aside from everything else that happened, the loss of money, the unfulfilled promises, the disappointment, the mere fact that all her friends knew about the jilting must have been a cruel blow. It certainly was for me.

Helen: Yes. I guess that added a great deal to my misery.

Director: John, in the role of Tom you had an opportunity to interact with Helen. Do you have any ideas or experiences to contribute?

John: I had one experience with a con man. I suppose many people do. A man very much like Tom sold shares in an oil-well to two of my friends. They each bought a one-sixteenth interest for $30,000. I would have bought a share myself if I had the money. He was very convincing and it seemed like a perfect opportunity to make money. The oil well was real and his interest was legitimate. Our lawyers checked it out. The only trouble was, as we learned later on, that the crook sold fifty-sixteenths of the well. He timed all the deals to close within a few days of each other. Con men are so darned convincing. I can see how any girl would be taken in by the deal suggested by Tom. He always had the right answers and she thought he was in love with her and wanted to marry her. She says she was stupid to fall for a man and his swindle. I don't think she was stupid. The con man just has a big edge.

Director: Henry, in the role of Sam you had an opportunity to interact with Helen. Do you have any observations you would like to share with us?

Henry: As Sam I could feel that Helen was suspicious of my motives. She didn't seem to believe me or trust me no matter how hard I tried to convince her that I loved her. I was married to a woman who's father deserted his family while she was still a little girl. Her mother poisoned her mind against me. She never believed me or trusted.me. In the three years we were married she constantly accused me of cheating on her. Eventually I did. Helen's attitude toward Sam reminded me a little of this. My former wife would have had difficulty trusting Sam. She would have been more likely to trust Tom because he offered what she wanted most; marriage, wealth and status. Most women want those things. They

pretend to want romance and love. What they really look for is money and status. Maybe I'm bitter. I'd like to hear what some of the women in the group have to say.
Director: Would any of the women here care to comment?
Joan: As a woman I certainly am interested in marriage, wealth and status. What's wrong with that? I married a man somewhat like Tom. I didn't have a great deal of money but we lived on what I had or earned. I supported him for two years until he finished college. When he got his degree and a good job he walked out on me. He never did a thing for me. In fact, I learned later on that he was even cheating on me. Yet, when he walked out, it was a blow. Later I realized I was lucky to be rid of him. I won't be taken again. I will never again allow myself to become involved with a man unless he has a good job and can provide me with a sense of security. If I had been in Helen's position the offer of security made by Tom would have trapped me. Helen is lucky that she did not marry Tom. All she lost was money and some of her pride. She could have lost three valuable years of her life like I did.
Director: Are there any other comments?
Betty: I always seem to be disturbed by what people think of me. My mother used to interfere with every relationship I had with a man by raising that question. What will people say about me going out with a married man? What will they say about me going out with an uneducated man? What will they say about—it was always that. For some reason I still listen to her. I wish I knew why. So I'm alone, an old maid, and everyone feels sorry for me. If I had been through Helen's experience it would not have been the loss of the money or the loss of the man that would have caused me the most grief. It would have been the knowledge that everyone felt sorry for me.
Director: You were about to comment, Dora.
Dora: My affair with my present boyfriend is a lot like the relationship between Helen and Sam. He is married and I often feel that he is taking advantage of me. He makes promises that he doesn't keep. I get fed up and threaten to break off. If I stay away from him for a few weeks, I get awfully lonesome for him. It seems that I suffer either way. If a fellow like Tom had pursued me I would probably have done exactly what Helen did. I'm grateful to her for showing me what can happen. Unmarried women are all vulnerable to the approaches of men like Tom.

Director: Do you have anything to contribute, Bill?
Bill: No, except I hate men like Tom. He must be an awful louse to take advantage of a real sweet girl like Helen. Fellows like me never make out with girls like her. They seem to be hard to get and I guess that I can't risk failure. It's the persistent guy, like Tom who gets the nice girls. It's a shame.
Director: Do you have something to say, Joe?
Joe: I have no personal experiences with con men. I do know a fellow who boasts about the way he puts things over on girls. I used to think he was clever. Now that I have seen the other side of it I don't think much of him. I have a great deal of respect for Helen. She is honest and decent. Decent people don't do well against con men and liars. It's really too bad.
Director: Helen, it appears that no one in this group considers you stupid. The general feeling is that what happened to you could well have happened to any woman under the same or similar circumstances.[1]
Helen: (to group) Thank you all for trying to help me.
Director: Helen, do you believe that they were saying nice things just to help you?
Helen: Yes, and I appreciate it very much.
Director: Would you like to know how they really feel about you, about Sam, about Tom and about your relationship with each of them?
Helen: I certainly would
Director: We have a technique in psychodrama for this. We call it the 'Behind Your Back' technique. You, Helen, sit on this chair in the center of the stage with your back to the group. (She does so) You (to group) reseat yourselves away from the stage. (group members comply) Now, Helen, everyone here will talk about you, Sam, Tom and your relationships. You will be able to hear what is said but you will not know which person is saying it. You will get some idea what people are saying behind your back, what they really think of you.
Director: (to group) Be honest. Say what you really think about Helen and the men in her life. (From this point on voices will be identified as F, for female and M, for male with comments coming in rapid succession).
F.: She is lucky she didn't marry a rat like Tom. He could have left her with a baby.

[1]The director is summarizing the feedback from the group.

F.: He could have wasted years of her life. She can't do worse than a man like Tom.

F.: The trouble is that this experience may embitter her. She may find it more difficult than ever to trust men.

M.: Tom wasn't a man. He was a thief. Even if he liked her a lot, loved her, he would still have to steal her money. That is the way he earns his living.

F.: Still, to her he was a man, an unfaithful, dishonest lover.

M.: She mustn't see it that way. It will make it impossible to trust another man if she sees Tom as a lover who she trusted. He is a thief who pretended to love her so he could steal. She should see him as a craftsman, like a pick-pocket or check forger.

F.: If an intelligent girl like Helen could be deceived we all can.

F.: Helen is fortunate to have Sam waiting in the wings. It seems to me that he would be only too happy to come back to her.

M.: I can't understand how she could be so mean to Sam. He must really love her. She knows that. If she wasn't in love with him why has she been taking him away from his family for three years?

M.: I don't see what Sam's family has to do with it. Sam would have nothing to do with his wife in any case.

F.: How do you know? Maybe if Helen weren't around he would become reconciled to his wife.

F.: She is unfair to Sam's family. If she is not sure that she loves him she ought to leave him to his family.

M.: Helen is attractive and intelligent. I wish she'd go for my type.

M.: I'd love to be in Sam's shoes. He'll go back with her any time she wants him.

F.: Before going back to Sam she ought to try someone else. That was what she was about to do when she was sidetracked by Tom.

F.: If she tries someone else she may lose Sam. He really loves her. She has a lot to lose.

F.: She will go back to daddy now.

F.: Yes. She treated Sam as though he were the daddy who abandoned her mother.

M.: Another woman analyst. I think she just wanted a husband and got tired of waiting.

F.: What's wrong with that?

F.: Nothing. But if she wants a husband why doesn't she stay away from married men?

F.: What if she really loves Sam?

F.: She is the only one who knows whether she does or not.

M.: If she knew she wouldn't have a problem. The fact is she isn't sure. She may be ambivalent.
M.: She ought to level with Sam. She can take him back and wait until he is ready to marry her. Why doesn't she? After living with a man for three years without a formal wedding what does one year more matter?
F.: I'll bet her mother objects to Sam.
M.: Her mother is probably against any man she chooses.
M.: She is old enough to decide for herself what she wants and who she wants.
F.: Are any of us really old enough for that?
F.: If I were Helen I would make up with Sam at the first opportunity.
F.: So would I.
M.: If I were Sam I'm sure I would go back to her if she would have me.
M.: So would I. She's a doll.
Director: Will everyone return to his or her former position. Helen, do you believe that the people here were honest in the expression of their opinions?
Helen: Yes, I do. I learned a great deal this evening.
Director: Of course, we must all remember that we have not seen Sam or Tom. We have only observed Helen's perceptions of them. We do know a great deal about Helen. It is obvious from what has been said that we all admire and respect her. She is a very attractive and intelligent woman.

(To Helen) At this point, Helen, you might benefit by a future projection. This technique permits you to project yourself into a situation in the future at a time and in a place of your choosing. First select a time, when some important change will occur in your life. When is it, one, two or three years off?
Helen: Two years from now.
Director: It is two years from now. Show us where you are, what you are doing and who is with you. Set up the scene.
Helen: I am in the living room of my apartment. The same one. Sam is sitting opposite me on the other easy chair. He has been promoted to principal. We have been married a year.
Director: Henry, will you please play Sam. (He moves to the stage opposite Helen.) Show us how you see things, Helen.
Helen: Did you have a hard day, dear?

Henry: (as Sam) The usual. How about you?
Helen: You know I went to the doctor today.
Henry: (as Sam) Is there anything wrong with you?
Helen: I don't know whether you would consider it good or bad, but I am going to have a baby.
Henry: (as Sam) I know you have always wanted a baby, dear, but it will create some problems right now.
Helen: You are not angry with me, are you?
Henry: (as Sam) Angry? Of course not, dear. It will be a bit difficult, but we'll manage.
Helen: I'm so happy.
Director: That is a most optimistic future projection. I'm sure everyone in the group wishes you all the happiness you hope for yourself.[1]

Analysis of the Discussion Phase of the Psychodrama

The director began the discussion by calling first upon the trained auxiliary ego, Sylvia. Since she was familiar with the objectives of a psychodramatic group discussion she could be counted on not to attempt to analyze the protagonist and to relate one of her own experiences to the problems presented by the protagonist, Helen. The director then called upon the other auxiliary egos for comment. Having been in the interaction with her they could be expected to be sympathetic with her. After that the directed questions were few. An effort was made to stimulate each person to make some comment but no pressure was exerted to extend the discussion. After each had had an opportunity to comment, Helen remarked that she felt they were being deliberately supportive. At this point the director introduced the "Behind Your Back" technique to give her an opportunity to be psychologically absent while the others were discussing her. The director then suggested that Helen enact a future projection. Ordinarily the future projection would have been presented as the final scene of the action portion of the session. Since the director did not see fit to use it at that time, he still had it available if the discussion indicated that it would be useful. It is obvious that the contributions of the members of the group in support of Helen were highly constructive. Whether or not other members of the group experienced catharsis as a result of the production and the discussion is a mat-

[1]The director then summarized the discussion.

ter of opinion. There is no question, however, that the discussion produced many clues to relationships of other members which could be explored at future sessions. Judging from the involvement in the discussion on the part of every member of the group, the production held the interest of everyone.

Each member of the group, in his own way, tried to help Helen work out the problems presented in her enactments. Each may have experienced catharsis and developed insights as he shared aspects of Helen's problems that related to his own. The application of the "behind your back" technique provided Helen an indication of how her behavior was perceived by the others, persons who were not emotionally involved with her. In a sense, she was afforded an objective evaluation of her patterns of behavior, by the "public." Others in the group witnessed an *evaluation of their own patterns of behavior* to the extent that these were similar to the ones evaluated.

Not all Psychodrama sessions are as dramatic as the Psychodrama of Helen. However, describing it here provides us with a clear understanding of the structure of a Psychodrama session. It also provides us with illustrations of some basic techniques employed by Psychodrama directors to provide a protagonist with opportunities of increasing awareness and considering alternative courses of action. In my opinion, there is no better opportunity for a person to experience existential validation than a Psychodrama in which he can reenact traumatic portions of his life experience, exposing his faults and weaknesses and find that members of the group sympathize, empathize and even love him as he really is. He need no longer question his acceptance by others with the "If they only knew" thought. The mask is off, they do know and they accept him with his faults.

Chapter 8

BASIC TECHNIQUES IN PSYCHODRAMA

According to reliable estimates, over two hundred Psychodramatic techniques have been developed by Dr. J. L. Moreno, members of the staff of Moreno Institute, and others who have employed Psychodrama over the years. Many of these have been described in detail in articles published in Group Psychotherapy and Psychodrama, the official journal of the American Society of Group Psychotherapy and Psychodrama, and Sociometry, a journal founded by Dr. Moreno, and now published by the American Sociological Association. In this chapter I shall describe the sixteen techniques most frequently employed by me and my associates. These are: Self-Presentation, Presentation of Other, Interview in the Role of Other, Role-Reversal, Double, Multiple Double, Aside, Alter Ego, Soliloquy in own Role, Soliloquy in Role of Other, Mirror, Magic Shop, Dream Technique, Blackout Technique, Auxiliary Chair, Behind Your Back Technique, and Future Projection. I shall also describe some of the techniques I use to increase the expression of feeling, and to deal with crisis situations. Where a particular technique was employed in the Psychodrama of Helen, its use will be explained. While these techniques have been developed for use in Psychodrama and Role Training sessions, some of them have been adopted by Gestalt Therapists, Transactional Analysts, and other professionals working with groups. Anyone participating in a Psychodrama session directed by a qualified person will experience applications of most of these techniques. In addition, some of them may be used to good advantage by persons applying them to an understanding of their own behavior and relationships. In this chapter, I shall describe each of the techniques, illustrate their use, and suggest applications to Socioanalysis.

Self-Presentation

This technique is generally employed before the first enactment of the protagonist. The individual is asked to talk about himself and tell the group what he considers important. As he presents himself, the director may ask the protagonist to describe the relationship as he sees it and explain how he proposes to seek a solution. I try to get the protagonist to state his objectives for the session at this time. The self-presentation permits the group to better understand and to evaluate the action, first by providing necessary information and secondly, by inviting attention to objectives. If the objectives are difficult or impossible of attainment I call this to the attention of the protagonist. I try, if possible, to arrive at some agreement as to the goals of the session.

The self-presentation usually leads to the selection of the first scene to be enacted. As the protagonist presents himself potential auxiliary egos have an opportunity to learn the protagonist's perception of the relationship. This helps to prepare them for playing the parts of other persons when required to do so in the action.

Presentation of Other

In the course of his self presentation the protagonist has described a relationship with at least one other person that he wishes to explore. Before setting a scene I then ask the protagonist to physically move to the other side of me and present the other person or persons. As Helen presented her father and mother the group and director were given her view of her family relationships.

Interview In Role of Other

While the protagonist is presenting another person. I ask several general questions such as:

What is your name?

How old are you?

What do you do for a living?

What is most important in your life at present? The interview has several objectives. It is intended, first of all, to get the protagonist to think as that other person. As he answers questions in the role of other he begins to develop empathy for that role. Hopefully, he may eventually begin to see himself from the point of view of the other. I try to initiate this process as early in the session as I can. The protagonist in the role of other, presenting that person, affords me the first opportunity to do so. As Helen, presenting her father and mother, tried to express their attitudes she was made increasingly aware that those attitudes and their relationship may have influenced her attitudes and behavior toward men.

Role Reversal

This technique, when used in a Psychodrama, requires the protagonist to exchange parts with the person with whom he is interacting on the stage. In the scene in which Helen met Tom for the first time, I asked her to reverse roles with John, the auxiliary ego who was playing the part of Tom. As director, I told her to play Tom for a while until John learned the part. I asked the two persons to physically change places and proceeded to interview Helen in the role of Tom. The dialogue was as follows:

Director: (to Helen as Tom) Tom, what do you do for a living?
Helen: (as Tom) I am an investment counselor.
Director: How is it that you came to this dance without a date?
Helen: (as Tom) I am from Cleveland. I arrived in New York a few days ago and wanted to meet some people. An acquaintance at my hotel recommended this dance.
Director: You have just met Helen. What do you think of her?
Helen: (as Tom) She is a good dancer. She'll do.

Such a Role Reversal at the beginning of an encounter has several important functions:

1. It gives John, the auxiliary ego who is to play the part of Tom some idea of the sort of person he is to represent. He is then able to portray him better when in interaction with the protagonist.
2. The interview with the protagonist in the role of other (Helen in the role of Tom) gives the protagonist, Helen, an opportunity to think as Tom. Let me emphasize that the Role Reversal does not necessarily present Tom accurately. Helen can only present *her perception* of Tom. As she does so in interaction, taking his role from time to time, that perception may change. Role Reversal, in my opinion is the most effective technique ever devised for developing and increasing both empathy and sympathy. This ex-

perience may help the protagonist take the role of other (place herself in the position of other) when in interaction with persons later on in an enactment and, what is more important, in real life situations in natural groups.

3. In the course of Role Reversal, even in the brief interview referred to above, the protagonist is given an opportunity to view *himself* or *herself* from the point of view of the other.

In addition to its use at the beginning of an encounter, Role Reversal may be employed at any time in the session to make the production more accurate. The protagonist is generally the only person in the enactment who was present in the original situation. If he expresses the view that the part of other is not correctly performed by the auxiliary ego, he may be given an opportunity to present the action of other through the use of Role Reversal. The director simply instructs the protagonist to reverse roles with the auxiliary ego and 'show us what really happened'. The director should bear in mind, however, that literal accuracy is not essential. Repeated role reversals inhibit the spontaniety of a session. The protagonist should be advised of this early in the session.

If, at any time, in the course of the interaction the protagonist asks a crucial question, roles must be reversed immediately so that the protagonist is placed in the position of having to answer it. For example, if the protagonist, in the interaction, asks, "Will you marry me?" there is no point in having the auxiliary ego respond. The only person present who is qualified to answer is the protagonist and roles must be reversed so that he is required to supply the answer.

If the director is of the opinion that the protagonist may have a distorted view of the attitudes or feelings of the other person he may have the protagonist perform in the role of other assisted by a double. A skillful or sensitive double may assist the protagonist in arriving at a better understanding of the other person. At the very least he will stimulate the protagonist into considering alternative possibilities. In each instance, a most important function of the Role Reversal is to assist the protagonist to increase his perception of his relationship with the person who is represented on the stage by an auxiliary ego. At one time or another, in the course of a Psychodrama, the protagonist should be encouraged to reverse roles with every person with whom he is in interaction on the stage.

The Double

Where the protagonist expresses views or attitudes or behaves in ways which appear to conceal or distort his thoughts and feelings, rather than express them, a double may also be used to explore the situation. A double may be used to stimulate the protagonist when he appears to be having difficulty expressing himself or is saying very little. The double, whether a trained auxiliary ego or a member drawn from the group, is an agent of the director. Where no trained person is available the director may and often does perform and act as the double. Although this practice is not encouraged it is used where a trained auxiliary ego is not available or where the director decides to move in a particular direction and there is no way of instructing the auxiliary ego without inhibiting the spontaneity of the session. One of the most important functions of the double is to give voice to the unexpressed feelings and thoughts of the protagonist. He begins by placing himself alongside the protagonist and duplicates his physical position to the best of his ability. He also speaks in the same manner and tone of voice as the protagonist. To stimulate the protagonist into expressing thoughts and feelings the double may express strong feelings in a particular direction, if he suspects that the protagonist holds such feelings. The protagonist is informed that he may disagree with or accept any expression or action of his double. If the protagonist does not object to the expression and attitude of the double he is presumed to be adopting them. The double technique may be used to further the following objectives:

1. To help the protagonist express thoughts and feelings that he may be deliberately concealing or distorting.
2. To stimulate the protagonist to review his attitudes and feelings by encouraging him to consider as many aspects of a relationship or situation as possible.
3. To stimulate the protagonist into expressing thoughts and feelings in areas he has not considered.
4. To encourage the protagonist to reexamine his relationship patterns and consider alternative solutions to his problems.

The protagonist and his double are supposed to represent two sides or aspects of *one* person. In the Psychodrama we have just described, Sylvia as the double and Helen as the protagonist, *both* were thinking out loud as *Helen*. The double begins by telling the protagonist that he may disagree or accept, and that any expression or action of the double is deemed to be *his,* the protagonist's, expression or action unless he objects. If the double is exploring the depth of the protagonist's feelings toward a person or situation, he begins by repeating the expressions of the protagonist and then extending them a just a little. He gradually escalates the expressions of feeling from mild to extreme until the protagonist gets off the escalator by rejecting an expression of feeling which he considers too strong for him. As he does so, the protagonist may arrive at a better understanding of his feelings and his relationships. To help provide such understanding is an important function of the double.

In Socioanalysis the principal function of the double is to increase awareness of alternatives. I therefore, use what I call a Stimulus Double. The *Stimulus Double* is a most effective tool because through its use the protagonist may be required to consider courses of action he has never faced before. He may also be required to respond to stimuli related to his attitudes, motives, and feelings. The Stimulus Double moves in every direction. This is particularly true when the double is used in conjunction with a soliloquy. The double provides the stimuli and encourages the protagonist to respond to them. Furthermore, since the double presents all sorts of possible solutions his comments are not likely to be considered as advice or guidance by the protagonist.

The double used to encourage a protagonist to express hitherto unexpressed feelings I refer to as a *Sensitivity Double.* The auxiliary ego serving as the Sensitivity Double tries in every way to duplicate the posture, behavior, and verbal expressions of the protagonist, and attempts to feel as the protagonist feels and express his feelings in words and actions. The effectiveness of this type of doubling depends on the empathic ability, skill, and training of the auxiliary ego employing it. When I use the Sensitivity Double I refrain from any sort of interpretation.

The Multiple Double

I use this technique when a protagonist does not express affect in a relationship and I believe that it exists. If I do not know whether the unexpressed affect is positive or negative I provide two doubles, one to express each. The intent is to stimulate the protagonist into an honest portrayal of his feelings. It is important, when this technique is employed, that the protagonist is frequently reminded that each of the auxiliary egos serving as double are merely attempting to stimulate him into expressing his real feelings. Unless this is done the technique may serve to confuse the protagonist. Since it is not unusual for a protagonist to be ambivalent in his feelings, the use of the multiple double technique may serve to give the protagonist insight into this ambivalence.

The following is taken from the Psychodrama of Mabel, a protagonist in interaction with Fred, an auxiliary ego playing the role of her husband, Bill. I shall call one of the doubles used Positive and the other Negative, a reflection of the attitudes they were to exhibit toward the marriage.

Mabel—I'm tired of being alone every evening, can't you find some time to stay home.

Fred—Well, I'm busy right now. We were together twice last week.

Mabel—I don't enjoy going out with you the way things are.

Fred—Why not? You seemed to be having a good time.

Mabel—Everyone seemed to know you didn't care about me.

Fred—That is only in your imagination.

Mabel—Well, they all know about you and Alice.

Fred—I'm married to you—What has Alice got to do with it?

Mabel—That's just it. You're married to me and you flaunt your affair with Alice.

Fred—You wanted to get married—You knew I wanted to continue relationships with other women.

Mabel—I thought you loved me, and that you would forget about other women.

Fred—I do love you but I need other relationships too. I need to feel free to have other women.

Mabel—It leaves me so alone.

Fred—I'm not stopping you from having an affair. It might be good for you.

Mabel—You don't care enough about me.

Fred—You're in another of those moods.

Mabel—I'm not happy this way. Unless things change I'll have to leave you.

Director: (to Mabel)—How did this scene end? Bring it to a conclusion.

Mabel—It never really ends—it just goes on that way until somehow we change the subject to dinner or going out or something.

Director: The scene is over and you are in your room thinking out loud about it. Chelley (Positive) and Ruth (Negative) will act as your doubles. You may agree or disagree with whatever either says.

(The following is a Soliloquy with 2 doubles)

Positive—Maybe I ought to try some other guy.

Mabel—I've tried that. It makes me feel like a tramp.

Positive—I love Bill. Maybe he'll get tired of Alice.

Mabel—He will get tired of Alice, then there will be someone else.

Negative—Bill doesn't love me. I'm just a convenience.

Mabel—He says he loves me but I'm not happy.

Negative—He avoids sex with me.

Mabel—Oh no he doesn't. I reject sex with him sometimes because I hate to follow another woman in bed with a man.

Positive—I love sex with him.

Mabel—I did but now I resent him at times.

Positive—I'm just trying to punish him.

Mabel—Yes, I just wish he'd drop the other woman.

Negative—I'll just have to leave him.

Mabel—I tried that before but I was too lonely.

Positive—I need Bill.

Mabel—I need my self respect. I'm too unhappy.

Positive—I can stay with Bill, then I won't be lonely.

Mabel—I'll have to leave if he doesn't change.

Negative—He won't change. I'll start looking for a new relationship—one I can live with.

Mabel—I'd like a real good relationship with a man.

Negative—I'm attractive, intelligent. I'll find one.

Mabel—Where?

Negative—I'll look around. Lots of men are interested in me.

Mabel—Yes, but for only one thing.

Positive—Bill loves me. The others just want my body.

Mabel—If Bill really loved me he wouldn't suggest that I have an affair.

Positive—But, I'm lonely and miserable without him.

Mabel—I'm miserable when I'm alone. What I need is a good relationship with a man.

Negative—I'll find a good relationship with a man and then leave Bill.
Mabel—That's right. If I found a good relationship I wouldn't need Bill.
Negative—I'll start looking now.
Mabel—That's right. I will.
Positive—I'll stay with Bill until I find a better relationship.
Mabel—That's right, and I'll start looking now.

The soliloquy ended here because it appeared to Mabel that she had reached a solution. The doubles helped her examine several possibilities, and increased the possibility of this decision.

Aside

At times it is apparent that a protagonist, for some reason, is not expressing his real feelings in the course of an interaction. For example, a protagonist may be reenacting a scene in which his father is berating him for some disapproved behavior. In the interaction the protagonist sits quietly, head down, taking the abuse without any verbal response or simply keeps saying; "Yes father" to each denunciatory comment. The aside technique may be employed to afford him an opportunity of expressing his real feeldngs. I instruct him to continue to respond as he actually did in the situation and in addition, turn his head *aside* in the direction of the group and say out loud what he is really thinking or feeling.

To illustrate:4

Father: You sit around listening to records when you should be studying. No wonder your grades are poor.
Jim: I'm just relaxing now.
Father: You're always relaxing. I never see you do anything.
Jim: Remains silent.
Jim Aside: There's no point in saying anything. He won't listen.
Father: When are you going to act grown up?
Jim: I'll start studying soon.
Jim Aside: He'll pick on me for something else. He's never satisfied with what I do.

Alter Ego

The Alter Ego technique is used in the same situations in which Asides are used. Where the protagonist does not appear to use

Asides when asked to, I say to him; Jim you keep on responding as you did in the actual situation. Bill, your Alter Ego will say to the group what you may be thinking or feeling. Bill sits alongside the protagonist and the encounter continues.

> *Father:* You're old enough to be responsible. Either you make good in school or get a job.
>
> *Jim:* I'll try to do better.
>
> *Bill: (Alter Ego)*—I wish he'd get off my back.
>
> *Father:* When I was 18 I worked eight hours a day and went to school at night. You have nothing to do all day and you can't hack school. You're lazy.
>
> *Jim:* Silent.
>
> *Bill: (Alter Ego)*—I wish I could get a job and get out of here.
>
> *Father:* If you don't make it in school you'll have to get a job or get out of this house. I'm not going to support you forever.
>
> *Jim:* Silent.
>
> *Bill: (Alter Ego)*—I hate his guts.

At this point, if Jim remains silent I might ask him if he has ever expressed anger to his father. If he indicates that he has difficulty expressing anger I encourage him to do it verbally in action. The way this is done will be described later in this chapter.

Soliloquy in Own Role

The director, when he uses this technique, instructs the protagonist to think out loud and say what is on his mind. He may be asked to soliloquize at the end of an interaction. In so doing he can express his feelings and attitudes, and examine them. As he soliloquizes, the protagonist may be furnished a double to stimulate him into the consideration of alternative perceptions of problems and alternative solutions.

In the Psychodrama of Helen, a soliloquy with a double was used in different ways and for different purposes. Sylvia, doubling with Helen, in a soliloquy about Sam was trying to get her to express her feelings as accurately and completely as possible. This type of double, a *Sensitivity Double,* requires the auxiliary ego to try as nearly as possible to simulate the action, thoughts and speech of the protagonist, extending them in the direction the protagonist is taking. When Sylvia doubled with Helen in her soliloquy, as she was considering Tom's proposal, she was engaging in a *Stimulus Double.* Here the double tried to get the protagonist in her soliloquy to deal with several likely alternatives and respond to each. In this form of doubling the auxiliary ego may offer conflicting stimuli to evoke responses. For example, Sylvia, as double, said: "I hate to leave New York." When this was rejected by the protagonist Sylvia said: "I'll be happy in Cleveland." The double was trying to get the protagonist in her soliloquy to deal with her feelings about going with Tom and provided the conflicting stimuli.

The double, in the soliloquy, after the suicide attempt represents a combination of the *Sensitivity Double* and the *Stimulus Double.* Sylvia, as double, tried to take the role of the protagonist, and extend it in much the same way as one does when employing the Sensitivity Double. However, in addition she provided stimuli by raising questions for the protagonist to answer.

I find it useful to employ a Soliloquy with a Double before and after each important encounter. It serves to prepare the protagonist and the auxiliary ego for action when used before the encounter. When used after the encounter it serves to summarize for the protagonist the effect of the encounter upon him including his feelings about the person with whom he was in interaction.

Soliloquy in Role of Other

At the end of an encounter I at times have the protagonist soliloquize (think out loud) in the role of the other person in the encounter. This is accomplished by having the protagonist reverse roles with the other person in the encounter and bring the scene to an end as that other person. The protagonist, ending the scene in the role of other is asked to soliloquize, with or without a double. To illustrate:

Jim (as father)—Jim is lazy. I wish he'd leave. *Bill (as double)*—Jim needs discipline. If I didn't show an interest in him who would?

Jim (as father)—He'll never amount to anything.

Bill (as double)—I want him to succeed. I really care about him.

Jim (as father)—I'd like him if I could be proud of him, if he succeeded at something.

Bill (as double)—A good father has to discipline his son if he is not achieving.

Jim (as father)—I don't really know what I expect of him.

Bill (as double)—I don't really know what I am supposed to do to help him make it.

Jim (as father)—I'm disappointed in him.

Bill (as double)—I very much want to be proud of him. He is my son.

Jim (as father)—The whole family, my brothers, sisters, and friends know Jim is not making it. I'm ashamed of him.

Bill (as double)—I would like to be proud of him. I love him.

Jim (as father)—I don't love him.

Bill (as double)—A man is not supposed to love another man.

When a protagonist engages in a soliloquy in the role of another person he is afforded an opportunity to think as that other person. If a double is used stimuli are provided. Ideally, his perception of the feelings and attitudes of the other person would increase. Perhaps in the above soliloquy with a double Jim might consider the possibility that his father was trying to further his career. He might also learn that his father just didn't know how to relate to him.

The Mirror

When I use the Mirror Technique I send to the stage a trained auxiliary ego or assistant to duplicate the behavior of the protagonist in a previous enactment or situation. Insofar as possible, the auxiliary ego as Mirror, uses the same words, posture, demeanor and movement that the protagonist did in the course of his performance. The protagonist, as he witnesses the enactment, has an opportunity to observe *his own behavior* as it appears to another person. If he believes that he has been misrepresented by the Mirror, the protagonist is asked to raise whatever objections he may have, either immediately following the application of the Mirror Technique, or in the group discussion. Seeing how he is perceived by others may help the protagonist to develop a more accurate perception of himself.

The Mirror Technique is frequently employed in an effort to establish communication with a non-communicating individual. When used for this purpose, the auxiliary ego, after carefully observing the behavior of the person to be mirrored, portrays him on the stage in his presence and in the presence of a group. As soon as the person being mirrored indicates an awareness that it is he who is being represented by the auxiliary ego, either by showing amusement or by verbal comment, the auxiliary ego *misrepresents him* in a startling manner. Use of profanity, inept performance, unprovoked aggression, or other action likely to be regarded as unfair by the person mirrored, may be used to provoke him to respond. This sort of gross misrepresentation by the Mirror provides a form of Psychodramatic Shock and results in the protagonist protesting to the director and to the group. When he does so the protagonist begins to communicate.

Under certain circumstances the protagonist may be asked to mirror the performance of another person. If, for example, the protagonist is being prepared on the psychodrama stage to encounter someone at a later time, he may be encouraged to examine a series of alternative courses of action. This is accomplished by having several members of the group play the part the protagonist is preparing to assume. The protagonist plays in the *other* role. Thus, if the protagonist is preparing for an encounter with his employer in which he will request an increase in pay, several persons may be asked to show how they would play the part of the protagonist. He plays the role of the employer. This pattern of action is called a Role Training Sequence. After observing Henry, John, and Joe perform in the role, Bill, the protagonist, may be asked to mirror one of them. The director instructs him as follows: "Bill, you have seen John handle the situation. His method may be no better than that of any of the others, but it might be useful to try to see if you can do it that way. Ask for the increase *exactly* the way John did it." The use of the Mirror in this way stimulates other members of the group to consider alternative courses of action and perform in the required role. In this way all members of the group participate in the action and may gain increased understanding of the relationship involved.

I often use an actual or simulated Mirror to have a protagonist describe his perception of himself. At the conclusion of a session in which the protagonist has tended to be unusually critical of himself, I have him, look into a mirror (real or simulated) and tell us what he sees, starting with the top of his head and going down to his feet. A protagonist who rejects himself tends to emphasize negative characteristics. A fairly attractive woman may note that her nose is too flat, her breasts too small or too large, her hips too narrow or too broad, her body too thin or too heavy, etc. Seldom will she refer to attributes making her worthy of admiration. What she is saying, in so many ways, is; "I am ordinary and unattractive. That is why no one can love me." Members of the group invariably pick this up in the discussion which follows. I also use a Mirror Technique to stimulate the expression of feeling. This will be described later in this chapter.

The Magic Shop Technique

The Magic Shop is defined as one that has things that are not available at any other shop. When using the Magic Shop Technique, I set up such a shop on the stage, and have a trained auxiliary ego play the role of 'shopkeeper'. I do not use this technique unless I have such a person available. The protagonist is asked to enter the shop as a customer and seek to purchase what he wants most. He is told that the shop is stocked with imaginary items representing values that are not for sale. They may be exchanged, however, for other values to be given up by the protagonist. No money or other material items are involved. This technique affords the protagonist and others in the group the opportunity to evaluate the price each is willing to pay for the things he wants the most. A hierarchy of values may be better defined and in the course of doing this the individual may achieve greater insight into the direction of his efforts. The Magic Shop Technique is most effective when employed early in the session as it results in producing many possible avenues for exploration. It may even be used as a warm-up.

I have used a version of the Magic Shop in dealing with husband-wife relationships where one or both of the parties was dissatisfied with aspects of the relationship yet each expressed the desire to continue the marriage if the other would change in some respects. The shopkeeper asks the husband the three changes he most desires in his wife. He then asks what the protagonist is willing to give up to achieve each change. The same procedure is followed with the wife. A price is established for each change desired. The parties are then placed back to back on the stage and asked to negotiate the changes. If an impasse is reached they are asked to make another deal with the shopkeeper. Once a deal is made the parties go into action in a scene in which each possesses the newly gained attributes. They may then find that they are not as happy with the changes as they had imagined or that the sacrifices they made did not result in pain.

In the following session the technique proved extremely effective. The protagonist, a woman, went into her relationship with her husband. She reenacted several situations in which her husband was portrayed as indecisive and wishy-washy. She, on the other hand, wanted him to be powerful and decisive. As the session progressed it became apparent that she loved her husband and did not want to dissolve the marriage. In the group there was a woman highly skilled in the use of the Magic Shop Technique. I had the protagonist enter the shop and try to negotiate a deal. She asked for a more aggressive and decisive husband. The shopkeeper asked if she were willing to give up some of his sensitivity. She agreed. I then had a very domineering powerful man play the changed husband. He came on real strong giving her orders and disregarding her objections. She was not satisfied. She was then asked to reenter the Magic Shop. After much negotiation she acknowledged that she had wanted her husband to change and become more assertive and aggressive, yet she was not willing to change in any respect. Furthermore, she wanted her husband to be much more aggressive, and at the same time, remain as considerate and sensitive to her needs as he was. She recognized that this represented a contradiction. The Magic Shop, she said, had made it all too clear to her.

Dream Technique

If a protagonist tells of having a dream, particularly one which recurs, I encourage him to reenact it. He is warmed up to the sleep situation and to the dream by being placed in a bed (simulated or real) on the stage, and encouraged to think about the dream. As director I then ask him to rise from the bed and act out the significant portions of the dream with the aid of auxiliary egos of his choice, or if he prefers, by playing all of the parts himself. The purpose of the enactment is to give the protagonist an opportunity to explore in action his relationships with others involved, directly or symbolically, in the dream. I do not offer any interpretation of dreams. In my view, only the protagonist can arrive at meaningful interpretations of his dream. Used in this way the dream becomes a projective device which the protagonist can use to increase his understanding of his relationships. The content of the dream is accepted at face value. I make no attempt to impose a symbol system on what is presented. If the protagonist interacts with another person in the dream I ask who that person is. I also encourage him to identify any object or person mentioned in the dream. Even when a protagonist identifies a person in the dream as his father, wife, or mother I refrain from any comment or interpretation.

The following enactment of the dream of Shirley will illustrate my way of presenting it psychodramatically. In the warm-up portion of the session Shirley stated that she had a nightmare a few nights before and that this was the fourth time she had this nightmare in a year. Shirley was chosen to be the protagonist. Shirley had been protagonist in a previous session and had examined her relationship with her husband, Rocco, to whom she had been married for three years. She was a physically attractive woman about thirty years of age. Rocco owned and operated an automotive repair shop for many years. Prior to marrying Rocco she had been his bookkeeper for two years and had been his mistress for most of that time. After the marriage Shirley quit working at the request of her husband who was anxious to have a family. As of the time of the session Shirley had not to her knowledge become pregnant.

In her self-presentation Shirley was asked what her objectives for the session were and she replied that she would like for the nightmares to end. The first scene was a reenactment of the events of the evening preceding the nightmare. The scene began on Monday evening at 7 P.M. when Rocco entered the house. The greeting was warm. At dinner the conversation appeared to be friendly. The auxiliary ego playing the part of Rocco presented many critical and negative stimuli to the protagonist but she rejected them. In his role, in the course of a Role Reversal, as Rocco, she was very warm and loving but also very tired. Shortly after dinner, Rocco went to bed, and Shirley watched T.V. for two hours and then went to bed. Before going to bed I had her do a Soliloquy with a double on what she was thinking at the time. In her soliloquy she expressed disappointment at not being pregnant, a desire to go back to work, and generally depressed feelings.

She went to bed without waking Rocco and then she was asked to enact the nightmare.

The Dream

Shirley was running down a street barefoot in her nightgown, pursuing a man. The man entered a building and she followed. She found herself in a garage like room without windows or furniture. There was another door to the room through which the man must have passed. The door was locked as was the door through which she entered. She beat on the door to the other room until she dropped to the floor exhausted, and terrified. At this point she awoke from the dream exhibiting all of the symptoms of extreme fear.

I asked Shirley to reenact the nightmare with an auxiliary ego playing the part of the man she was pursuing. I stopped her while she was running and asked her where she was. She could not identify the street, but did say that there were residences on both sides of the street. She could not identify the man she was pursuing. When she entered the room I asked her to describe the walls, floor, and ceiling. As she described it she remarked that it was very much like her living room but without furniture. I then asked her to open the door to the adjoining room and tell us what she saw. She proceeded to open the door. The only person in the room was her mother-in-law. I asked her when she had last seen her mother-in-law. It was the Sunday afternoon preceding the nightmare, when she and her husband visited for a weekly Sunday dinner. We reenacted that scene. Mother-in-law was polite but subtly rejecting. She would say something and then remark to Shirley, "You wouldn't understand. Only an Italian would know what I mean." Shirley in a soliloquy with double, after leaving her mother-in-law's house, expressed negative feelings toward her mother-in-law. Rocco was always running to her and away from Shirley. Both he and his mother were disappointed in her because she was childless, and did not become "Italian" in cuisine or culture. She then interpreted her dream as follows: "My husband was running to mother and I was trying to catch up with him and keep him. He got to her and I was left out, locked in another room, trapped. I love my husband and can't leave him but his mother keeps him from being mine."

We then ran a Psychodrama session with Rocco and Shirley during which their relationship was reexamined and Shirley's fears examined. Thier relationship was greatly improved and the nightmare did not recur.

The Black-Out Technique

The director, when using this technique, causes all of the lights to be extinguished while the action continues. If, while observing the protagonist, I see that he is visibly moved or is starting to cry, I dim the lights or put them out to enable the protagonist to go through a series of what may be painful experiences, unobserved by others in the group. The Black-Out is usually maintained until the protagonist regains his composure. A variation of this technique that is widely employed involves the dimming of the lights as the protagonist moves into a meaningful interaction. The dimming of lights takes the protagonist further away from the group into deeper involvement into his private world. There is a tendency on the part of some people to see crying as a sign of weakness. They respond by rushing up to the protagonist with handkerchief or tissues and offering sympathy. In my view this sort of attempted 'support' is uncalled for. It is like attempting to treat cancer with a bandaid. I do everything I can to encourage a protagonist to express feelings and explain to the protagonist and the group that the ability to cry and otherwise express feelings is a sign of strength, not weakness. I have seen men and women cry for several minutes on the psychodrama stage and emerge much stronger after the experience. The blackout affords a measure of privacy to the protagonist while he gives expression to this emotion.

The Auxiliary Chair

When this technique is applied, a chair is used to represent a person and the protagonist is instructed to address his remarks to the chair as if he were speaking to that person. In a modification of this technique, the director may use two chairs and instruct the protagonist to play himself when in one of the chairs and the other person in the interaction, when in the other chair. The protagonist engages in a dialogue by moving from chair to chair playing the required roles. This technique is used when the director is of the opinion that an auxiliary ego would have difficulty anticipating the responses of the other person. The proposal sequence in which Helen was responding to Tom's proposal and he to her reservations provided the occasion for use of the two chair technique.

The use of an auxiliary chair permits the director to halt the action and focus on one aspect of behavior. In this way a specific action or behavioral pattern may be emphasized and even exaggerated. When using the chair technique the director may move and speak for the persons symbolized by the chairs. I, however, prefer to have the protagonist act and speak in all of the roles in each chair.

I use this technique when a protagonist repeatedly corrects the auxiliary ego and appears intent on fidelity of production. Obviously, an auxiliary ego cannot supply the exact responses given by the person portrayed by him. If a protagonist insists on accuracy he may achieve this by playing both roles. I find it particularly useful when the protagonist is self-conscious, or shy, and has difficulty confronting a person.

The Behind Your Back Technique

This technique is employed in the discussion phase of a Psychodrama if the director feels that a face to face confrontation of the protagonist and the group members would inhibit honest discussion. It is also used if the protagonist questions the sincerity or honesty of the comments made by the group members in the course of the discussion. The director applies the technique by asking the protagonist to turn his back to the group and asking the other members of the group to change seats and then discuss the protagonist and the problems he presented honestly and sincerely. In this way members of the group may express views they might be reluctant to verbalize when face to face with the protagonist because of fear of embarrassing him. Since the protagonist is not present (psychologically) members of the group may make adverse comments without directly offending him. He can, however, benefit by their comments because he is able to hear them and thus, get some idea of what people say about him and his relationships. He is, in a sense, eavesdropping on gossip about himself.

I use this technique when it is apparent from the action portion of the session that the protagonist has a low self-image and that the group will very likely make favorable comments about him. Favorable comments might be interpreted as people being kind or reluctant to make him feel bad. If positive statements are made to his face, such a protagonist is likely to discount them. Comments made behind his back are more likely to be believed.

Future Projection

This technique is frequently employed as the last scene of the action portion of a session. The protagonist is asked to create the situation he expects to be in at some specified future time and enact a portion of it. It may be employed for the following purposes:

1. To give the protagonist insight into some of his goals.

2. To give the protagonist, the director and the group some indication of his view of the future. Does he see himself as married to his wife or divorced? Does he see himself as a success or failure in his career? Does he (an addict) see himself still using narcotics? Does he (a homosexual) see himself involved in heterosexual relationships? Does he see himself (a mental patient) out of the hospital leading a normal life? The ways in which such questions are answered in a Future Projection tells us a great deal about the image the protagonist has of himself and his prognosis for the future.

3. To afford the protagonist an opportunity to experiment on the stage with a new course of action so that he, with the help of the group, may examine its applications. In the group discussion that follows his new situation may be evaluated by the group.

I frequently use Future Projection to encourage a protagonist to develop new goals. For example, if a protagonist expresses dissatisfaction with things as they are, and sees little hope for improvement in the future, I ask him to create on the stage the situation in which he would like to be at some time in the future. I do so by posing the following questions:

Director: What important change would you like to see in your life one, two, three, or five years from now?

Protagonist: I would like to be engaged in some meaningful occupation, one in which I could derive satisfactions.

Director: When do you believe such a change may occur?

Protagonist: I don't believe it will ever occur.

Director: Let us examine the possibilities. It is now June 1980 (five years from date of session). You are now engaged in a meaningful and satisfying occupation. What is your occupation?

Protagonist: I am a Social Worker.

Director: This is your office. Show us what it is like.

Protagonist: Arranges office and describes it.

Director: Here is Mr. Smith. (an auxiliary ego) Show us how you deal with him.

The Future Projection consists of an enactment of a scene that could take place in the office of a Social Worker.

I then have the protagonist assume the role of an occupational counselor and prepare for a Role Training Sequence. I initiate this by inviting the other members of the group to participate in an effort to help the protagonist determine the likelihood of his becoming a Social Worker and the steps necessary for him to achieve that goal. This is accomplished by the following instruction to the group members. "David would like to become a Social Worker in the next five years. This may or may not be possible. We would like now, to have him consider the steps necessary to achieve this objective. David will play the role of an occupational counselor. Anyone coming up will play the role of David. Ask the counselor any questions you deem appropriate and offer any information you consider relevant."

After several "interviews" I have the Protagonist assume his own role and then ask him whether or not he still considers it impossible to become a Social Worker. If he still considers it impossible I ask him to choose another occupation he would like to consider and proceed to another Role Training Sequence.

Expressing Anger

Very frequently in the course of a Psychodrama, it becomes apparent that the protagonist has difficulty expressing anger to either a male or female authority figure. In the situation selected to illustrate a soliloquy in the role of other Jim acknowledged that he had difficulty expressing anger to his father. When this occurs, I suggest that the protagonist try to do so in action. His father is not present and cannot be directly affected by what is said. Jim agreed. I set the scene for expression of anger as follows:

I have the auxiliary ego playing the father seated on one side of the stage. I place a table between the auxiliary playing the father and the protagonist. On the table I place a heavy cushion removed from an upholstered chair. The protagonist *stands* on his side of the table and is asked to express his anger. The auxiliary ego playing the father is instructed to use two sentences as stimuli, both put downs.

"You're just a little boy."

"You're a stupid little boy."

To get the protagonist to feel and express anger I have the auxiliary ego face him with consistent, frustrating stimuli. I do not want a debate between the auxiliary ego and the protagonist. That would serve little purpose. If, despite this precaution, the protagonist still has difficulty expressing anger, a double tries to stimulate him. If this effort proves unsuccessful I use a mirror technique.

To illustrate:

"Jim, you still seem to have difficulty expressing anger to father. It is not easy to do something you have not been able to do before. I am going to express anger verbally and loudly and I shall pound the pillow as I do. You do exactly as I do *whether you agree or not*. Pounding the pillow in a standing position will activate your body from the abdomen on up."

After these instructions to Jim I respond to the put-downs coming from the auxiliary ego as follows:

Auxiliary Ego: You're just a little boy.
Director: I'm not a little boy.
Jim: I'm not a little boy.
Auxiliary Ego: You're just a little boy.
Director: I'm a man.
Jim: I'm a man.
Director: Again and louder.
Jim: I'm a man.
Auxiliary Ego: You're a stupid little boy.
Director: I'm not stupid.
Jim: I'm not stupid.

The put-downs continue and I continue to contradict them and encourage Jim to mirror me in a form of assertiveness training. After a while I shift to an escalation double which goes as follows: (I make each comment as double and wait for the protagonist to repeat it.)

I wish you were 100 miles from here.
I wish you were 500 miles from here.
I wish you were 1,000 miles from here.
I wish I didn't have to see you more than once a month.
I wish I didn't have to see you more than once a year.
I wish I never had to see you agin.
I wish you were dead.

At some point the protagonist may get off the escalator, by denying a statement. For example, he may say, "I don't wish him dead."

I then point out the ambivalence and end the scene. I then have the auxiliary ego and the protagonist stand facing each other holding both hands in non-verbal communications. Lights are dimmed and the auxiliar takes the protagonist in his arms. What started with hate and anger frequently ends with tears and love.

Persons having difficulty expressing one emotion generally have difficulty with others. It is easier for me to work on the expression of anger and I find that it is useful in that it helps a protagonist to realize his ambivalence and to express love.

Dealing With Crisis Situations

I am not going to offer any particular techniques for dealing with crisis situations as it is obvious that the situations are varied and the techniques require a great deal of expertise. In general, if someone is depressed, I seek in a Psychodrama to find some significant other who may may be a suitable target for the expression of anger. If a situation presents itself I have the protagonist express the anger in much the same manner as described in the last few pages. I vew depression as a form of aggression directed at oneself. My goal in Psychodrama is to have the depressed person externalize his aggression. To play with batacas or beat pillows in isolation does not, in my opinion, provide adequate catharsis. I seek in a Psychodrama a significant target for the aggression and then encourage the protagonist to get it out.

Each of the techniques described in this chapter is designed to increase awareness of alternatives by the protagonist. It is he who is the explorer and researcher. Proper use of these techniques and assistance of auxiliary egos afford him an opportunity to examine any of his relationships on the stage without danger of reprisal. What he says to his auxiliary wife is not likely to destroy his family relationships. What he says to his auxiliary employer is not likely to cost him his job. In the Psychodrama laboratory he may experiment with alternative courses of action in all sorts of problem situations. The techniques described facilitate this sort of exploration. The group, representing the world at large, can provide him with some basis for evaluating his patterns of behavior and his relationships and considering possible alternatives. This sort of exploration may be undertaken with a minimal risk of trauma. As he becomes aware of additional alternatives and has an opportunity to experiment with them, the spontaneity of the protagonist tends to increase. Other members of the group also increase their awareness of alternative courses of action and relationship patterns. The psychodramatic techniques may thus, in addition to providing insights into factors that limit spontaneity by increasing understanding of available alternatives, directly increase spontaneity.

Psychodrama has been particularly effective in socioanalysis because:

1. It increases the ability of people to express their feelings toward others. The verbal expression of such feelings as love and friendship are as difficult for some people to express as are feelings of anger and hate for others. Inability to verbalize negative feelings may result in physical aggression being directed against others and in some instances against oneself.

2. It reduces the isolation of people by helping them to establish and maintain satisfying relationships with others. In the course of psychodramatic sessions people learn to place themselves in the positions of others and view things from the perspectives of others. This enables them to understand better how others think and feel toward them. They develop the social skill necessary to make themselves more acceptable to others and the understanding that makes others more acceptable to them. They are, thus, prepared to abandon isolation for meaningful relationships.

3. It assists persons in improving their social relationships by either modifying their patterns of behavior to the extent necessary to achieve satisfactory responses or by substituting relationships with other persons for those presently frustrating them.

4. It develops spontaneity. Spontaneity is related to readiness for action. In psychodrama the protagonist is constantly facing new situations or experimenting with new solutions to old problems. To a considerable extent, therefore, psychodrama provides training for spontaneity.

5. It helps people to solve problems arising in social relationships by:

a) Better equiping them to recognize the existence of such problems.

b) Enabling them to recognize the existence of alternative solutions to their problems.

c) Providing them with practice in choosing between available alternatives.

d) Improving their ability to take action, once having chosen between available alternatives.

Chapter 9

TOTAL INVOLVEMENT TECHNIQUES IN PSYCHODRAMA

In the previous chapters I have described warm-up techniques designed to result in the emergence of a protagonist or protagonists from a group. The basic action techniques were then made available to the protagonist so that he could examine his relationships, express his feelings, and experiment with possible change. The focus was always on the protagonist and his problems. The other members of the group became involved if they could identify with a portion of the enactment. They also had an opportunity to involve themselves in the discussion portion of the session by sharing experiences. In thousands of sessions with all sorts of groups protagonists emerged and became deeply involved in the exploration of their life experiences and relationships. Other members of each group also related to what was being enacted and appeared to benefit by sharing and catharsis. Nevertheless, I am convinced that there were always some members of each group who were involved peripherally or not at all. In the course of directing sessions in the Alcoholic Rehabilitation Program of the Navy in Long Beach, California, I found this to be particularly significant. I would direct a session with forty or more navy people in a large room. No matter what warming-up techniques I employed most remained indifferent, or apathetic. When a protagonist emerged the session revolved around his relationships and difficulties with little or no sharing by the majority of those present. This troubled me greatly. I experimented with all sorts of Psychodramatic techniques without securing much greater involvement. I did not limit my efforts to the Alcoholic Rehabilitation Program. As I developed more effective techniques I tested them at sessions of the California Institute of Socioanalysis, in classes at California State University, Long Beach, and at seminars and workshops of Role Training Associates of California. The resultant techniques, those I found most effective, I refer to as total involvement techniques. The ten I shall describe in this chapter, in the order presented, I strongly recommend as ideal for use in an Alcoholic Rehabilitation Program with adults. They have also achieved total involvement when used with my college classes and at workshops with professionals. Rochelle Haskell has employed several of them with considerable success in her Psychodrama Program at the Federal Prison for Men, Terminal Island, California. As you begin reading the description of these ten sessions, bear in mind that the principal objective is to get every member of the group involved at some level in the relationship problems of others as well as of himself. Additional objectives are to increase self-respect, self-image, and self-direction.

The Initial Session

The objectives of a total involvement technique used as the first session of an ongoing group are no different from those of the initial session described in Chapter 7. Getting people acquainted with each other, presenting themselves in front of the group and learning a little about the Psychodramatic Method are the principal goals. In a total involvement session there is the additional goal of having everyone involved on some level. To stimulate involvement of persons who are reluctant to communicate on a verbal level, I have developed a form of non-verbal communication.

In the warm-up talk I start by discussing non-verbal communication in our culture. I point out that from his first day at school on the child is pressured into verbal communication. All non-verbal communication is discouraged and eventually inhibited. By the time we are adults we have forgotten how to communicate non-verbally. Also, we are so in the habit of emphasizing negative things about ourselves and others that we neglect positive communication. If the group consists of twenty-four persons or less, I have twelve chairs arranged in a circle as depicted in Figure 3. I invite half the group to seat themselves in the chairs. Persons in the remaining half are instructed to each station himself in front of a seated person. Each standing and sitting person is told to communicate the things he likes about the other, non-verbally and without physical contact of any kind. Communication may be by

Figure 3.

PLACEMENT OF SUBJECTS FOR NON-VERBAL COMMUNICATION

= person standing.

= person seated.

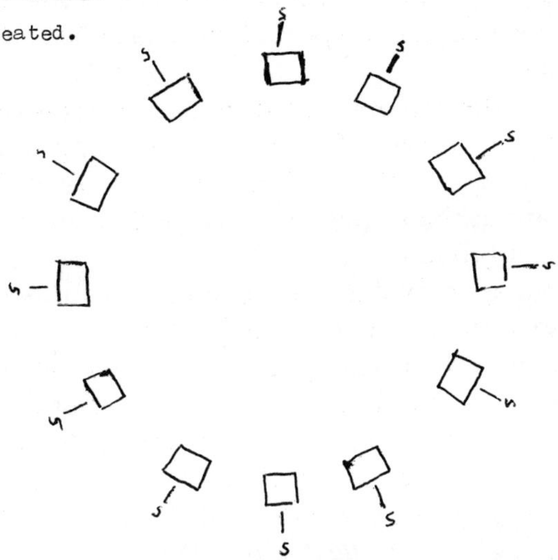

When used with classes of forty ten chairs are placed at each side of the room. Ten students are seated in them and ten begin the session standing in front of them.

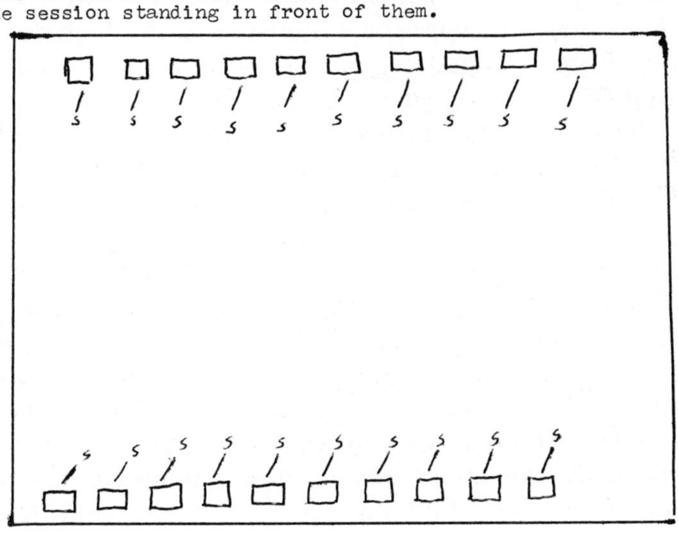

movement of hands, legs, head, body, and facial features. No words—no touch. After 50 seconds I ask the people to move one space clockwise and continue positive communication; non-verbally. This process is repeated until each has returned to his initial position.

I then have the persons seated change places with those standing and repeat the process. The persons standing are then asked to move back several feet and those seated to rise. The members of the group are asked to pair off each with *someone he knows least about,* and get acquainted.

Let me pause to explain the session up to this point. The purpose of the non-verbal, no touch communication emphasizing positive attributes has two purposes. First, to create *structure hunger.* People are not accustomed to communicate non-verbally. They find it awkward and difficult as they fumble for a structure. Timing proved extremely important. If I allowed 30 seconds between moves most people did not develop any structure. They did nothing and on the next move did not get started. Allowing more than a minute was equally ineffective. People would start communicating, run out of techniques and quit. The optimum time was between 45 seconds and one minute. By the time the 45 seconds were up each had begun some form of non-verbal communication. When he moved he repeated the technique used in the previous experience and added a little. By the fourth or fifth move everyone was doing pretty well. The communication focused on positive attributes to get the subjects to begin to communicate in positive terms.

By the time I had the persons seated change places with the persons standing there was no longer any structure hunger. Each had some way of communicating non-verbally. However, as the process continued *stimulus hunger* was building up. There was a need to speak, to say something to add to or explain the non-verbal communication. After moves subjects were asked to pair off with *someone they know least about.* The semantics are very important. When we tried the "milling" method asking people to move around until they paired off some people would experience repeated rejections as others looked at them and went elsewhere. When I asked people to pair off with some one they would most like to know many felt rejected. The language I am recommending produced few if any anxieties or feelings of rejection.

Five minutes after the group has divided itself into pairs and gotten acquainted, I ask each subject to tell his partner the three things he likes most about himself. Before doing so I usually point out that in our culture we are not supposed to talk about things we like about ourselves. We always emphasize the negative. Yet each of us has many qualities and in this session they are being emphasized.

After about five minutes I walk over to one pair and tell them that we are forming groups of four. I then ask if they would mind joining two other persons. (I point to another pair) If they agree I then suggest to one of the pair that he introduce his partner and form a group of four. I continue the process until six groups are formed. Subjects are asked to continue discussing the three things each likes most about himself giving reasons.

After about ten minutes I approach each group and ask one member to turn his back to the group. The other three are to discuss what they like most about him. He may listen but not participate in the discussion. This process is continued until every subject has heard himself discussed. The process takes ten to fifteen minutes. I then invite each pair to come before the entire group and introduce his partner telling what the group liked most about him.

I consider this an ideal way of forming a group. I started with a dyad, two people getting acquainted, then each telling his partner what he liked about himself. Then I built groups of four with as little trauma as possible. Two people approached two others, were introduced by one of them, and proceeded to discuss positive characteristics. Sitting with one's back to three others and hearing himself discussed is a pleasant experience. However, a person with a low self-image might not believe the positive things said about him. When he turns around and joins two others in discussing a third, he becomes a decision maker. Not only does his role take on importance but he begins to realize that he does see positive traits in the others, and that they probably honestly described the positive traits they saw in him. This was our most successful initial session. Each person was involved, each was in a sub-group discussing himself and others, and finally, each came before the entire group and addressed it.

If the group consists of highly verbal persons I omit the non-verbal communication portion of the session. Such people do not require stimuli to get them to talk. However, in an Alcoholic Rehabilitation Program creating structure hunger and stimulus hunger proved an effective way of starting good verbal communication. When using non-verbal communication with 16 year old boys, I ask them to communicate non-verbally what sport the other would be best at. Communicating positive affect may be too threatening.

Session 2

The Structured Scene in Occupational Roles

In any ongoing group I find it best after the initial session to move into occupational roles. People appear less reluctant to examine their relationships with fellow workers, foremen, colleagues or employers than they do their problems in relationships with members of their immediate families. In our culture one is supposed to love his father, mother, brother, sister, husband, or wife. If these relationships are somehow imperfect we are taught to regard this as some deficiency of ours. The directed warm-up already described, when focused on any occupational role will usually result in a session around that role. However, most of the group may remain uninvolved. The total involvement technique I find most effective is a *Structured Scene*. I have used this in the classroom, in management training, and in sales training, and found it to be an ideal second session for an Alcoholic Rehabilitation Program.

In my warm-up talk I discuss the importance of such occupational roles as getting along with colleagues, employers, supervisors, clients, etc. I then ask the members of the group to pair off with someone they know least about and discuss some serious occupational problem they have experienced or know about. I emphasize that it need not be a problem in which they were personally involved. The problem of a neighbor, a friend, or a colleague will suffice. After allowing from five to ten minutes for the presentation of problems in the dyad, I start the formation of groups of four, as described in the initial session. Groups of four are asked to consider the problems presented by each.

After about ten minutes I approach each group separately and ask them to select one problem to be presented to the group. I explain that the person who has presented the problem selected by the group does *not* perform in any of the roles. He becomes the *resource person,* selects persons to play the parts, and instructss them on their roles. When the problem situation is enacted the resource person can correct any deficiencies in performance by standing behind the person whose actions he wishes to correct or supplement, and so doing.

After each group is prepared to place a problem situation into action, usually about ten minutes, I have them begin the enactments. The resource person begins by describing the problem situation. The other members of his group act it out. If additional persons are required to play roles the resource person selects them from other groups. The action continues until the problem is readily identifiable.

Example—The Resource Person described the following problem situation. A young woman employee, Miss Jones, found that Miss Bates, an older woman on the job was unjustly complaining about her work to the supervisor, Mr. Harris. The supervisor would then criticize her. She was afraid of losing her job and didn't know what to do. After the enactment, the Resource Person is asked whether he would like to work on having the young woman, Miss Bates, deal with Mr. Harris. The Resource Person selected the relationship with Mr. Harris. At this point, the Resource Person, the only one present who knows anything about the problem, is asked to play the part of Mr. Harris. I then began a Role Training Sequence by inviting other members of the group to play the role of Miss Jones. After several ways of dealing with Mr. Harris are presented, if the Resource Person so desires, he may then proceed to deal with improving the relationship between Miss Jones and Miss Bates. The Resource Person would be asked to play Miss Bates and the other members of the group invited in a Role Training Sequence, to show how each, playing the part of Miss Jones, would deal with her. After either or both of these enactments, the group discusses the problem and possible alternative courses of action.

Each of the five groups is given an opportunity to enact the problem situation it had selected. I have found that there is not sufficient time to complete more than two problem situations in one session, and that I can usually complete the other three at the next meeting of the group. When working with adolescent groups I use problem situations at school, as school roles are the occupational roles of adolescents.

Session 3

The Structured Scene in Community Roles

In the warm-up talk discussing community roles, I try to relate to the problems and interests of the group. When dealing with an adolescent delinquent group, I discuss problem situations involving police, probation officers, merchants, older people in the community, social workers, and any others in the community they may have problems with. In an Alcoholic Rehabilitation Program with an adult population I used a very general sort of warm-up asking them to discuss any problem situation involving others in the community. All sorts of problem situations were selected. The ones that came up most frequently involved neighbors, getting acquainted with strangers, and going out with others without drinking.

After the warm-up the group pairs off, moves into groups of four and selects problem situations for enactment in much the same way as in the Structured Scene in Occupational Roles. However, there was one important difference. While in the second session most problem situations selected were those of persons other than themselves, in the third session in virtually every problem selected the Resource Person presented a problem situation in which he was directly involved. This is some indication that the members of the group had developed confidence in the method and were more willing to explore problems and relationships of their own in front of a group.

Even when the Resource Person presents a situation in which he is directly involved, I have him select someone to play his role. He continues as the Resource Person. In the Role Training Sequence that follows the enactment the Resource Person plays the role of the person presenting him with the problem. Others play his role. For example, if the enactment revealed a problem the Resource Person, Bill, had with a neighbor, John, he, Bill, would play the part of John, the neighbor for twenty minutes or thereabouts, while others approached him in the role of Bill. This is the first attempt to provide extensive empathy training. Session 3 is seldom completed in less than two meetings and may take three.

Session 4

The Structured Scene in Family Roles

While in the Protagonist Centered Psychodrama described in a previous chapter, it is not unusual for a protagonist to be involved in exploring intimate relationships with mother, father, or some other member of his family at the first meeting, following an initial session, such relationships are carefully avoided in a total involvement series. I found that in the Alcoholic Rehabilitation Program if I directed a session involving intimate personal relationships early in a series, the action was inhibited for several succeeding sessions. Members of the group appeared afraid to go into the difficulties they had in such relationships. For this reason, until the fourth session which might actually be the sixth or seventh meeting of the group, no mention is made of family relationships.

Even in the fourth session I avoid intimate family relationships of group members. In warming up the group I talk about problems in family relationships, difficulties people have with husbands, wives, children, and parents. I then ask the members of the group to pair off with a person they know least about and discuss a *"serious family problem you know about, not in your family."* "The problem could be one involving your neighbors, friends, colleagues, or any one you know about." If a group selects a problem directly involving one of its members and he, as Resource Person insists on enacting it I permit it. However, I do not encourage it. The process of forming groups of four, selecting a problem situation for enactment, and putting it into action is much the same as described in session two. So is the discussion that follows. However, participation in the Role Training Sequence is far greater, the sessions last longer, and the discussion is more animated. The five or six enactments are generally spread over three meetings of the group.

Session 5

Happiest Moment

This is the first session in which I ask the members of the group to involve themselves in their own life experiences. By this time, however, most of them have done so either in an occupational, community, or family problem situation. In the warm-up for this session I talk about happy moments we have had that we experienced with another person or persons. I point out that we tend to remember the unhappy moments, the trauma, and the suffering, but appear to put aside or forget the happy moments. Yet, we can learn a great deal about ourselves by reliving the happy moments.

I then ask the members of the group to pair off, form groups of four, and select the happiest moment of one member of each group to put into action, in much the same way as in Session 2.

There is one important difference, however. Once the group selects a member to put into action his happiest moment *he becomes the protagonist,* not a Resource Person as in the previous three sessions.

I, as director, have him come before the entire group and describe the situation. I then have him enact some of the events immediately preceding the happiest moment and the moment itself, employing whatever Psychodramatic techniques I consider most effective at making the enactment most useful to the protagonist.

Example—A woman who was having serious marital problems was selected to examine her happiest moments. Her husband, who was present, had no objection to her doing so.

The first happy moment she described was when, after receiving her discharge from the Woman's Army Corps after World War II her fiance, now her husband, returned from Asia. I had her reenact the evening before his arrival. In a soliloquy with double she went into her anxieties. He had not written often. His letters were very brief and unromantic. Had he found someone else? Was he going to break off their relationship? Did he really intend to marry her? These were all questions that were unresolved in her soliloquy the evening prior to his return. Then we reenacted his return with an auxiliary ego, chosen from the group, to play her husband. He told her how much he loved her (she played his role in a role reversal) and asked her to marry him. This was the happiets moment in her life. She then did a soliloquy on her feelings that night. She was loved, she was happy, her life was going to begin with the man she loved. The couple then left on their honeymoon.

She then reenacted the next happiest moment when her first child was born. In a soliloquy on the night before she indicated many anxieties. Would she have a healthy baby? She was almost thirty. Would she survive the childbirth? Would her husband like the baby? When the happiest moment came, the time she and her husband both held the baby she was ecstatic. In the soliloquy following this scene she was overjoyed because the birth was easy, the baby healthy and her husband happy with his new born son. The third happiest moment came five years later when her daughter was born. The situation was similar to the first birth. There were anxieties and joys when they were relieved.

After this enactment the protagonist asked "Would you like to see my last happy moment?" When I replied in the affirmative, she reenacted a scene that occurred in 1968, a year before the Psychodrama. It was the graduation from high school of her youngest child, her daughter. Her husband was in the construction business and because of tight money business had been bad. He drank a great deal and their relationship had deteriorated. She planned a surprise graduation party for her daughter but was holding it at a church social hall to avoid the embarrassment of her husband barging in drunk. She returned home from the party at 6 P.M. The place was in disarray as she had left it but whiskey bottles were on the floor. Her husband walked in at 6:15 dead drunk. There was a verbal exchange and he beat her up badly. She was hospitalized for nearly a month. She had not spoken to him since except in a lawyer's office regarding a divorce. They had come to an open session of Psychodrama on recommendation of the court marriage counselor.

After this enactment I asked the husband if he wanted to enact his version of their relationship. He came on to the stage and an auxiliary ego was selected from the group to play his wife. He started by saying that the happiest moments his wife had reenacted were all among his happiest moments. The decision to marry, the honeymoon, the birth of the children were among the happiest events in his life. Then he remarked that he came to the stage to show us his version of the graduation scene.

He acknowledged that business had been bad, that he was drinking heavily and had been a bad husband. He decided that he would throw a surprise party for his daughter on her graduation. He had planned to pick her up at 3 P.M. on the day he had set for the party and had invited his friends to come to his house for the party at 4 P.M.

He came home at noon. The house was a mess and no one was home. He inquired at the neighbors but no one knew where his wife was. He waited until 2 P.M., then went to school to pick up his daughter. She did not meet him. He returned home. No one was there. At 4 P.M. his friends arrived. He was embarrassed and told them the party was off. He then started drinking. He finished a half bottle of whiskey and some vodka that was in the house. He then left and was in a saloon until after 6 P.M., his normal homecoming time. When he entered the house his wife greeted him as follows: "You drunken bum. Did you know that your daughter graduated today? Couldn't you behave decently just once?" He responded violently and later regretted it, but his wife would not let him near her, nor would she let him explain.

I ended the session by having the husband and wife stand on the stage holding hands in non-verbal communication. He took her in his arms and both wept. The first words spoken were; "when did we stop communicating with each other?"

Session 6

Splitting

This is the first session in which the warm-up involves each individual in his intimate family relationships. In the warm-up I talk about how many of us are irritated by our responsibilities, and annoyed by the fact that our spontaneity is inhibited in so many ways, We often think of how good it would be if we could just go off and do our thing. Get away from it all. If we did leave in most instances, someone would be deeply affected by our departure. I point out that if I left my wife would be affected. We have been married a long time. So many of our activities, pleasures, and pains are shared that our lives are intertwined. I would certainly be affected by her departure.

I then ask the members of the group to pair off with someone they know least about. Each is then asked to assume the role of the person most affected by his departure. To make sure that each is in the right role I question them.

Director to Bill: Who are you?

Bill: I am Bill.

Director: No. Bill is gone. You are the person affected by his going. Who are you?

Bill: I am Mary, Bill's wife.

This process is repeated until I am sure each person is in the role of the person left behind. I then give each person the following note:

Dear

When you read this letter I shall be gone. I do not know exactly where I shall be or why I am leaving. All I know is that I am tired of the routine nature of my existence. You know I have been unhappy for some time. I'm not blaming you or anyone else.

I must have some excitement and adventure, and I am leaving in a search for a new life. I shall be gone at least a year, maybe longer. I may never return. In the meantime, don't expect to hear from me.

Goodbye for now.

I ask each to discuss the departure with his partner, another person who has received a similar note, answering such questions
Why did he go?
What did I do to drive him out?
What could I have done to prevent his leaving?
Will he come back?
Do I want him back?

I then form groups of four in the same manner as in the initial session. I give each member the following message and ask them to discuss it and answer the questions raised.

Three months have passed. The situation remains the same.

1. What changes have come into your life during the past three months?
2. Would you want him or her to come back?
3. What, if any, conditions would you lay down for accepting such a return?
4. What meaningful relationships have you developed to replace him or her?
5. How would his or her return effect your new relationships?
6. What are your plans for the future?

After about ten or fifteen minutes I give each subject the third message and ask them to discuss it.

A year has passed. You are now certain he or she will not come back.

1. How do you feel about him or her now that you know the break is final?

2. How are you getting along?

3. What were the most serious problems you encountered over the year?

4. How were these problems resolved?

5. What person or persons did you call upon to help you?

6. What do you intend to do with your life now that you know it will not include him or her?

When a group has completed the discussion of the third message I instruct each to assume his own role. Each group then is asked to select one person to enact a return home.

The enactments are presented in much the same way as those in the fifth session, beginning with a soliloquy on the day before the return. In this soliloquy with a double the protagonist goes into where he has been, why he left, and why he is returning. The return is then enacted. The protagonist is asked to reverse roles with the auxiliary ego playing the role of the person left behind. In that role he is asked his reaction to the returning party (himself). At the conclusion of each enactment I ask the protagonist if the "splitting" was pure fantasy or if he really would like to examine his relationship with the party left behind. If he elects to do so I direct a Psychodrama around that relationship.

This session generally takes three meetings of the group and is perhaps the most effective session in the series. For one thing, *every member of the group is involved* playing the role of someone close to him for thirty minutes. This represents a considerable amount of empathy training. Also, each has an opportunity to examine his relationship with that person. Whether he does so in action or not he deals with that relationship with the help of others at the session, and by himself after the session.

Session 7

Aspirations

I developed this session in the 1950's for use with adolescents in the Berkshire Farm for Boys, Aftercare Program and limited its use to adolescents over the years. In the Alcoholic Rehabilitation Program of the Navy I learned that adults in the military found it very useful. The response from college students was equally favorable. In Rochelle Haskell's Psychodrama Program at the Federal Men's Prison, Terminal Island, it was also well received. In each instance, the warm-up should be different. It must be designed to interest the group. For example, when working with adolescents the warm-up emphasizes occupational goals. The questions raised are; What do you see yourself doing when you are in your twenties? What would you like to be? How do you expect to make it? In the Alcoholic Rehabilitation Program of the Navy the emphasis was also on occupational choice. For the older men the applicable questions were; What do you expect to do when you leave the Navy? What kind of career are you hoping for? What are you doing now to prepare for it? How do you expect to make it? When used with college students, the warm-up is directed at educational goals and ultimate choice of a career. Some of the questions raised are; How long are you going to continue your education? Will you go for an M.A. degree?, a Ph.D.?, What, if any, profession have you chosen?, How do you expect to make it?

In a Prison setting this sort of session takes on particular significance. The "present" of inmates of a prison is very unpleasant and little can be done to change it. Most therapy programs go into the past and seek to give insight into deficiencies in character, personality, and/or life style. The thrust of this sort of session is on surplus reality, the reality of the future. Questions raised are; What do you want to be in life? What obstacles do you foresee? What can you do to overcome them? What can you do while in prison to further your objectives?

After the warm-up talk the members of the group pair off and discuss their aspirations. Then groups of four are formed as in the initial session, and members discuss their aspirations and the obstacles anticipated. Then, as in the initial session, one member of each group turns his back to the group and the others discuss ways of achieving his objectives. This process is continued until each member of the group has had his aspirations considered. Then each group selects one person whose objectives are considered most difficult to attain. The person selected presents his objectives and his proposals for attaining them. A Role Training Sequence follows in which each member of the group is invited to present ways of achieving the objective of the protagonist or alternative proposals if he considers those stated by the protagonist to be unattainable. In the discussion portion that follows members of the group discuss aspirations, obstacles and attainable objectives. This session is usually completed in two or three meetings.

Session 8

Demands on Others

This is the first session that challenges the American myth of "rugged individualism" and independence. In the warm-up I point out that few people can make it on their own, that we are interdependent, and that most people need help from others. Furthermore, many people fail in our society, particularly those who are required to succeed without the assistance of others. Many people are [1](delinquents), (alcoholics), (unemployed), (inmates of prison), because they did not have the cooperation or assistance of others when they needed it. I end my warm-up talk by saying; "In this session we shall focus on the cooperation and assistance we need from others if we are to succeed in our endeavors and be happy in our lives".

The total involvement process described in Session Two including pairing off, forming groups of four, and discussion of the need for cooperation and assistance of others is discussed. One person in each group then turns his chair while the others discuss the ways in which each can get others to meet their demands for cooperation and assistance. When each person has had his demands discussed each group selects a protagonist to go into action. Each protagonist presents his demands and the person or persons on whom he proposes to make them. A Role Training Sequence follows in which the Protagonist plays the role of the person on whom he proposes to make demands. Other members of the group enact ways of getting him to fulfill them. The action portion of the session is followed by a discussion of our dependency needs and how they are fulfilled.

This session was very productive when used with groups of Alcoholics, inmates of a prison, and patients in a mental hospital. In my view, persons in all of these categories are taught in the course of their socialization that a person must succeed on his own. Somehow, it is wrong for him to ask for help from others. To do so is an acknowledgement of inadequacy and possibly in-

[1]Select the one that is applicable to your group.

feriority. Escape via alcohol, drugs, and "mental illness" may be steps some people take because they cannot face life as inferior beings. Learning that there is nothing magical or inherently good about a competitive society and that we are all interdependent may counteract these feelings of inadequacy. This session is useful because it emphasizes our needs and our right to depend on others.

Session 9

Pressures on Us

In the course of my warm-up for this session I point out that a great many of our difficulties, our wanting to escape from it all may be attributed to the fact that others are not satisfying the demands we make on them. Why do we make these demands? Why are so many of our needs not satisfied? We have already examined our aspirations and our unsatisfied demands in privious sessions. In this session I propose that we deal with pressures others put upon us, demands they make of us that we cannot or do not wish to satisfy. Who is putting pressure upon us? Why do they bother us? What do we do about these pressures? What else can we do about them? These are some of the questions we may consider.

The process of pairing, forming groups of four and discussing pressures put upon us is exactly the same as in session eight. A member of each group turns his back and hears the other three discuss ways in which he can deal with the pressures put on him. Each member of each group goes through this experience and each group selects one member to go into action as protagonist, just as in session eight.

In the course of the action portion of each session, the protagonist plays the role of a person exerting the pressure he experiences while others act out ways of dealing with him. In this way each person gains in empathy for the person exerting the pressure and learns a variety of ways of interacting with such a person.

Session 10

Terminating a Relationship

In the warm-up I point out that almost as important as establishing relationships is the ability to terminate them when they no longer serve a useful purpose. Many of us maintain relationships with people who bore us, in some instances annoy us, and often subject us to unbearable pressures, yet we have difficulty breaking with them. Some people date, and may even go steady with members of the opposite sex although they know they are not happy in each other's company. In extreme cases people may stay married to each other for ten years or more although they know after a few months of marriage that they have made a mistake.

Why do we continue relationships long after they have become non-functional and even disfunctional? In some cases because we liked the person in the past, and hesitate to hurt his feelings. In many cases, however, we continue a relationship simply because we are afraid to break it off. We just don't know how to do it without hurting others, and we don't want to hurt others. We may also be afraid that we will be lonely or in some other way suffer if the relationship is dissolved. Because the effect of breaking a relationship is uncertain, those afraid to take risks continue destructive relationships far too long. In this session we are going to consider ways in which unproductive or destructive relationships may be terminated. By examining the varied ways in which members of the group deal with such situations we may acquire a repertoire for getting out of such relationships.

Members pair off, form groups of four and discuss relationships they would like to terminate. The process is identical with that used in session nine. One member with his back turned to a group consisting of three others hears them discuss ways in which his destructive relationships can be broken. After each member of the group has this experience, one is selected as protagonist to enact the break in relationship. The protagonist then plays the part of the person who is being terminated and others play the role of the protagonist showing how they would terminate it.

After this Role Training Sequence I have the protagonist reenact the termination taking into consideration the different ways presented by others in the Role Training Sequence. I then ask the protagonist to consider the break final.

Example

Director: Donna you have made a final break with Joe. He is no longer a part of your life. Show us a Saturday night in your life after the break. Where are you? Who, if anyone, is with you? Enact a scene with or without another person in it.

After the enactment I have the protagonist do a soliloquy (think out loud) about her situation without Joe. She may, in the course of the enactment, decide that she is happier without him. She may, on the other hand, come to the conclusion that she would miss him far too much. If she should decide that she needs Joe, we would then work on improving the relationship with him. After all, the break was not irrevocable. It occurred only on the Psychodrama Stage.

The above described ten sessions I consider an effective Alcoholic Rehabilitation Program. The group may have to meet twenty or more times to complete the sessions and it may be desirable for some people to continue working on their relationships for a longer time. However, in the course of the ten sessions people do greatly increase their understanding of their relationships, learn how to improve them, and how to terminate the destructive ones. These same sessions with minor variations have been demonstrated to be effective in a prison setting, in college classes, and with professionals at workshops and seminars. They provide a genuine growth experience for participants and most everyone present becomes involved on some level. An inexperienced director with a little study and practice can direct the first five sessions. To direct the last five takes considerable training in Psychodramatic Role Training.

In addition to the ten sessions described above, I have used total involvement sessions with adult groups around the following problem areas:

Your daughter (son) (sister) is on drugs. How can you best relate to him or her?

Your father (mother) (brother) is an Alcoholic. How can you best relate to him or her?

Your father (son) (brother) is unemployed for a long time. How can you best relate to him?

Your son (daughter) (brother) has no goals in life. How can you help him or her develop meaningful goals?

It should be obvious from the description of the total involvement techniques in this chapter that they can be applied to any of these and countless other problems occurring in school, industry, the community, and family life. All one has to do is prepare an appropriate warm-up and apply them.

PROJECTIVE TECHNIQUES

In addition to the verbal techniques described in previous chapters and the largely verbal ten total involvement techniques described in this chapter, there are a great many projective techniques which may be used as warm-ups to both Protagonist Centered Psychodrama, and Total Involvement sessions. In this chapter, I shall describe three: Person Projections, Music Projections, and Poetry Projections.

Person Projections

I use this technique to stimulate the projection of guilt, fear, anger, or any other feeling or emotion.

The stance of persons and my accompanying remarks provide the stimuli. To project guilt, for example, I have a woman seated, head down, with back to the group. I make the following remarks; "You see seated here Rochelle, my associate. You all know her. In this scene, however, she represents a woman in your life with whom you have some unfinished business. She may represent someone's wife, mother, girlfriend, sister, or any other female. Who would she be in your life Bill?

Bill: My mother.

Who would she be in your life, Sam?

Sam: My former wife.

Who would she be in your life, Mary?

Mary: My older sister.

I continue the process asking the same question of every member of the group. If I want Bill as the protagonist, I ask Rochelle; "Can you be Bill's mother?" She replies in the affirmative, and we have a Protagonist Centered Psychodrama, with Bill as the protagonist. On the other hand I may have the group vote on a protagonist and proceed with a Protagonist Centered Psychodrama, the protagonist selected by the group.

If I use this warm-up for a total involvement session, I have the members of the group pair off and discuss the unfinished business with the person each projected. I then form groups of four as in the initial session and have each group select one person to act out his unfinished business, with either Rochelle or a female selected by him from his group to play the part of the woman.

To project fear I have a male auxiliary ego stand in front of the group with a strap in his hands. My accompanying talk goes something like this; "You see before you Barney, a member of our staff. He is holding a strap in a threatening manner. In this scene he represents a man in the life of each one of you, one whom you may have been afraid of in the past. He may represent your teacher, father, big brother, husband, or some other man in your life. From then on the session may proceed in any of the ways described above in the projection of guilt.

To project anger I have an auxiliary ego, male or female, sitting or standing in front of the group with a contemptuous look on his or her face. My accompanying talk goes something like this; "You see before you Barney, a member of our staff. In this scene he represents a man in the life of each of you who has treated you with contempt. He is, by his very expression, putting you down. He may represent your father, brother, husband, teacher, or some other man in your life." The session may then proceed in any of the ways described in the projection of guilt. Once a protagonist is selected I have him examine his relationship with that person in several situations. When we arrive at one evoking unexpressed anger, I encourage the protagonist to express it in the manner described in the previous chapter.

Music Projections

I have recordings of popular songs that I play to the group as part of the warm-up. Many of the blues songs sung by the great Billie Holiday provide excellent stimuli. One that I used quite often is a song that was very popular in the early 1970's, "Help Me Make It Through the Night". I have recordings of the song made by one male singer and two different female singers. I start by playing a recording by a female singer whose style is declaratory and clear. The key lines are; "I don't care who's right or wrong. I won't try to understand. Let the devil take tomorrow. Tonight I need a friend." It ends with; "Help me make it through the night."

After the first play through I point out that the song represents a call for help in time of need. I ask the members of the group to listen to a replay concentrating on times each called out for help—to whom they called out—and the response to the call. In my alcoholic group many were moved to tears in the course of the replay in a darkened room. After the replay I tell the group that I shall play the recording once more. I ask each to concentrate on times when others called out to them for help and they did not come. The third recording is the most emotional. The male singer ends with cries of; "Help Me, Help Me, Help Me."

I then ask each member of the group if he has thought of a situation when he has called out for help or someone has called out to him. A protagonist is selected in one of the ways described in the use of a Person Projection. If a total involvement session is planned the process is similar to that described in the fifth session. A person from each group is selected to be the protagonist. Once a protagonist is selected I have him act out the call for help and the response and then, if he wishes, go into an examination of his relationship with that person. In almost every session involving alcoholics the resulting sessions were highly productive. The dependence on the "helper" was clearly indicated as was the guilt over the disappointments suffered by wives, mothers, and children of the alcoholic.

Poetry Projections

A great many poems and essays have been used effectively to warm up a group for a Psychodrama. The following prose-poem published anonymously in a church paper usually involves many persons:

I'd Pick More Daisies

If I had my life to live over, I'd try to make more mistakes next time. I would relax. I would limber up. I would be sillier than I have been this trip. I know of very few things I would take seriously. I would be crazier. I would be less hygenic. I would climb more mountains, swim more rivers and watch more sunsets. I would burn more gasoline. I would eat more ice cream and less beans. I would have more actual troubles and fewer imaginary ones. You see, I am one of those people who lives prophylactically and sensibly and sanely, hour after hour, day after day. Oh, I have had my moments, and if I had it to do over again, I'd have more of them. In fact, I'd try to have nothing else. Just moments, one after another, instead of living so many years ahead each day. I have been one of those people who never go anywhere without a thermometer, a hot-water bottle, a gargle, a raincoat, and a parachute, If I had it to do over again, I would go places and do things and travel lighter than I have. If I had my life to live over, I would start barefooted earlier in the spring and stay that way later in the fall. I would play hooky more. I wouldn't make such good grades except by accident. I would ride on more merry-go-rounds. I'd pick more daisies.

I have a tape recording of "I'd Pick More Daisies" in both a male and female voice. Before playing the recording I introduce it by saying: "Many of us, as we grow older, regret not having done some of the things we would have liked to do. For most of the people here it is not too late to do some of those things, to fulfill ourselves. As I play this recording, think of those things you would have liked to do that you did not do in the past." I am going to play this recording again. This time think of the things you are not now doing that you would like very much to do. After the second go around, I ask each person if he regrets having omitted doing something in the past or if there is something he would like to do that he is not doing. A protagonist is then selected in the same manner as in the Person Projection or, if a total involvement session is planned, I proceed in the manner described in the fifth session. Once protagonists are selected, they reenact scenes selected by them.

Many poems dealing with relationships may be used as warm-up techniques. Virtually every poem in Moon River Anthology lends itself to such use.

Whether we use projective techniques, verbal techniques, or total involvement techniques, an important objective of the warming-up process in Psychodrama is to have a member of the group come forward as protagonist. In Socioanalysis we are particularly interested in having the protagonist examine relationships in action. The more techniques we develop for encouraging people to undertake such explorations the more likely we are to succeed. Verbal techniques may stimulate some people, projective techniques may stimulate others, and total involvement techniques do what the name implies. They involve everyone participating in the session.

Chapter 10

ROLE PLAYING AND ROLE TRAINING IN SOCIOANALYSIS

Role Training is used in this book in a specialized sense. It refers to a form of role playing employing psychodramatic techniques in which the emphasis is on the reenactment of past experiences. Role Playing, the more inclusive term, is defined as a temporary stepping out of one's own present role *to assume the role of another individual* or of one's self at *another time.* Moreno has described three categories of roles: Psychosomatic Roles such as the sleeper, the eater, etc.; Psychodramatic Roles such as a mother (mother of the protagonist, for example), a teacher, etc.; and Social Roles such as the mother, the teacher, etc.

In a psychodrama we may deal with all three types of roles. Every role in which the protagonist functions is open to investigation. We may examine his psychosomatic behavior. Much of the current research in sexual behavior involves an examination of the psychosomatic role of sex partner. We may, and usually do explore psychodramatic roles of the protagonist as evidenced by his relationships with *his* mother, *his* wife, *his* teacher, or with any other person if he wishes it. If we examine relationships with teachers in general or with employers in general we are dealing with social roles. Role Playing and Role Training afford us with opportunities to observe how individuals in given positions behave, the ways in which they carry out or fail to carry out the requirements of the positions.

Before we take any action in an interaction with another person, we often consciously "take the role" of other. That is, we *mentally* place ourselves in the position of the other person and adjust our action in accordance with our estimate of that person's reactions. We are so in the habit of doing this that we are generally unaware of the fact that this process of examining or anticipating the behavior of another exerts a tremendous influence on our actions. The position that the other person occupies in itself influences our action. It symbolizes for us a range of appropriate and inappropriate actions. Symbols we employ take on different meanings as they relate to persons occupying different positions. A non-verbal symbol such as a pat on the back means different things when administered by a man to his child, to an employee, or to a strange man, or to a strange woman. So would the verbal symbol "I'd like to know you much better" when addressed to the various persons referred to above. A classic example of the way the same verbal symbol may have different meanings was provided by the great entertainer Maurice Chevalier, in his performance of the song "Ca Va." The only verbal symbols used in this act are the words "Ca Va." He walks into a store and looks at some merchandise, the store keeper and sales person say to him "Ca Va?" and he replies, "Ca Va." In the context of this interaction the verbal symbol used by the sales person means "Is this satisfactory?" The response "Ca Va" by the customer means "It is satisfactory." The same dialogue takes place when Chevalier greets a young woman; he walks over to her and asks "Ca Va?" and the young woman replies: "Ca Va." In this context the verbal symbol offered by Chevalier means "How about it?" and the response of the young woman means "o.k." n fact, in this latter dialogue, Chevalier enthusiastically concludes the conversation with another, "Ca Va" which means "great." It is clear from this illustration that the verbal symbol takes on an entirely different meaning when used by the salesman, the customer, the young woman, and the man on the make. In each case the meaning of the term is greatly influenced by the role of the person using it and non-verbal symbols that accompany the words such as voice inflection, smile, shrug of shoulders, movement of hands, etc.

To understand a role fully, we must consider the nature of the interaction and the person with whome the individual is interacting. Thus, for example, we are all acquainted with the role of doctor and we are also acquainted with the role of nurse. The situation in which they find themselves at any given time will greatly influence the interaction of the two persons and the expectancies we would have relative to their behavior. Knowing the roles of doctor and nurse would help us predict the ways in which they would interact in the doctor's office or in an operating room but would not help us much to predict their interaction on a date on New Years Eve. Obviously what has happened is that they are not in the professional roles on their date although their professional roles may influence their interaction. *Role* refers to the behavior of the person rather than the position that he occupies. A person, therefore, enacts a role and performs in a role but does not occupy the role, he occupies a position. Social role refers to the behavior that is appropriate for one occupying a particular position. It is the behavior that is expected as distinguished from the manner in which the role is actually enacted in the specific situation. The latter is referred to as the role performance or role enactment. In role playing or role training we have an opportunity to observe the role performance. We can see how an individual interprets the appropriate ways in which to behave. According to available research the performance in the role playing situation provides a reasonable approximation of the behavior exhibited in "real life" situations.

"Role Taking" or "taking the role of other" involves an imaginative construction of the other's role. It is a mental process. Role playing, however, constitutes an overt enactment in which one demonstrates the way he believes one should behave in relation to others in a given situation. Role taking proceeds from identifying a position. That is, once we recognize an individual as a postman, we identify the position and assume that the person will behave in a certain way. He will play the role of postman. The behavior we anticipate from that individual is influenced by our definition of his position. We may also infer the position from the enactment, that is, by listening to his comments or by observing what he does we may guess that he is a postman. Ways have been devised to measure empathy, the relative ability of a person to take the role of other. One way is to have an individual predict what the other is thinking or feeling about a given situation and then finding out what the other is thinking or feeling about that situation. The accuracy with which the individual predicts reflects his empathic ability. The Social Perception Test described in Chapter 3 provides some measure of empathy. When we attempt to take the role of other, we are, in a sense, involved in a social act because we are modifying our behavior by what we believe the other person will do in the situation. It is relatively unimportant that his estimate of the situation may be inaccurate. We can take the role of other by imagining how we would behave if we were the other person or we can base our interpretation of the role of other on past experiences with him or with people like him.

An individual who takes the role of another may identify with the role of the other person. He does not necessarily become more sympathetic or kindly. The development of empathy need not result in the elimination of differences with others. It is possible for one to place himself in the position of other, take his role quite well, and still hate him and totally reject his behavior. The conficence man, a professional criminal, is often successful because of his ability to identify accurately the feelings and attitudes of the other person with whom he is dealing while completely avoiding any involvement or sympathy. In taking the role of others he is better able to manipulate them.

Reference group behavior greatly influences performances in a role. The term reference group is used here to refer to a group whose acceptance one seeks and in which he obtains recognition, sustenance, approval, and appreciation for just being "himself". The desire to be accepted by others in a group is the mechanism which leads to the adoption of the values and perspectives of that group, and in that way makes it one's reference group. One then assumes the role of a member of the group and adopts the group way of looking at things as one's own. The precess works in this way: 1) an individual desires acceptance by a particular group; 2) he assumes the role of a member of the group, that is, he tries to behave in ways acceptable for membership in the group; 3) as he does so, he becomes accepted by the group and he then takes the points of view of the group with respect to situations with which he comes into contact as a group member. For example, if he wishes to join a gang, he observes the members of the gang and he tries to behave as they behave. In this way, he comes to see things from the point of view of a member of the gang. Acceptance in the gang is important to him. Once accepted he continues to see things from the point of view of a gang member. This standpoint will influence his attitude toward police, toward courts, toward stealing, etc. The gang member sees his role performance observed and evaluated by other members of the gang and he is concerned about the evaluations and expectations which members of the group hold toward him. He "takes the role" of the gang and is influenced by what they think about his behavior, about his attitudes, and about him.

Thus, if we observe the individual in interaction in a Role Playing situation, we may recognize his identification with a particular Reference Group. Also knowing something about an individual's reference group will help us predict the behavior he will exhibit in an interaction both in a role playing scene and in a real life situation.

Role conflicts arise when incompatible demands are placed upon an individual because of his relationship with two or more groups. Reference group pressures are great when two groups are in conflict and exert strong pressures. For example, the boy who is a gang leader and accepts the rights and obligations of gang leadership is also a member of a family and may accept, to a certain extent, the rights and obligations of son. A role conflict results. The gang members and mother make incompatible demands upon him. He feels obligated to meet the competing demands and faces the threat of sanctions from each reference group. Most young people placed in this position attempt to retain both positions, their place in the gang and their place in the family. There is no clear-cut decision to abandon either. The one that exerts the most influence at a particular time influences the action at the time.

Frequent observations from real life attest to the influence of role enactment on other aspects of behavior. People's attitudes and perceptions tend to shift toward greater consistency with the roles they play in life. The lawyer tends more and more to see such things as "no fault" auto insurance from the point of view of the lawyer. The real estate broker tends more and more to see housing segregation from the point of view of the real estate broker. Prolonged occupancy of any position in the social structure affects the individual's attitudes. Frequent performance in a role by the occupant of a position makes him see this role more favorably. During and after a role enactment there is often some reinforcement from other persons. This invariably occurs in a role training session. An individual who performs a particular role and receives the approval of other members of the group for his performance is likely to have that particular performance reinforced. Role enactments before audiences that show approval serves to reinforce the behavior exhibited. Likewise, the enactment of a role which supports an attitude *contrary* to one's private belief may lead to change in that belief if the *enactment* is approved by an audience.

The direction of attitude change is likely to be toward the position expressed publicly during the role enactment. Thus, role playing and role training may be used to encourage people to experiment with roles that are new to them. A gang boy who has tended to reject occupational roles may begin to accept them if in a role training group he consistently wins approval for his performance in those roles. In the course of Role Playing and Role Training sessions the participants become aware of many alternative courses of action. Differences in spontaneity as evidenced by the ability to recognize alternatives and to choose between them *may* become apparent.

The behavior of persons low in spontaneity is characterized by a failure to choose between available alternative courses of action. They tend to act as though there is only one solution to a problem and always offer that solution when faced with the problem. If, after one or more efforts, it becomes apparent to them that the solution they have selected does not produce a desired effect, they respond by inaction. One would conclude from their behavior, and often from their verbal appraisals of the situations, that they consider the problems insoluble. To the observer they appear either indifferent or apathetic. Even when alternative courses of action are pointed out to such individuals they may not be able to choose between such alternatives or to act on them. Verbal instruction is not very effective in getting people to learn alternative courses of action. Role enactments and performances in a role, are forms of action that are learned. The way an individual performs in his occupational roles, school roles, family roles, and community roles are all part of a repertoire he acquired in action. The patterns are not unalterable. In the course of learning them he may not have come into contact with alternative patterns or may have selected his present patterns over all others he was aware of. Nevertheless, the person has learned to perform in various roles and may learn to select alternative ways of performing in them.

A person is not likely to function satisfactorily in a society unless he has learned the roles appropriate to the significant positions of the society. Most particularly, he cannot function adequately unless he knows the rights and obligations connected with his *position* and the positions in which he may find himself. In other words, he has to know the roles in which he will be required to function.

The better the person knows his role the more satisfactorily he will perform in the part, and, if he does perform in a manner more acceptable to others, he is more likely to be rewarded. The less he knows about the role, the more likely he is to deviate, that is, the more likely he is to make "errors." In other words, he is likely to do things that others do not expect him to do and perhaps do not approve of. If he deviates in such a way as to offend others or shock them, he is likely to meet with rebuffs. Knowing the role will enable a person to face each situation with a minimum of trauma and with the greatest possibility of reward.

We shall now consider various ways in which persons can learn more about the roles in society, particularly the one's involving them. All of these should be useful to one attempting to increase his spontaneity. Also learning as much as one can about his own roles and those of persons he interacts with are important to one's Socioanalysis.

Role Playing Distinguished from Theatrical Performance

Role Playing differs from performances in the theater. Although some of the principles are drama principles, the individual in a Role Playing session presents *himself* in action. His enactment influences the impressions others form of him as a person. The kinds of things he may and may not do while playing in a role do not differ significantly from those he is permitted to do in real life situations. In the theater the actor performs in the "make believe". On the stage one actor presents himself in the role of a character to other characters represented by other actors. The audience is present to be entertained. Members of the audience do not usually interact with the actors, and see them only as performers. In Role Playing as in "real life", the part one individual plays is influenced by the performances of others present and the audience. Nevertheless, playing a part in a theatrical performance may be useful for persons low in spontaneity. Performing in roles other than their own, in interaction with others, in front of an audience, should increase their ability to relate to others and also increase awareness of alternative patterns of behavior. A mental hospital in New York State cast non-communicating patients as actors in a play with considerable success. Many began to communicate verbally with others in the play and also with the audience and staff members—after their performance on the stage.

The Skit as a Training Technique

There are several ways in which Role Playing is employed as a teaching or a training technique. One way which has been used in industry and by the police in various jurisdictions is to have experts enact a "skit", from a prepared script while a group of learners sit in the audience and watch. For example, in preparing trainees for the duties of policeman, veteran policemen may act out a skit perporting to illustrate the correct way of making an arrest. The students watch the actors perform and then are asked to replace the actors and imitate the action that they have observed. A discussion period is then used in which the group comments on the performance. The principal objective of the skit and the role playing scenes that follow is to get the students to perform in the role as nearly as possible in the manner in which it was portrayed by the experts. The assumption is that the experts know exactly how to perform in the situation and that the trainees will benefit by witnessing the enactment and imitating it. There is the additional advantage that the experts have an opportunity to observe the students perform in the situation. This sort of role playing has very limited uses. It is most effective where the response can be reasonably anticipated. For example, it may be useful in training bus drivers to accept fares from passengers, preparing ticket-takers at theater windows to sell tickets and make change and in preparing people for other relatively standardized roles in which the response of others can be accurately predicted.

Role Playing in a Structured Situation

Role Playing in a structured situation permits slightly more spontaneity. In this type of role playing, the director sets up a scene by instructing the actors in their roles and asking them to perform in it. For example, in training salesmen the director might set up a scene in which he instructs the individuals participating on the general requirements of their roles. He may say, for example, "You, Sam, are a salesman. You are entering the house of Mrs. Jones and are attempting to sell her a vacuum cleaner. Let us see how you go about it?" In this sort of a situation, the person performing in the role of Mrs. Jones has a prepared role, that is, she acts as an assistant to the director and she presents the same or similar responses to the trainees whose task it is to sell her a vacuum cleaner. In this sort of role playing each salesman enters the scene, and attempts to sell the vacuum cleaner in the way he thinks best, based on his experience, what he knows about salesmanship, or possibly what he has learned in the course of instruction that he has just completed. After three, four, or five presentations in which different trainees act out the way they would attempt to sell the vacuum cleaner, the director leads the group in a discussion and an effort is made to arrive at a consensus on the best approach to making the sale. When they agree on the best approach the students are permitted to act out the sales attempt in the approved or accepted manner. This sort of role playing permits greater creativity than the skit and it does permit the various sales people or trainees to witness alternative courses of action. To that extent they are better prepared for the role of salesman. Furthermore, as they become more aware of alternative courses of action and increase in their ability to choose between them it is likely that their spontaneity is increased. Having been exposed to several alternative approaches to the customer and having witnessed a number of possible responses of the customer to different sales presentations, they are better prepared for future encounters. Because they are better prepared they are likely to be less anxious when in the "real" situation and may be more spontaneous. They should, therefore, be able to cope with customer responses they would not have been able to handle prior to the training sequence. This sort of role playing has been used for instructing people to perform roles in industry. It is used widely in foreman training, in sales training, and for other limited objectives. In the prepared skit the trainee is in effect told: "This is the approved way of doing it, the closer you approximate this way of doing it, the more successful you are likely to be in performing in the role." In the structured situation he is allowed greater freedom. The director, in effect says: "Let us explore several ways in which you people would do this based on *your* experiences". He then gets the group into a discussion and tries to lead them to a consensus. There is the implication, however, that there is a correct way of doing it and the group is trying to arrive at this correct way.

Role Playing as a Warm-Up for Group Discussion

Role Playing may be employed with both children and adults as a warm-up for a discussion group. When used in this way it is an approach to discussion which attempts to get the maximum participation of all the members of a group by having a few members of the group present an example of the problem in action. The other members of the group watch and observe the performance. When the Role Playing is over all members of the group join in a discussion of the specific example and the general problem. It has been the experience of those that use this technique that Role Playing stimulates members of the group to express their ideas and raise questions about the problem under discussion. The Role Playing is considered successful to the extent that it involves and stimulates all members of the group. Used as a stimulus to discussion the procedure is as follows:

1. The director in a ten minute talk comments on many problems that might interest the group. He then asks the members of the group to suggest the ones that they consider most important. These are listed and the members are then asked to vote to select a topic for discussion.

2. After the problem is decided upon the group is encouraged to formulate a concrete situation in which the problem might arise. The director then assigns members of the group to perform in roles required to enact the situation. The director may ask the group to select persons to play each role, or, if he wished, the director may ask people to play in specific roles. The people who are selected to play the roles are given time to warm-up to the roles. They learn the names of the persons they are playing and the part they and others are expected to play.

3. Those members not involved in the actual Role Playing are instructed to act as observers. They may be assigned to watch particular role players or to watch for important clues which come out in the role playing.

4. The Role Playing lasts approximately twenty minutes. The director may stop the production at any time if he believes that the basis for a meaningful discussion has been provided.

5. As soon as the action ends the immediate reaction of the role players is elicited. They are asked how they felt in their roles and how they reacted to others. Participants are addressed *in their roles*, not as students or trainees. To address them otherwise might give them the feeling that they are being evaluated.

6. The members of the group are then asked to give their impressions as well as question the actors. They may comment on the

performance, on mistakes, or omissions, and are also encouraged to suggest ways of improving the action. The director may, at times, invite a member of the group to show how he would perform in a role he has criticized. A series of performances in each of the roles secures greater involvement of the individuals in the group and may present alternative courses of action. In re-playing a scene the original players may be asked to try a different approach to the problems. However, it is advisable to get different persons from the group to present different approaches to a problem. The advantage of this is that members of the group, in discussion, can refer to the action as "the way Joe did it", "the way Bill did it", "the way Sam did it". If we have Joe do it in four different ways the discussion becomes complicated.

7. The actual Role Playing is intended to be a stimulus for participation of the entire group in the discussion. The comments on a specific problem can at that time be related back to the more general problems under consideration. The director, in his summary, touches upon the principal points illustrated in the Role Playing and the comments elicited from other members of the group.

The problem should be clear and specific, and not too complex. It should be one that can be dealt with by the persons chosen for the enactment. The emphasis in this sort of Role Playing is on the discussion that follows the enactment. Success is measured by the extent of involvement in the discussion and the number of alternatives presented in both the action and the discussion.

Role Playing to Change Attitudes

Role Playing has been successfully employed as a means of changing attitudes. The director assigns an assistant, an auxiliary ego, to present a particular attitude and defend it consistently. For example, he may be asked to present and defend a racist attitude toward minority groups. In his warm-up talk the director discusses the attitude in question, and problems resulting from it. After the warm-up a protagonist emerges who undertakes the task of changing the attitude of the auxiliary ego.

After one person has made the attempt others are invited to assume the same task, that is, to attempt to change the racist attitudes, defended by the auxiliary ego. The director leads the group in a discussion and an attempt is made to arrive at consensus.

This from of Role Playing has proved effective in changing undesired attitudes. It has been demonstrated experimentally that persons who have repeatedly presented a particular position in Role Playing sessions tend to support that point of view in future situations. I have also found this type of Role Playing useful as a form of Assertiveness Training. When seeking to increase an individual's ability to assert himself, I assign him to defend an unpopular attitude with the aid of an auxiliary ego who serves as a double. As others in the group attempt to change his attitude, he learns how to say no effectively, to defend his position, even an unpopular one, and to assert his individuality in other ways.

In the 1950's I directed Psychodramatic Role Training workshops for clergymen who were going to take positions in Southern States. One of the techniques found most effective by the clergymen involved Role Playing of the type described above. I had a capable and resourceful auxiliary ego play the stereotyped role of a segregationist chairman of the board. We gave him the name of Mr. Calhoun. However, instead of portraying Calhoun as a person hostile to the young minister, our auxiliary ego presented what turned out to be the sort of person encountered in the southern churches. Our Calhoun greeted the young minister with warmth and sympathy, invited him to his home, introduced him to all the important people and was in every respect kindly and friendly. Even on the subject of integration he appeared to have an "open" mind. All he asked was that the young minister wait a year before introducing any change. After all he was new. If he were to be effective he had to make friends, get people to like him and understand him. All this would take time. Our charming Calhoun was devastating. The young ministers were ready to deal with "red neck" southerners, hostile board chairmen, rabid segregationists. They had no idea at all of how to respond to a warm, friendly man who defended a position to which they were opposed and asked for understanding. In the course of our sessions they learned how to give Calhoun love and understanding and still move toward integration of his church.

Role Playing a Problem Relationship

There are individuals who experience difficulties in certain types of relationships. Role Playing may be used to prepare them to deal with people in such relationships. For example, if a group is assembled and the problem is how to deal with hostile people, an assistant to the director, an auxiliary ego, or therapeutic assistant, plays the hostile role. Members of the group who have experienced difficulty in dealing with hostile persons are placed in interaction with the auxiliary ego. He or she displays hostility to each protagonist in turn, voicing disapproval of his behavior, attitude, or point of view, making every effort to dominate. The problem given each protagonist is to overcome his fears and successfully avoid a submissive role.

Others in the group who do not find it difficult to deal with such persons are then asked to show how they would accomplish the objective. At the end of the enactments a group discussion follows in which the differences and advantages of the various ways of dealing with hostile persons are discussed. An attempt is made to reach consensus.

This type of Role Playing is useful in preparing people to deal with persons presenting problems such as; Authoritarian Father, Overprotective Mother, Disobedient Daughter, Drug User Son, and others who are domineering, continually seeking attention or recognition, excessively dependent or negativistic. To the extent that it prepares people with alternative ways of coping with such problem relationships, the Role Playing is useful in one's Socioanalysis and contributes to an increase in spontaneity. It is also useful in training people to be more assertive.

Role Playing for Leadership Roles

In many instances,particularly when dealing with younger people, the director has the task of helping them improve their ability to perform in certain roles. For example, it may be that we are preparing persons to assume specific roles in groups to which they will belong, such as leadership roles.

A leadership role may be defined for the group as one requiring an individual to offer new ideas and start new activities. Persons being prepared to function in leadership roles are instructed to try to understand the needs of the group, and show how they would meet those needs. Persons in action are given leadership tasks such as; increasing communication within the group, achieving agreement on courses of action, and stimulating activities. Role Playing used in leadership training of this sort involves having members of the group perform in a situation in which each is assigned a specific task. Other members of the group are placed in interaction with the protagonist and are instructed to obstruct his endeavors. In this way, an individual is prepared to cope with resistance to his leadership efforts. After five or six people attempt the leadership roles a group discussion follows in which the several approaches to achieving the objectives are discussed, and, if possible, consensus arrived at.

I have used this type of Role Playing to prepare young people to function in cooperative roles (role of fellow worker), subordinate roles (the junior man on a job), and roles involving initiating relationships (the new boy on a block, the minority group member entering a previously segregated church group, etc.)

Role Playing a Problem Situation

Role Playing may be used to help people to learn how to cope with a specific problem. Here the protagonist is encouraged to act out a relationship problem that he has experienced. The director draws from the group other people to play the roles required by the role player or protagonist. He is asked to avoid situations in which he has problems with persons emotionally close to him; his parents, his wife, his children, his sweetheart, etc. Problems involving intimate relationships can best be explored in a Psychodrama. An ideal problem for Role Playing is one that is common to members of the group. In training policemen, for example, Role Playing might be used to present a problem a policeman has had in giving a traffic summons to a woman. He would act out the experience that he had, and others would show how they would handle the situation. A Psychodramatic technique always used in these instances is Role Reversal. Using this technique the protagonist is placed in the position of the person getting the ticket, and others play the role of policeman. This technique affords the protagonist and the group an opportunity to examine many ways of dealing with a situation, and permits it to explore alternative courses of action.

I have used this type of Role Playing to deal with such diverse problem situations as a minority group member faced with a racist fellow worker or foreman, a foreman faced with a hostile minority group member, a female secretary dealing with sexual advances made by a supervisor, and a husband or wife dealing with a jealous spouse.

Role Playing to Develop Skills

Role Playing and Role Training may be used to prepare people for developing specific skills in relationships, such as getting acquainted with strangers, meeting members of the opposite sex, asking for a date, preparing for an interview, applying for a job, etc. If a skit is used, it should be made clear to the group that is is not presented to demonstrate the correct way to function in the relationship. Since one cannot predict the response of other to any approach presented, the director should explain that the purpose of the Role Playing session is to familiarize participants with as many alternative approaches as possible. An ancillary objective is to give people an opportunity to interact with others in an approximation of the situation for which they are being prepared. The structured situation in which the members of the group prepare and play parts in accordance with their selections is preferable to the prepared skit because it permits members of the group to focus on areas they consider important, and allows greater spontaneity.

In deciding which type of Role Playing session he will lead, the director must take into consideration the spontaneity level of the members of the group. If he is leading a group whose members have had little or no experience in dating and who tend to be shy and withdrawn (indicating a deficiency in spontaneity in this area) he might use a carefully prepared skit illustrating an approach which is uually successful. As each member plays a part, some increase in his spontaneity no matter how slight, may result.

If the members of the group lack experience in this area but are otherwise fairly spontaneous the director may structure a situation and have the members play the roles as they see fit. With a still more spontaneous group he might have the group create the scenes, assign the roles, play in them and present alternatives. With people who have had experiences in the role, whether satisfactory or unsatisfactory, I prefer the Role Training approach described in the next section of this chapter.

Multiple Role Playing

Multiple Role Playing may be used to prepare people to deal with a problem area in which several different roles are in conflict and it is desired to view them in interaction. In this form of Role Playing the director starts the session with a warm-up in which he speaks about a particular problem or problem area. He does not describe a situation in detail nor does he structure a situation. He calls upon members of the group to volunteer to perform in a situation involving the problem which he has outlined. He may select two, three, or more persons to perform and ask them to leave the room for a few minutes and prepare a situation involving the problem. The situation is then enacted and then the topic is discussed. In multiple role playing the roles may be assigned by the director but ideally the members of the group should distribute the roles among themselves and enact the situation. This is very similar to Sociodrama. After the enactment, members of the group are asked if they would like to substitute themselves for anyone in the performance and substitutions are made as desired by the group members. The following is an illustration of the way in which this type of Role Playing may be employed in a classroom of 11 year old children. The problem selected for the Role Playing is how to relate to children of a minority ethnic group who have recently moved into your street. The teacher, after speaking on the subject of getting to know strangers asks for five volunteers to set up such a situation and enact it. The five volunteers are sent out of the room to prepare a skit. If considered advisable the teacher may designate one of the children as leader. The children enact the skit when they return. The presentation is then discussed under the direction of the teacher. During the discussion the teacher refrains from criticism of the performance of any of the children. If a child is critical of the performance of one of the actors he is told "let us see how you would do it" and then the skit is replayed with him in the role he selects. An effort is made to permit as many substitutions as time permits. At the conclusion of the action and discussion the teacher summarizes the session mentioning each alternative presented by the children. Again the teacher should avoid introducing his or her preferences. To do so would inhibit the spontaneity of the children in future performances. They would tend to play the roles in such a way as to satisfy the teacher's preferences and would be less likely to experiment with their own. In Piaget's terms, the children in interaction with each other are engaging in reciprocal cooperation and are moving toward the formal operations stage of their development in which they agree on the rules of the game and apply them. They should be permitted to settle whatever differences that arise and develop increasingly complex rules on their own. To interfere with this process in our judgement, inhibits spontaneity. Everything published by Piaget and Moreno would lead to this conclusion.

The role of the director in the role playing situations described above is to help the protagonists perform in the various roles, select the other players, suggest the action and guide the discussion in which the audience actively participates. At times the action sequences are planned in detail by the director with the aim of helping the participants gain an understanding of a particular relationship. At other times the objective of the director is to help them cope with a specific problem, a relationship with aggressive people, for example. The persons with the problem may be asked to act in the role playing sequence or, they may be assigned relatively minor parts, that is, they may remain in the audience while some other person or persons enacts the roles. The scenes may be carefully structured in every detail or the situations may be vaguely defined and the actual enactment left to the creativity of the trainees. Usually, each protagonist plays himself, and the trained assistant plays the person with whom he is in interaction, that is, the prospective customer, the foreman, or the aggressive person. However, in many instances others in the group perform in the auxiliary roles. The protagonists gain self-confidence, as they learn to cope with increasingly challenging situations. It is suggested, however, that the director explain that the objective of the Role Playing is not to arrive at an ideal way of performing in the role but rather to consider many alternatives of performing in it.

There may be a reluctance on the part of some members of the group to participate in the action because of fear of ridicule. Some of them may hesitate to perform in a role because of the risk that their inadequacies might be exposed in front of a group. To minimize these anxieties, the director must create a warm permissive atmosphere in his warm-up. If the director wins the cooperation of the group in the course of his warm-up, and succeeds in having the group choose the protagonist or protagonists, fears and anxieties are greatly reduced because the protagonist moves into action knowing that he has the support of the group. In my experience as a director, I have found that when a group chooses a protagonist it remains sympathetic to him throughout the session including the action portion and the discussion. The discussion portion in particular should not be permitted to be turned into an attack on the protagonist or protagonists. The director should emphasize at all times that in the discussion people are, insofar as possible, to call upon their own experiences and relate them to the production.

All of the forms of Role Playing described above have as their objective in some way to increase spontaneity, that is, to prepare the trainee to act adequately and quickly. The efforts are to preserve and increase flexibility rather than to train precision. Performance in Role Playing sessions of the types described above is considered more effective than counseling in increasing spontaneity. The director can not be completely isolated from the protagonist, who in turn, cannot be isolated from the roles of others with whom he is in interaction. There is an interrelationship of all the roles and the ways in which they are learned. The Role Playing situation may to some extent approximate the real life situations that the individual has faced or will face. However, the approximation is not so complete as to represent the real situation. The protagonist is free to experiment in ways of performing in roles in order to gain skill in dealing with situations involving these and other roles in future situations. He also learns a great deal about relationships, learning that is important in Socioanalysis.

Role Training

As used in this book, Role Training is defined as a form of Role Playing in which the emphasis is placed on the reenactment of past experiences. All Psychodrama techniques considered appropriate may be employed. The warming-up techniques and the instruments used are similar to those employed in Psychodrama. Every effort is made to encourage people to perform in roles rather than to narrate their experiences in roles. The warm-up phase is over when the group decides on the situation or role-relationship to be examined. The first protagonist is then selected to enact or reenact an experience. The action portion of Role Training in many respects resembles the action portion of a Psychodrama. The protagonist is moved from the group to the action area where he describes the situation he is about to enact. Auxiliary egos are chosen and the action begins. However, there are some important differences between the action portion of a Role Training session and that of a Psychodrama. While in the latter the action sequences revolve around *one protagonist*, and as many relationships as he wishes to explore, in the former, the *Role Training Session*, the focus is on *one role.* If, for example, the Role Training is in the role of worker in relation to foremen, each of several members of the group may enact *his experiences* in that role. Each, thus, becomes a protagonist. A Role Training Sequence is employed when a problem in a role is uncovered. The use of this technique involves placing the protagonist in the role of other. The protagonist, a worker reenacting an encounter with a foreman is placed in the role of foreman, and as many others in the group as wish to do so come up to play the role of worker.

There are also differences in the way discussions are handled. In Psychodrama, the discussion is limited to a sharing of experiences, whereas in Role Training members of the group are often encouraged to offer their solutions to the problems presented. Furthermore, in a Psychodrama, only after the action portion is over does the group begin to discuss the problems and relationships presented. In a Role Training session discussions may take place after each enactment with members of the group being invited at any time to present alternative ways of performing in the role.

A Role Training session is, in a sense a Sociodrama. The emphasis, however, is on a particular social role and the diversity of ways in which persons perform in that role. The Role Training session includes acting out as many problems as possible encountered in the performance of the Role under examination by members of the group. An immediate objective of Role Training is to increase awareness of the limitations placed by society on performance in social roles. Since one of the major premises of Socioanalysis is that security in a role permits the individual to become more spontaneous, a long range goal of Role Training would be to maximize security in social roles, and in that way increase spontaneity.

Each society and group, through its culture or subculture, sets limitations on virtually every role required by it. In Role Training the focus or emphasis is on basic roles to which all members of the society have some relationship and on which most are required to function at one time or another. They may be grouped into three major categories: occupational roles, family roles, and community roles. It is hypothesized that for the individual each of the three role areas constitutes a problem area and that success or failure in

Figure 4

The Patterning of Social Roles

Normative Performance (Success)	**Deviant Performance (Failure)**
Acceptance of Culturally defined goals and Socially approved means.	Rejection of Culturally defined goals or Socially approved means.

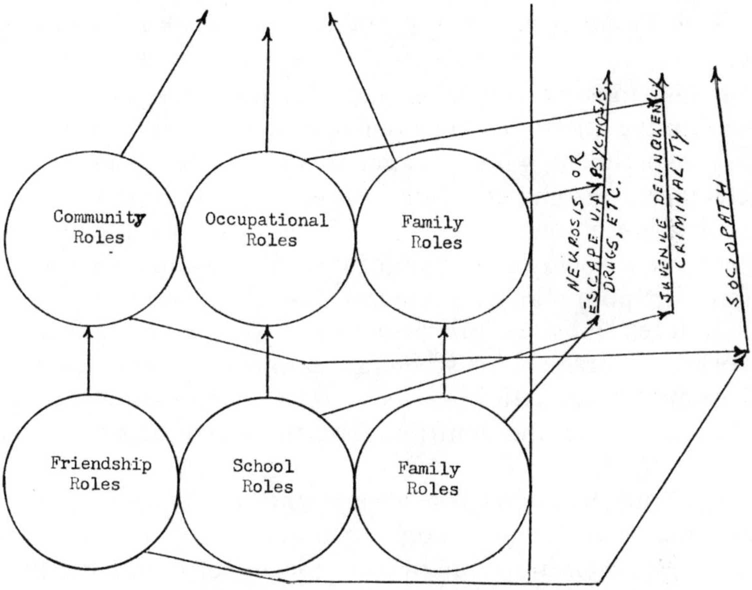

Diffuse Relationships	Specialized Relationships	To Other Sex Relationships

Circles represent problem areas, lines represent movement.
If through inadequacies in role performance or other deficiency, the individual fails in a problem area he moves toward rejection of the culturally defined goals or toward the use of deviant means.

Failure in one problem area contributes to failure in the other two.
Failure in a problem area as a child (lower level) contributes to failure in that problem area as an adult.

one significantly affects chances of success in the remaining two. Figure 4 illustrates this interrelationship. The Role Training session provides the group members with a laboratory in which each can reexamine old patterns of behavior, experiment with new patterns and observe others in diverse situations. Experiments, as they occur, are relatively without risk to the experimenters. The immediate goal is to develop social skill that comes with security in social roles. The ultimate objective is to develop spontaneity, the ability to provide novel solutions to problems.

Role Training has been particularly effective in helping people to:

1. Get jobs by preparing them for job interviews. They learn most of the questions they are likely to be asked in interviews and they experiment with answers. Such problems as how to get references, recommendations of former employers, and school records are among those solved. For young people and persons from lower socio-economic groups, this amounts to the preparation of a "poor man's resume".

2. Keep jobs by preparing them to get along with fellow workers, foremen, customers, employers, and unions. The development of satisfying social relationships on a job makes it more attractive and contributes to the willingness to continue in employment.

3. Aspire to higher educational and training goals. As the individuals learn what it takes to obtain better jobs not only are levels of aspiration raised but means of attaining them are developed.

4. Develop satisfactory relationships with professionals, teachers, school administrators, shop-keepers, landlords, police, and others in the community. This is particularly useful to young people who lack "caretakers". adults who can help them to succeed in the competitive struggle for occupational and social status.

5. Improve relationships with mother, father, siblings, spouses. and other family members. Learning more about the roles of these people has contributed toward an understanding of their behavior. As the individual learns what others expect of him he learns to distinguish between rejection of himself as a person and rejection of his behavior.

The emphasis in Role Training is on Spontaneity. We recognize that the individual has a great need for new experience, a need for experimentation, a need for self-expression. When he tries to satisfy these needs impulsive behavior often results. With Role Training the individual acquires knowledge of the permissible limits in a role. He learns the consequences of deviance, and he can better anticipate and anticipate with greater accuracy the responses of society to his actions. He becomes more spontaneous as he widens his range of responses and experiments with new methods and techniques. The emphasis in Role Training is not on an analysis of his behavior, but on action. In a truly warmed-up group, the protagonist represents the group and moves into action as a part of it. Others in the group become involved in the action. If the individual is preoccupied with an analysis of his actions, his ability to respond adequately is inhibited. He cannot be spontaneous. In the Role Training scene he can experiment with all sorts of behavior without risking serious injury. The content of the session is relatively unimportant, what is important is the development of spontaneity, and this is obtained by the learning of many alternative courses of action, learning that there are alternatives and developing an ability to respond. The concern is with the problem as a whole and the way people deal with it, not with a particular solution "the right way". What we are after is to expand the dimensions. The atmosphere for a Role Training session is open and unthreatening. The director avoids correcting under any circumstances and in his instructions to the group emphasizes his desire for people to present alternatives. He makes it clear that no alternative is necessarily correct and none is necessarily wrong. The director does not attempt to deal with each attitude or feeling as expressed. He gets the feelings out into the open in action, and encourages people to experiment. Negative points of view are dealt with in feedback or summary but not during the action portion of the session. The individual learns by doing, acting, and involving himself. It is in this way that he increases his spontaneity.

Chapter 11

OTHER EXPERIENCES USEFUL IN SOCIOANALYSIS

Even before he begins his Socioanalysis one is likely to recognize the existence of some problems in his social relationships. Early in Socioanalysis one learns to recognize alternative solutions to these problems. Throughout the Socioanalytic process one increases in one's ability to choose between available alternatives. One also increases in his ability to act on available alternatives. However, all of these abilities increase in synthetic groups; Socioanalytic Groups, Psychodramatic Groups, and Role Training Groups in which one prepares to deal with significant persons in natural groups. He still may not apply this learning to his behavior in his natural groups including his wife, children, parents, employers or others in his social atom. He may need to experiment in here and now groups in which he has no serious involvement. In this chapter I shall discuss four such groups; Spontaneity Theater, Sensitivity Groups, Encounter Groups, and Psychodrama Growth Groups.

Spontaneity Theater—1975

According to Dr. J.L. Moreno, its founder, the principal objective of the Viennese Theater of Spontaneity between 1921 and 1923 was to change theatrical production by first eliminating the playwright and the written play. The goal was a "theater without spectators with everyone in the audience a participant and actor." The play, actions, motives, words, and encounters were improvised and spontaneous. In place of a stage separating actors from audience he established the open stage—the space of life and life itself. Spontaneity Theater met with resistance from the public and the press. When productions were superior, critics believed them to have been rehearsed. When they were bad, critics concluded that real spontaneity was impossible. Because the public lost interest in Spontaneity Theater, Moreno shifted his interests to "Living Newspaper" and later to Psychodrama. In 1929

Moreno brought Spontaneity Theater to Carnegie Hall, New York, and in 1930 to the Civic Repertory Theater, also in New York City. Both of these efforts achieved temporary successes but were not continued for long. Moreno explained the failure of Spontaneity Theater to take hold as follows: "The theater of 'one hundred percent' spontaneity however, faced enormous difficulties first of all from the audiences. They had been brought up in all departments of living, the sciences and the arts, to use and rely upon cultural conserve and not to trust their own spontaneity".

In 1974, taking into consideration Dr. Moreno's experiences with Spontaneity Theater in Vienna and New York, I experimented with and ultimately developed another form of Spontaneity Theater. Audiences in Long Beach, California in 1974 were somewhat different from those Moreno encountered in Vienna in the 1920s or in New York in the 1930s. They were similar in one important respect. They appeared to fear and resist spontaneous action on a stage. I agreed fully with Moreno's thesis that the locus of the self is spontaneity, that when spontaneity is at zero the self is at zero, and that when spontaneity declines the self also shrinks. If the self is a function of spontaneity then we can expect the self to expand as spontaneity grows. Ideally, if the spontaneity potential is unlimited then the self potential too, is unlimited. My goal in Spontaneity Theater was not merely to give people an opportunity to be spontaneous but to increase and develop the spontaneity of the people in my Long Beach, California audience. I also sought a vehicle for Socioanalytic experimentation. One in which a person could begin to risk interaction with others on a here and now level with diminishing fear of reprisal.

To achieve these objectives I decided to use spontaneity players, people specifically trained to warm up the action and participate in interaction with members of the audience. The task set for the Spontaneity Players was to help increase the spontaneity of members of the audience. To achieve this I inhibited the spontaneity of the Spontaneity Players. The format was as follows:

A Warm-Up talk by the director in which I spoke on the objectives of Spontaneity Theater and introduced the first scene.

Scene 1—Two of the Spontaneity Players acted out a skit. They did not have a script but they were asked to prepare to take a fixed position in a clearly defined role.

To Illustrate: A quarrel between husband and wife, in which one advocated open marriage and the other strongly objected. The spontaneity players were instructed to play these roles and to polarize their actions taking extreme positions. This action, lasting five to ten minutes was used as a warm-up for the audience. Members of the audience were then invited to come up to the stage and support, criticize, or otherwise interact with either or both of the players. The players were trained to take a position somewhat in the manner of "I'm O.K., You're O.K.," and try to increase the spontaneity of the group member. Under no condition was a player to reject, humiliate, or in any way criticize or put down a member of the audience, who moved into action.

For example—An audience member moves to stage to criticize wife advocating open marriage.

Audience Member—Why get married if you want lots of men?

Spontaneity Player—No one man can satisfy me in every respect. Why shouldn't I have a husband if I need such a relationship.

Audience Member—If you go to bed with any man you like, you're a whore.

Spontaneity Player—I like my life style. Why do you want to change me?

No matter what the audience member says, the spontaneity player respects his view, maintains her position, and asks the audience member for understanding.

After about twenty minutes of interaction, the director warms up the group for scene 2, usually dealing with a social issue. After another twenty minutes of interaction, the director warms up the group for scene 3, dealing with another relevant relationship; sexual, social, or political. The same procedure followed in scene one was employed in scenes 2 and 3.

The three scenes lasted between sixty and ninety minutes. Then, prior to a fifteen minute intermission, members of the audience were asked to suggest skits for improvisation. While the Spontaneity Players prepared their skits, members of the audience were invited to have coffee and get acquainted. The Spontaneity Players then put on two or three improvised skits, dealing with topics suggested by the audience. These were used as stimuli in the same way as the three scenes in the first portion of Spontaneity Theater.

Spontaneity Theater was advertised as entertainment and was well received in Long Beach, California. The following are comments excerpted from a review of Spontaneity Theater by Samuel Whitman, a distinguished semanticist:

"The audience, via what seemed a majority of those present, addressed itself tranchantly to the various aspects of relationships that emerged on stage, evoking basic, gritsy, articulate reactions from all who concerned themselves with this issue, setting off roars of laughter and waves of hearty applause—which, on reflection, was really looking amusedly at themselves, at the corny ridiculousness of their life styles and at the now ever dimming prospects of any self-satisfying solutions."

* * *

The long held, reinforcing fact that impressed me most deeply, was the evidence that the opportunity for vocal expression is a basic, human need. The affording of such opportunities in greater number must be one of society's future commitments, now obviously inadequately recognized."

Patricia de Luna, a staff newsperson, in a review of Spontaneity Theater wrote:

"Spontaneity Theater is not to be confused with ordinary theater where the audience is expected to sit straight with appropriate smiles and frowns washing over each face and hands poised to applaud. Nor is it to be mistaken for improvisational theater where the audience does little more than suggest a theme then sits back while the actors take it from there.

"Oh no! With spontaneity theater, there is little room for such passivity. You can be on your toes, or on your feet, or best of all, up on the stage."

* * *

". . . the Spontaneity Players are here to present scenes 'relevant to all'. And you—if the spirit moves you—are encouraged to 'react, talk back, express your ideas and give vent to your feelings'."

At the annual meetings of the American Society of Group Psychotherapy and Psychodrama we did a demonstration of my version of Spontaneity Theater before an audience of about six hundred persons. In the course of the presentation some sixty people, about ten percent of those present, moved to the action area to express themselves to our spontaneity players. Involvement was clear and strong and the spontaneity of those moving to the action area increased by the minute.

As far as I know none of the people in the audience were involved in Socioanalysis. However, if there were any, Spontaneity Theater presented an excellent opportunity for them to express their real feelings to another person. No one was put down or rejected. A series of such experiences would be very helpful for one experiencing difficulty in taking action once he had chosen a course of action.

Sensitivity Training and Encounter Groups

Encounter Groups usually meet over a weekend at some facility providing room and board. Persons participating vary from 12 to over 30 with as near a sexual balance as possible. These groups do not usually meet on a continuing basis, however, most leaders schedule groups once a month or more often. One is not likely to meet many of the same persons at succeeding sessions.

The emphasis is on open and honest relationships between the persons present in the here and now of the weekend. In virtually every group people are encouraged to confront others and expose weaknesses and dishonesty. Self defeating behavior patterns are attacked. The principal goals are self-awareness, emotional experiences and change in behavior patterns. Persons of all sorts and with every kind of problem may participate. Since there is a sizeable fee most participants are middle class.

Among group leaders one finds Psychiatrists, Psychologists, Social Workers, and some nonprofessionals with little or no training. The techniques employed, verbal and non-verbal, vary greatly depending largely on the skills, training and philosophy of the leader. Psychoanalytic, Psychodramatic, Gestalt Therapy, Transactional Analysis, and many less sophisticated approaches are employed. In most sensitivity or encounter groups the leader assumes no responsibility toward the participant. Each is considered responsible for what he does and what happens to him. Dr. Frederick Perls, the founder of Gestalt Therapy summarized this view in his book, Gestalt Therapy Verbatim as follows:

"Sir, if you want to go crazy, commit suicide, improve, get turned on, or get an experience that would change your life, that is up to you. You came here of your own free will."

It is for this reason that I do not recommend participation in Sensitivity Training or Encounter Groups until one has reached a point in Socioanalysis where he has decided on the direction of change. The sensitivity training or encounter group experience will afford him opportunities to experiment with change in the here and now, confronting others and being confronted.

The Psychodrama Growth Group

The Psychodrama Growth Group is similar to a Sensitivity Training Group and an Encounter Group in that it too provides an experience in which a participant relates to others in the here and now. As Moreno saw it, the *encounter* is the sum total of interaction in the here and now involving both physical and psychic contact. Persons meet to experience one another, as actors, each in his own right. The encounter is extemporaneous, unstructured, unplanned, and unrehearsed. Any of the techniques employed in Psychodrama may be used with a growth group. The major difference between sessions of a Psychodrama Growth Group and those of a classic Psychodrama is that in the classic Psychodrama session protagonists examine relationships in their natural groups (persons not present) while in the Psychodrama Growth Group relationships examined are with those persons present. Also, other members of the growth group may move into action any time they see fit to do so. They may spontaneously interact with the protagonist or anyone else on stage, or they may double with the protagonist or anyone else to get him to express himself more fully and honestly. I, as director, use an alter ego technique, having another member of the group follow the protagonist around saying what he believes the protagonist is really thinking. I also use Role Reversals, Doubles, Auxiliary Chairs, Mirror Technique, Behind the Back, and other techniques I consider appropriate. The Psychodrama Growth experience provides a person in Socioanalysis with an opportunity to interact with people who can confront him, oppose him, and expose him. In the Protagonist Centered Psychodrama the auxiliary egos are generally agents of the protagonist or of the director. They often represent persons not present and confrontation or attack are not permitted.

As members of the group challenge one's actions and expressions of feeling a participant is compelled to defend or abandon the courses of action he has decided upon in Socioanalysis up to that time. Also, in the process which emphasizes openness, honesty, and expression of feeling to others, one develops increased trust in others and in one's ability to act on his own behalf. We expect that in the course of his Socioanalysis a person will develop sufficient self-esteem and self-direction to act on alternatives available to him and enter into relationships of his choice. The Psychodrama Growth experience affords him an opportunity of testing his increased ability to make choices and act in accordance with the choices he has made.

The Personal Reference Group (PRG)

A PRG as we have noted, is a group in which an individual receives sustenance, recognition, approval, and appreciation for just being "himself". It consists of those persons with whom the individual wants to associate in a person to person way and with whom he values emotional relationships. The family is the first such group of which a person is a member. How long it remains his PRG may depend on how well it performs the functions described above. The case loads of psychiatrists, psychologists, and social workers are filled with people whose families have failed to provide the needed recognition, approval, or appreciation. Much therapeutic effort is aimed at giving the "patient" insight into the deficiencies in his early development in the family. It is assumed by many that once an individual gains such insight his troubles are over.

The large extended family of the past was able to perform the functions of a PRG. The small nuclear family prevalent in the urban industrial society is not. Yet, I am convinced that each individual needs to be part of a group in which he can achieve a measure of self-direction (be himself) without fear of loss of approval. He needs recognition and appreciation if he is to survive as a person in the face of blows sustained in occupational and other roles. He needs to be part of a PRG. Furthermore, I am convinced that it is often impossible for the family as now constituted, to be his PRG. Neither, historical regression nor insight can change the objective situation, a small helpless nuclear family in an indifferent world. That is why, in my opinion, most psychotherapeutic approaches result in failure or lead to an acceptance of the hopelessness of man's fate.

Socioanalysis can provide the answer. Each individual can learn which others he wants to relate to and which others want to relate to him on a person to person basis. He can then join with these people to form a PRG. Why bother learning to love a younger brother you have hated for years? Why seek love from a father who does not know how to give love? Why fight for independence from an overprotective mother? Let them be. They cannot or will not change. They cannot or will not satisfy your needs. There are other "older" brothers who understand you as an "older" brother and like you. All you have to do is find them and join with them. We have discussed at the conclusion of Chapter *IV* ways in which a PRG can *be* formed.

In a PRG you can move toward self-direction, being yourself. As you can act without fear of rejection by those you like, the security achieved will make you more spontaneous, more capable of seeking and enjoying new experiences. In such a group you can also learn to love yourself because you will be with people who can give you unconditional love. Before one can give love to others one must first love himself. If you do not love yourself you place those who love you in a double bind. If someone expresses love for you you lose respect for him and cannot reciprocate. Why? Because anyone who loves you, "the worthless individual that you are", cannot be much good. If he does not love you he is another indifferent or rejecting person. Only those who have learned to love themselves can appreciate people who express love for them and can reciporcate in kind. Once you have learned to love yourself you will recognize people who love you to be giving, constructive, and good people. The ideal PRG consists only of such people. Sociometric research clearly indicates that choices tend to be reciprocated. Thus, we would expect that in a PRG one who gives love will in all probability receive love. Loving your neighbor as you do yourself becomes a meaningful principle only if you love yourself. In a PRG, with the support of people who can give you unconditional love; recognition, appreciation, and approval, you can be more spontaneous and creative. You can also contribute to the spontaneity and creativity of others.

The question then arises; what do you do in such a group? You can, with others who like you and who you like, discuss creatively ways of leading fulfilling lives, potentials and ways of realizing them, objectives and ways of achieving them. You can explore ways of improving your neighborhoods, cities, and countries. You can establish liaison with other PRGs and form networks for political and social action. The PRG can become the extended family of the future and joined with other PRGs create a healthier society. Socioanalysis represents an important first step toward that goal. The development of millions of PRGs is the second step. The formation of networks of PRGs can lead us to the ultimate goal set by Dr. J.L. Moreno, *"a therapeutic society."*

BIBLIOGRAPHY

Borgatta, Edgar F., Robert Boguslaw and Martin R. Haskell, "On the Work of Jacob L. Moreno," *Sociometry*, March, 1975.

Haskell, Martin R., *An Introduction to Socioanalysis* (Long Beach: California Institute of Socioanalysis, 1967). 2nd Edition, 1972.

———*The Psychodramatic Method* (Long Beach: California Institute of Socioanalysis, 1967) Fourth Printing, 1973.

———"An Alternative to More and Larger Prisons: A Role Training Program for Social Reconnection." *Group Psychotherapy*, March, 1961.

———"The Berkshire Farm After-Care Program: Role Training and Job Placement," *Group Psychotherapy*, September, 1959.

———"The Contributions of J. L. Moreno to the Treatment of the Offender," *Group Psychotherapy and Psychodrama*, Vol. XXVII, 1974.

———"Role Training Applied to Inmates of a Correctional Institution." Co-author, H. Ashley Weeks. *Journal of Criminal Law, Criminology, and Police Science*, February, 1960.

———"Socioanalysis and Psychoanalysis," *Group Psychotherapy*, July, 1962.

———"Techniques of Group Psychotherapy." *Group Psychotherapy*, September, 1968.

———"Toward a Reference Group Theory of Juvenile Delinquency." *Social Problems*, Winter, 1961.

Haskell, Rochelle J. and Alfred L. Larr, "Psychodramatic Role Training with Stutterers," *Group Psychotherapy and Psychodrama*, Vol. *XXVII*, 1974.

Inhelder, Barbel and Jean Piaget, *The Growth of Logical Thinking*, New York: Basic Books, 1958.

Jennings, Helen H., *Leadership and Isolation*, (New York: Longmans, Green, & Co., Inc. 1953).

———"Leadership and Sociometric Choice," *Sociometry*, 10, 1947, pp. 32-49.

Lippitt, Rosemary and Anne Hubbell, "Role Playing for Personnel and Guidance Workers," *Group Psychotherapy*, Vol. 9, 1956, pp. 89-114.

Mead, George H., *Mind, Self, and Society*, Chicago, Ill: Univ. of Chicago, Press, 1934.

Moreno, J. L. *The Theater of Spontaneity*, Beacon, New York: Beacon House, Inc., 1973.

———*Psychodrama: Volume I*, Beacon, New York: Beacon House, Inc., 1946.

———*Who Shall Survive?* Beacon, New York: Beacon House, Inc., 1953.

———(Ed.) *The Sociometry Reader,* Glencoe, Ill.: The Free Press, 1960.

Moreno, Zerka T., "A Survey of Psychodramatic Techniques," *Group Psychotherapy,* 1959, 12, pp. 5-14.

Piaget, Jean, *The Moral Judgment of the Child,* London: Keagan Paul. 1932.

Verny, Thomas R., *Inside Groups,* New York: McGraw Hill, 1974.

Weiner, Hannah B., "Treating the Alcoholic with Psychodrama," *Group Psychotherapy,* March-June, 1965, pp. 27-49.

Yablonsky, Lewis, *Robopaths,* New York: Bobbs-Merrill Inc., 1972.

Two entire issues of *Group Psychotherapy* have been devoted to bibliography: Vol. 9, No. 3, November 1956, and Volume 17, No. 4, December 1964. The following books contain extensive bibliographies including the works of J. L. Moreno and Jean Piaget:

Back, Kurt W., *Beyond Words,* New York: Russell Sage Foundation, 1972.

Blatner, Howard, (Ed.) *Practical Aspects of Psychodrama,* (Department of Child Psychiatry, Stanford Univ. Medical Center), 1968.

Flavell, John H., *The Developmental Psychology of Jean Piaget,* Princeton, New Jersey: D. Van Nostrand, Inc., 1963.

Greenberg, Ira A., *Psychodrama and Audience Attitude Change,* Beverly Hills, Calif.: Thyrsus Pub. Co., 1968.

Greer, Valerie J. and James M. Sacks, *Bibliography of Psychodrama,* Valerie J. Greer, 505 West End Ave., New York, 10024, 1973.

Who Shall Survive?, contains an extensive bibliography of relevant material published prior to 1953.